More Praise for *The Collaboration Economy*

"When it comes to solving complex environmental and social challenges, cross-sector collaboration clears a path forward. *The Collaboration Economy* shows how to nurture cross-sector collaboration for the benefit of the public, private, and civil sectors."

—Tim Brown, president and chief executive officer, Nestlé Waters North America

"Eric Lowitt is highlighting one of the most important human behaviors for our beneficial common future: collaboration. In my experience, working with some of the largest companies and governments in the world, this sphere of activity is time and again proven to be the best and fastest path toward clarity of purpose, effective paths for integrated innovation, and sustainable growth: three things that we need to assure a positive, abundant future for all. It's about taking forever; and it's about taking us all together—that's the point."

—William McDonough, chairman, McDonough Advisors

"A very timely and relevant book! Eric Lowitt shows in an eloquent manner—with numerous excellent examples—how saving the world can be good business for all. I hope this book encourages all stakeholders to check their old assumptions and to experiment new collaborative business models for a better world."

—Mikko Kosonen, chairman, SITRA, Finland's Innovation Fund

"The Collaboration Economy provides original thinking on a vitally important question: How best to create cooperation in a world that badly needs it. Today, we face a shortage of both effective global leadership and a shared sense of urgency to address a lengthening list of problems without borders. Eric Lowitt offers valuable ideas on how business, government, and civil society can work together to pursue their individual interests toward a common goal."

—Ian Bremmer, president, Eurasia Group

JB JOSSEY-BASS™
A Wiley Brand

The
Collaboration
Economy

How to Meet Business, Social, and Environmental Needs and Gain Competitive Advantage

Eric Lowitt

WILEY

Published by Jossey-Bass
A Wiley Brand
One Montgomery Street, Suite 1200, San Francisco, CA 94104-4594—www.josseybass.com

Jossey-Bass books and products are available through most bookstores. To contact Jossey-Bass directly call our Customer Care Department within the U.S. at 800-956-7739, outside the U.S. at 317-572-3986, or fax 317-572-4002.

Wiley publishes in a variety of print and electronic formats and by print-on-demand. Some material included with standard print versions of this book may not be included in e-books or in print-on-demand. If this book refers to media such as a CD or DVD that is not included in the version you purchased, you may download this material at http://booksupport.wiley.com. For more information about Wiley products, visit www.wiley.com.

Library of Congress Cataloging-in-Publication Data
Lowitt, Eric, 1972–
    The collaboration economy : how to meet business, social, and environmental needs and gain competitive advantage / Eric Lowitt.—first edition.
        pages cm
    Includes bibliographical references and index.
    ISBN 978-1-118-53834-0 (cloth)
    ISBN 978-1-118-57332-7 (ebk.)
    ISBN 978-1-118-57335-8 (ebk.)
    ISBN 978-1-118-57336-5 (ebk.)
    1. Competition. 2. Consumption (Economics)
3. Sustainable development. I. Title.
    HF1414.L69 2013
    658'.046—dc23
                        2013002430

Printed in the United States of America
FIRST EDITION
HB Printing   10 9 8 7 6 5 4 3 2 1

Contents

Preface

It has been an eventful time for me since the publication of *The Future of Value*, my previous book, in fall 2011. I have given numerous talks on the subject of sustainability and competitive strategy at conferences, corporate events, and universities both in the United States and abroad.

Along the way, I've had the privilege of holding conversations with many leaders from the private, public, and civil sectors. These conversations inevitably led to the question, "Will we make it?" Will we collectively change our path, invest in urban infrastructure, alter our behaviors, and set the world on a sustainable course? My answer was always the same: "Yes. I believe in the human spirit's desire to survive and outpace the logic of Malthusian economics."

But a vague concern began to gnaw at me. For a long time, sustainability consultants, including me, counseled our corporate clients to focus on getting their houses in order. Focus on what you can control. Lower your energy, water, and materials consumption. Reduce your greenhouse gas emissions. Sure, we'd provide stakeholder engagement advice, but usually along the lines of "listen to what the NGOs have to say about your business activities."

Over time, my vague concern began to take shape. Am I giving my clients incomplete or, worse yet, bad advice by having them focus on getting their house in order? Would this goal, if accomplished by every company worldwide, enable the world to achieve a state of sustainable development? My answer was no.

This realization led to another question: What *would* enable the world to achieve a state of sustainable development?

For some reason, I then recalled an experience from my college days. I studied in Japan and lived with a host family near Osaka. A neighbor was a senior executive at a big Japanese trading company. One day, this neighbor invited me for dinner. He wanted to help me understand his business philosophy. At the time, the Japanese economy was running like a well-oiled machine. He was excited about the prospect of imparting wisdom to an American. So he placed two dominoes face down on his kitchen table.

"How many dominoes are on the table?" he asked me.

"Two," I said without hesitation, curious to know what I was missing.

"No, try again" he replied.

I thought my Japanese was wholly inadequate, so this time I put two fingers up. Again he said no. In feigned disgust, he put the dominoes away.

Nearly twenty years later, in 2012, I finally began to understand his thinking. He wanted me to say, "It depends." That is, if the two dominoes represent competing companies, then the likely outcome could be zero or one. Zero-sum competition between rivals rarely leads to the two rivals still standing after a period of time. But if the two dominoes represented partners, then there would be no limit to what they could do together. So in this case, the outcome would be "At least three."

This lesson led me to wonder whether the same conceptual thinking could be applied to the sustainable development question. What if a company collaborated with public and social sector counterparts? And what if this group added more like-minded organizations from all three sectors? What could we then accomplish?

The Collaboration Economy is for leaders young and old who truly want to bring about a better world today and a better future tomorrow. It is essential that you, the reader, put aside preconceived notions of collaborations and partnerships—they take too much time, they create a camel when we wanted a horse—and instead read *The Collaboration Economy* with an open mind.

If you do, then I am sure you will come to the same conclusion that the companies and organizations featured in this book have reached: collaboration is our best shot at achieving sustainable development. And if aimed at the most vexing issues held in common—environmental and social challenges—collaboration across sectors (and yes, even within industries) can lead to something else: increased prosperity for all. In this way, our efforts can bring about a new economic model, one that aligns prosperity with sustainable development: the Collaboration Economy.

April 2013   Eric Lowitt
Needham, Massachusetts

Acknowledgments

Like any endeavor that requires great effort, this book is the result of the combined contributions of many individuals and institutions.

The Collaboration Economy would not exist without the kindness of strangers-turned-colleagues and colleagues-turned-friends. I reached out to a select number of companies that I truly believe are integral to our current economic system's transformation into the Collaboration Economy. I was not sure what the response would be to my offer to collaborate on a chapter of *The Collaboration Economy*. To my pleasant surprise, I came into contact with experts in the fields of strategy, sustainable development, consumer behavior, investment policy, and public sector activity who were delighted to jointly develop content. In particular, my eternal gratitude goes out to Muhtar Kent, Bea Perez, Jeff Seabright, Greg Koch, Allyson Park, and Nelson Mumma at Coca-Cola; Kim Jeffrey and Michael Washburn at Nestlé Waters North America; Chris Bartle and Robert F. Kennedy Jr. at Keeper Springs; Mark Vachon, Lindsay Lorraine, and Jodi Groth at GE; Petter Heier at Grieg Green; Paul Polman, Jan Kees Vis, Karen Hamilton, Enrique Arceo, and Flip Dotsch at Unilever; Hal Hamilton at the Sustainable Food Lab; John Replogle at Seventh Generation; Walter Robb at Whole Foods; Judith Merkies MEP of the European Union's Parliament; Erik Hormes, who supported Judith Merkies's research into the development of a lease society; and Roope Mokka at Demos Helsinki. Thank you for working with me to craft the sector chapters of *The Collaboration Economy*!

Along the way, I had the privilege of getting to know the experts-turned-friends at Maine Pointe, a Boston-based consulting firm specializing in operations, logistics, and procurement effectiveness. Maine Pointe afforded me the opportunity to test content in *The Collaboration Economy* with both its executives and its clients. Thank you to Steve Bowen and Bill Forster.

Cherie Potts and Pat Steffens at Wordworks continue to amaze me. This sister team once again did yeoman's work, quickly turning interviews into consistently flawless interview transcripts. Often I submitted interview recordings to Cherie and Pat without advance warning. They always sent back verbatim transcripts within the shortest possible time frame, handled with the utmost confidentiality. Once again, please consider yourselves partners in this book!

Several friends provided advice throughout the research and work for *The Collaboration Economy*. Among them I thank Ian Bremmer of the Eurasia Group; Eric McNulty, Kelvin Thompson, and Jodi Kaelle at the RoseMont Institute; Tim Mohin; Will Sarni; Yossi and Dana Raucher; Dr. Will Li; Mark Johnson; Pauliina Valpas; Paul Gardner; Susan Blesener; Carolyn Panzer; Maung Min; Suzanne Reed; Lonnie Reed; Sherryl Kuhlman; Joanne Spigonardo; Ingvild Jenssen; Santiago Gowland; Kevin Decker; Tim Damon; Barbara Kimmel; Roberta Barbieri; Bonnie Nixon; Brad Zarnett; Dan McGinn; Caroline Holtum; James Boyle; Sherry Frazier; Beth Wilson; and Cameron Schuster.

This endeavor began with intensive research and ended with a book. For their help in getting it there, I continue to be indebted to my editor at Jossey-Bass, Kathe Sweeney, and her dedicated colleagues, including Alina Poniewaz-Bolton and Jeanenne Ray. Kathe truly helped shape *The Collaboration Economy*, championed the book from the outset, and, most important, always believed in me. Thank you, Kathe!

Finally, I owe my deepest gratitude to my family. In particular, my daughter, Dana, and son, Alex, who put up with me as I worked on the book. I want to share a quick story. Dana came home from school with her friend Ian in fall 2011. Dana and Ian were so proud to share their idea to "save the world" with me: they wanted to design an electric car and post signs about the car at local gas stations. Their innocent dedication to saving the world motivated me throughout this project.

To my extended family, especially my parents, brother, sister-in-law, niece and nephews, and in-laws, I owe my deep appreciation for your support, inspiration, and encouragement.

And to my wife, Allegra, whose love and never-ending belief in me served as the foundation for this effort, I dedicate *The Collaboration Economy* to you. Please know I am truly blessed to have you in my life—I remain the lucky one!

The Collaboration
Economy

INTRODUCTION

There once was a time when we rose to overcome great challenges . . .

The Collaboration Economy is a book about health and healing. Our planet is sick; so, too, are our economic, water, energy, food, resource consumption, and societal development systems. It is essential that we heal each of these systems, that together our planet and global economy are healthy providers for today, tomorrow, and in perpetuity.

Achieving this state of healthiness is a goal that can be met only through collaboration. Not just through an industry association or regulatory policy that requires compliance, but through honest and authentic collaboration nurtured across the private, public, and civil sectors. (Please note that for clarity, the combination of citizens' and nonprofit organizations is referred to in this book as the "civil' sector." Occasionally the term "social sector" will be used when relaying a quote provided by an executive who used "social" in place of "civil." Both terms are used to refer to the same thing: the combination of citizens and nonprofits.)

Visionary companies, social entities, and public sector administrators are beginning to pave the path toward global health and healing. Such companies as Coca-Cola (water), GE (energy), Unilever (food), Nestlé Waters North America (recycling), and Grieg Green (responsible shipbreaking) are embracing their role as orchestrators. They are pulling together networks of collaborators from the private, public, and civil sectors to assess the health of specific systems, charting a course toward addressing challenges within these systems, and carrying out plans that can heal these systems. In the process, these orchestrators are encouraging entities the world over to test their most closely held assumptions about our economy, our relationships, and our purpose for being.

Core to these orchestrators' efforts is a belief that the word *company* is a verb, not a noun. There is no longer an entity known as "the company"; boundaries that once governed the company's sphere of responsibility no longer exist. In their place is an ethos that resides at the center of fluid coalitions of the willing, dexterously employing these coalitions' tools and skills in order to heal our planet and ourselves.

Make no mistake: the pursuit of margin will continue to entice entities to invest in specific goods, services, and initiatives. But orchestrators also understand that without mission, there cannot be margin. So the purpose of *The Collaboration Economy* is to both entice and equip entities throughout the private, public, and civil sectors to work collaboratively in order to heal our systems today for an ensured future for generations in perpetuity.

With this goal squarely in mind, let's start the healing process with this premise: our current economic model is broken. We've financed the present by borrowing from the future, placing a significant burden on generations to come. We've consumed way beyond our means for far too long. We have poached from the natural environment to create an asset without documenting an offsetting liability on our balance sheets. The divide between the rich and the poor has grown to an unsustainable, if not unacceptable, extent. And our governments have maxed out their credit cards—they can no longer financially "save" us.

Individual consumption is responsible for between 60 and 70 percent of global GDP. Over the years, as consumptive demand grew, production supply expanded in lockstep. Production expansion led to growth, which led to more consumption, more jobs, and more optimism about the future. Borrowing capacity grew, which in turn enabled individuals to consume beyond their income levels.

Two mind-sets became pervasive: owning stuff is a status symbol, and stuff can be freely discarded for better stuff. Neither mind-set is sustainable. Whereas the first is psychological and will not likely change any time soon, the second can and must change. Case in point: our global level of consumption requires the equivalent of 1.3 Earths every year in order to continue in perpetuity. By most forecasts, global population will increase by three billion people within a relatively short time period—just thirty-five years. Highly populous countries such as China and India, long focused on gaining an influential and lucrative seat at the global economic table, are in the process of unleashing the consumptive ability of their two billion–plus citizens in order to sustain their pace of economic development.

As consumption increases, the reuse of the consumed products' materials, including the packaging materials, highlights the battle between smart economic development and, well, wasted opportunity for economic development. Consider this: in the United States alone, every year $11.4 billion of packaging material that could be reused is instead simply discarded as if resources were infinite and free.[1] This mind-set must change.

The math for our current behavior just doesn't work; something simply has to give. The ethos behind our current global economic model is no longer aligned with our global interests. The system that earned us our place at the proverbial dance will now prevent us from succeeding at the dance. We must transition away from what I've come to call the Waste Economy, which has been created by our cycle of need for external validation, subsequent overconsumption, and a corporate zero-sum competitive game mind-set.

But all is not doom and gloom. Whether by design or happenstance, our global economic model is undergoing a transition with far-reaching implications.

The transition to a new economic mind-set, the Collaboration Economy, is under way. In the Collaboration Economy, the private, public, and civil sectors work together for their own good and for the collective good. The unifying goal is clear: kick-start a new era of prosperity by pointing our collective best capabilities in the direction of solving the most vexing environmental and societal challenges we jointly face. These challenges are numerous, ranging from overstressed water systems to energy systems that do not properly balance economic and environmental considerations.

Why This Book, and Why Now?

Prominent events organized by the public sector intended to catalyze a response to our global challenges are proving at best ineffective and, at worst, counterproductive. Indeed, following the Rio+20 event in June 2012, I've witnessed, read, and heard increasing negativism and skepticism about the public sector's globalized efforts to pull us out of our ever-deepening mess. There clearly is a leadership vacuum when it comes to sustainable development.

Our significant challenges require even more significant responses. But our largest sources of central funding—our governments—are fully tapped out. Together we're staring at the abyss of sustained austerity just to get back to even. There is not a single sector that alone can fund the infrastructure, resource, and development work ahead of us. We need more creative, more collaborative solutions. It seems to me (and many of the largest entities worldwide) that smartly applying our best capabilities in tandem, across sectors, is an approach that deserves significant attention and exploration.

Even if we were to solve the "where-will-the-desperately-needed-funds-come-from" debate, we would still face considerable obstacles to further economic development. The set of vexing environmental and social challenges we collectively face affects everyone. So it seems appropriate that we all contribute to the creation and implementation of the portfolio of solutions required to set our ship on the course of sustainable development.

Collaboration across sectors and fueled by the human spirit for survival is the direction in which we are headed. This concept is not new. What *is* new is the emerging collection of stories, best practices, and challenges encountered by a trailblazing set of private, public, and civil sector entities as they attempt to turn capitalism into an engine for sustainable development.

Driving these organizations' efforts is a perfect storm of regulation, stakeholder pressure, and understanding that there's profitability to be gained by embracing sustainability as the basis for competitive strategy. This storm will have particular implications for the private sector. The need to internalize the external costs of businesses' activities is coming, will be disruptive, and, as a consequence, will require changes in how companies operate individually *and* how they compete jointly. The term *external costs* refers to the impacts on and subsequent costs from companies' activities on the environment. The categories and root causes of these external costs are common within industries, typically fall under existing regulation, and greatly affect civil society. So working together to reduce or eliminate these external costs makes sense both financially and in terms of sustainable development.

Consider this perspective from Michael Washburn, vice president of sustainability at Nestlé Waters North America. Washburn is tirelessly building a coalition of private, public, and civil sector entities to introduce a new industry-level model of recycling to the United States:

> We need to move to a rational model where waste is seen as value, systems are organized around markets rather than political boundaries, and companies are held accountable for the external costs of their packaging. If we move to a proven

model, extended producer responsibility, we can reduce waste management costs and reveal the value available in recovered and recycled materials.

The benefit of dramatically increasing recycling would include source-reduction, which will pay back dividends from both a climate perspective as well as reducing dependence on limited nonrenewable resources. Critical to our success will be getting all companies—including my company—to internalize the external costs incurred by business activities.

Many of these external costs occur as a result of crumbling infrastructure—recycling systems woefully underdeveloped, energy systems that are not scalable in an environmentally conscious manner, food systems that fail two out of every seven citizens worldwide. And that's before we consider the depth and breadth of societal changes—how employees are treated, how prosperity is distributed, and how citizens are governed.

Given the scale of these infrastructure inefficiencies, the *only* way to lower or even eliminate these external costs is through collaborative thinking, financing, and acting. This book starts the conversation about the need for change to the very business models that drive commerce.

Again, Michael Washburn:

I think there are two great big two-by-fours that are hitting companies that choose to behave like it's 1950. The first is social activism that is putting tangible pressure on companies' activities, decisions, and investments. Simply put, society won't allow companies to get away with subpar and non-inclusive actions any longer.

The second two-by-four is best described as "resource constraints." If your company survives the next ten to twenty years without proactively embracing sustainability, then you're going to hit the wall when your fuel and materials costs rise to unprecedented levels and your rare earth metals are suddenly simply not available. So you pick it. Do you want to internalize your externalities now when it costs less to do so? Or do you want to hit the wall and then scramble to merely survive?

As companies internalize their external costs, two things will happen. First, the global economy will shift from an economic model in which waste is waste and in which zero-sum game competition is the norm, to the Collaboration Economy, where business and social dimensions are combining both to place a recognized and fungible value on waste in all its forms and, ultimately, to change what is considered by stakeholders to be acceptable value creation by companies.

As the private sector begins to embrace the ethos of the Collaboration Economy, it will evaluate the rules of engagement with competitors. Said simply, problems held in common will require solutions developed and agreed on in common. This is the second aspect of business activity that will change as companies grasp, embrace, and internalize the enormity of their external costs.

The global economy itself is morphing from one that sees waste as an acceptable by-product to one that sees waste as squandered financial resources. This shift will align the interests of the public sector, the private sector, and society writ large. Smart companies will strengthen this alignment and find ways to profit as a result.

Why You Should Read This Book

The Collaboration Economy will primarily cover the private sector's role in this evolution. Chief among findings is that the private sector alone cannot force this transition to occur. Acting ahead of the coming curve, a small but growing group of stalwart companies, enterprises with massive and far-reaching scale, are altering their business models to embrace the need for cross-sector collaboration, and to invest in it. The one common theme among their individual actions is a deep-set intention to renew how their respective industries create value for their stakeholders, including shareholders, employees, and supplier partners. Although the corporate sector is the focus of this book, the public sector and our global society will heavily influence our dialogue.

The Collaboration Economy equips companies of all sizes to change their industries' business models by detailing replicable adjustments in three areas of business activity: competitive strategy, corporate culture, and operations. The first area focuses on how companies craft competitive strategies that embrace, not ignore, social conditions and dimensions. Gone are the days when a company can succeed in perpetuity on the back of a competitive strategy whose success requires only "in-house" resources. Said differently, competitive strategies must now reflect an ever more interconnected world, with problems much larger than any one company's resources can solve. In this book, you will learn how to craft these types of competitive strategies, in part by better understanding how to piece together, manage, and enhance today's sustainable "value chains."

Much as a boat needs to be primed before it can be painted, a company's culture must be altered before the company can execute its new competitive strategy. *The Collaboration Economy* will detail the various mind-set shifts companies need to make if they are to build coalitions, view all vendors as partners, and share financial burdens in order to split the spoils of collective efforts with rivals. In the culture section of *The Collaboration Economy*, you will learn how to identify and overcome a variety of institutional mind-sets that prevent sustainability- and competitive strategy–oriented change from taking hold not only within your company but also within your industry.

Experience has shown that if left unexecuted, even the greatest competitive strategies are not worth the paper on which they were written. That's why the third area is operations. The global push toward achieving a state of sustainable development has made the internalization of externalities a nonnegotiable part of companies' financial performance and fiduciary responsibilities. Reduction of these external costs represents a vital reason why it is in rivals' collective best interests to work together upstream in the supply chain, not just downstream in consumer market development. *The Collaboration Economy* will equip you to alter your procurement, logistics, and operations activities to lower and manage not only these external costs, such as the economic cost of sending waste to landfills, but also the partnerships with vendors, rivals, local communities, and other strange bedfellows in the process.

Certainly there have been books written about how competitors can collaborate. Primary among these books is Brandenburger and Nalebuff's *Co-opetition*,[2] although obviously others also exist. We can build on the lessons from these books by exploring intra-industry collaboration *upstream* (that is, supply chain management). Because the vast majority of external costs that companies create occur upstream in the supply chain, a guide to reduce these costs through influence, not unilateral command and control, will make a valuable contribution to the business literature.

To be clear, the scope of collaboration we will explore encompasses all three sectors. But whereas the public and social sectors have worked together for the common good before, we are in the early phase of the journey that now integrates the private sector into the collaboration calculus.

The three sectors' actions over the next decade will determine the quality of life our descendants will experience. Muhtar Kent, CEO of Coca-Cola, calls this group of sectors (private, public, social) the Golden Triangle: "Given the complexity of today's issues, it's challenging for a single company or industry to make a material difference on its own. Instead, we have to rely on partnerships that basically connect across what I call the 'Golden Triangle': business, government, and civil society. It is only then can we leverage the power of all of those to then make a sustainable difference." The only way we can meet our separate but interdependent goals of growth and sustainable development is if the Golden Triangle creates a beautiful jazz ensemble of blended actions.

The Collaboration Economy's Structure

The Collaboration Economy consists of three parts. Part One shows why and how the transition from the Waste Economy to the Collaboration Economy is happening. The one chapter in Part One brings the Collaboration Economy to life. In the first half of Chapter One, we will explore the various roadblocks industry must navigate to simultaneously achieve greater prosperity and global sustainable development. The chapter's second half provides a replicable framework for all to use in order to nurture cross-sector coalitions.

Part Two consists of six chapters. Each focuses on a particular industry or system of our global economy. These systems— energy, recycling, food, shipbreaking, individual consumption, and water—form the foundation not only for the global economy but for our collective survival as well. Each system faces at least one vexing environmental or societal challenge it must resolve in order to sustain itself over the long term. Therefore, it is not surprising that these six areas are transitioning to a cross-sector collaborative approach to their business models in order to create value not only for shareholders but for all stakeholders. As you read through each chapter, look at how the entity featured builds on and uses the Collaboration Economy framework introduced in Chapter One.

Numerous senior public and private sector leaders have joined me in the development of The Collaboration Economy. This approach afforded me access to not only these leaders' steps but also their mind-sets—access that one cannot glean from one or two interviews alone. Most chapters in Part Two are the product of coauthorship with one or more senior leaders of the global economy. Each chapter delves into a particular set of actions under way, driven by the leader(s) with whom I coauthored the chapter, intended to bring the system in question to a new stage of vitality.

Part Three consists of three chapters. Chapter Eight deals with the question of CEO leadership in the Collaboration Economy. This chapter discusses the most salient lessons learned and leadership traits culled from in-depth conversations with many of the world's top leaders. Chapter Nine details the specific and replicable tactics the companies featured in *The Collaboration Economy* are employing to integrate social dimensions in their strategies, their corporate cultures, and their business operations. Chapter Ten offers a glimpse into the future of the Collaboration Economy.

Call to Action

Whether you believe in the science of climate change or the ethos of sustainability is now moot. Our world, including the business world, is changing, **right now, this minute.** A perfect storm comprising myriad elements has formed to agitate for lasting change in the corporate sector. Among the elements of this perfect storm are a crumbling urban infrastructure, consumption far outstripping the Earth's ability to keep pace, and rampant poverty as some of the many reasons behind society's drive to challenge the status quo. Indeed, social dimensions are becoming as critical to corporate performance as corporate strategy itself.

Although *The Collaboration Economy* explores sustainability's impact on the global economy, the book will focus on the industry-level business-model changes brave individual companies are supporting. These changes are altering the traditional rules of competitive strategy. In this way, *The Collaboration Economy* is at its core a treatise on competitive strategy.

These brave companies will benefit financially from their efforts. The benefits will in part derive from the inevitable reaction of the corporate masses, who will wrongly deem such change either nominal or ineffective. But as I learned so many years ago, there's a fool in every game of poker. If you don't know who the fool is, it is probably you. The brave few agitating for and driving change will benefit in ways that will ultimately make the many envious. You are faced with a choice: Which future will you support: prosperity or economic obsolescence?

Part One

WELCOME TO THE COLLABORATION ECONOMY

I

THE COLLABORATION ECONOMY: PROSPERITY AND SOCIAL DIMENSIONS ALIGNED

If you want to go quickly, you walk fast and you walk alone. But if you want to go far, you walk with others.

—African proverb

The Swiss village of Zermatt is situated in the German-speaking section of Valais, one of the twenty-six member states of Switzerland. Home to about fifty-eight hundred residents, Zermatt has an economy that relies on tourism—for good reason. Zermatt is located at the base of the Mattertal, a gorgeous valley at the bottom of many of Switzerland's tallest mountains. Visitors seeking to climb, ski, or otherwise enjoy the fabled Matterhorn often start their journey in Zermatt.

Among the features visitors will appreciate about Zermatt are its crisp mountain air and its very quiet modes of transportation. The village is an internal-combustion-engine-free and car-free zone. Just about every vehicle in Zermatt is battery powered . . . and completely silent. Zermatt takes pride in keeping the air, and the view of the Matterhorn, as clear as possible.

One way to view the Matterhorn is from the windows of the Matterhorn Glacier Paradise Restaurant. Built nearly four thousand meters high up on the peak of the Klein Matterhorn (meaning "little Matterhorn"), a brother mountain to the Matterhorn, the restaurant offers patrons once-in-a-lifetime views of the surrounding area. From the Klein Matterhorn, visitors can on a clear day view forty peaks, each standing over thirteen thousand feet. On any given day, patrons can dine on a choice of Asian cuisine as well as traditional specialties.

But if not for two events, neither the Matterhorn Glacier Paradise Restaurant nor the Monte Rosa group of mountains, which include both the Matterhorn and the Klein Matterhorn, would exist. The installation of a cable car connecting the Klein Matterhorn to the cable car system starting in Zermatt was vital to the eventual existence of the Matterhorn Glacier Paradise Restaurant. Between its completion in December 1979 and 2005, over fourteen million passengers used the "Suspensionlift Trockener Steg." Prior to the installation of this cable car, visiting the Klein Matterhorn was nearly impossible.

The second event was purely natural: the advance and subsequent retreat of glaciers that both provided the materials for and subsequently carved the Monte Rosa group of peaks. Without the glaciers that formed the Matterhorn, Zermatt might not have become the well-trafficked ski resort it is today. There would not have been a business opportunity for the Matterhorn Group to develop the Matterhorn Glacier Paradise Restaurant.[1] And there certainly would not have been the need to install the Suspensionlift Trockener Steg. In other words, it is fair to say that this particular set of glaciers changed not only the physical landscape but also the business landscape of the Valais canton (member state) in southern Switzerland.

In the same way that the glaciers changed Switzerland, the sustainable development movement (SDM) is changing the business world today. That is, much as glaciers built themselves up over a period of time, the SDM built itself up over time, with Rachel Carson's 1962 publication, *Silent Spring*, providing the movement's first watershed moment. Glaciers brought rocks, soil, and other materials to the landscapes they covered; the SDM has brought new regulations, new markets, and new accepted types of partners to the commercial landscape. Over time, the glaciers receded, revealing new physical boundaries (such as the Matterhorn) and weather patterns that carved and otherwise altered the landscape the glaciers left behind. The SDM's impact is also coming into view. In particular, the SDM has forever altered the boundaries of business competition as well as the very means by which business develops and disperses value to shareholders and stakeholders.[2]

The enormity of the tasks at hand dwarf the kinetic energy one company or organization alone can unleash. Leading every wave of disruption is a group of companies that blaze a trail to a new era of prosperity. Today the most agile of these companies are doing what they have always done best . . . they're adapting again. They are evolving into what I call *orchestrators*.

Welcome to the Collaboration Economy

Orchestrators are managing a portfolio of initiatives and initiative structures to achieve their collective goals. Consider the Coca-Cola Company. Coca-Cola has made and documented a commitment to place water stewardship at the center of its enterprise strategy. We will explore its specific set of initiatives in Chapter Seven. For now, it is worth noting that some of the company's initiatives are conducted unilaterally, some are business-to-business, some are executed with nongovernmental organizations (NGOs), some are with government entities in the form of public-private partnerships (PPPs), and many are conducted alongside a mix of government entities and NGOs.

Orchestrators are leading and shaping the evolution of our current economic system. It is time that such leadership emerged, because the human hand in waste and climate change is no longer acceptable. Inaction is no longer acceptable. Underinvestment in infrastructure is no longer acceptable. Acting alone when the common interest is at stake is no longer acceptable. Said simply, orchestrators are working with unique sets of partners in order to fight these battles.

Transitioning from the Waste Economy to a Better Economic System

But what are we evolving our economic system into? The best way to view the differences between the business world pre- and posteconomic evolution is to look at the ongoing transition from what I've come to call the Waste Economy to the Collaboration Economy.

The Waste Economy is an economic system in which growth is dependent on ever-increasing levels of consumption. There are few, if any, costs associated with the disposal of unwanted materials and products. The civil sector seeks instant gratification, the public sector acts in terms of short-term election cycles, and the private sector is fixated on feeding the quarterly earnings beast.

The Waste Economy is driven by unsustainable consumption. That is, our consumption of natural resources is far exceeding our recurring supply of resources. The math behind our current global economic model is rapidly approaching its natural limits. The awareness of and care for these natural limits is a by-product of the sustainability "glacier" I described earlier. Every year, we use the equivalent of 1.3 to 1.5 Earths to satisfy our demand for and use of goods. Considering that our global population is forecast to exceed nine billion by 2050, it is not a stretch to say that at our current consumption rate, we would consume roughly four Earths annually by 2050.

The Collaboration Economy is an economic system in which smart growth, fueled by collaborative initiatives, serves as a vehicle to accelerate the journey toward sustainable development. Consumed resources are viewed as fungible building blocks of sustained success. The private, public, and civil sectors balance short-term needs with scales of thoughts, of plans, and of actions that occur over the long term.

This notion of collaboration across sectors and within industries might sound like an idealist's dream. But given our broken global economic model, now is not the time to simply dream of moral victories. Our future is dependent on tangible action *today* that yields a steady stream of meaningful impacts. Given our limited financial and natural resources, we must carefully consider our decisions about which initiatives to bring to scale for global impact.

Can the Kind of Collaboration We're Exploring Truly Make a Positive Impact on Our Global Economy?

To answer this question, let's first agree on a definition of *economy*. For the purpose of our discussion, an economy consists of the collective output of a region's labor, capital, land resources, manufacturing, trade, production, distribution, and consumption of goods and services.[3]

This definition implies a linear relationship between production and consumption. That is to say that the definition does not value *circular* economic activities, such as actions to reclaim and reuse materials postconsumption. A linear model of production through consumption can last in perpetuity only if we assume an infinite flow of resources, materials, and satisfied workers.

But we *know* that these resources are finite. Add in our capital constraints, and it is obvious that we have limits to growth. Indeed, this subject was well covered forty years ago in the watershed book *Limits to Growth*, by Donella Meadows and others. The accuracy of their predictions in 1972 is demonstrated by our failure to provide even the most basic goods and services to many of the seven billion people today, let alone well over nine billion. The global energy, food, and water systems are stressed for a variety of reasons, all of which we'll discuss in subsequent chapters.

Some will ask whether we *even need growth*. What if we collectively targeted a 0 percent growth rate? Wouldn't this "neutral growth" help us at least manage our resource consumption rate so that we would not need to change our production-consumption pattern? Some experts have persuasively argued for a "steady-state" world—a world where we have no additional economic expansion, a world where we legislate limits on consumption.

This won't work.

Put aside the obvious humanistic challenges to achieving such a steady state. Even if the existing population consumed at its current level, the addition of two-and-a-half billion people over the next four decades alone necessitates growth. So for the foreseeable future, whether or not these experts approve, the pursuit of "necessary growth" will remain an essential ingredient in our global economic system.

How Can Growth Accelerate the Journey to Sustainable Development?

So the question then shifts from *Do we need growth?* to *How can growth support our sustainable development goals and aspirations?* To tackle this new question, let's first define the elements of growth. In no particular order, the sphere of growth includes increased levels of consumption, enabled by expanded levels of employment, raised living standards, and a steady stream of start-up entities and related new ideas, all supported by affordable investment capital.

Growth has come with a serious price: lasting and ever more obvious ethical, environmental, and social impacts. Few would disagree that our challenges are many and seemingly overshadow our significant financial, technological, and human resources.

But I don't believe that we will experience a global case of Malthusian economics. This isn't our first dance with the abyss. We've faced times of great struggle before. The Great Depression. World Wars I and II and their aftermaths. In each time, the human spirit has persevered. It fueled our survival; it spurred us to greater heights. The human spirit still exists today. So, too, does the desire for a better life, not only for us but also for our children and grandchildren.

The human spirit and the desire for a better life are a powerful one-two combination that once again will lead us out of our global mess. For in front of the entrepreneurs, the activists, the financiers, and the many among our elected officials truly committed to collective greatness stands a new mountain to climb: ensuring that our future generations will have water, food, energy, and resources in abundance, with nominal to no damage inflicted upon the Earth as a result of the consumption of these resources. To achieve this vision, technology must advance beyond our wildest dreams; financial roadblocks must be overcome creatively and ethically; partnerships with strange bedfellows must be forged; and new behaviors must be adopted.

Let's stay with our theme of "necessary growth" for a moment to illustrate the differences between the two economic models. As our population expands, the global food system will be asked to feed more people. Growth in this case is inevitable; the question thus becomes, *How can we grow the food system's scale to meet these additional needs?* As we will explore in Chapter Four, experts believe that a vital part of the solution rests in our ability to integrate farmers with small agricultural plots—so-called smallholders—into the global food system. Unilever is leading the way in bringing these smallholders—and their agriculture yields—to the food system. As a result, Unilever is preparing itself to grow alongside the market, while improving smallholders' lives by equipping these farmers to achieve a higher living standard.

In time, will all growth be additive to the sustainable development journey? Certainly not. Then should conspicuous consumption (excessive consumptive demand satisfied by products not sustainably produced) be shunned, if not regulated against? I leave this to the collective wisdom of the Golden Triangle—of which we're all a part—to decide.

The Collaboration Economy Will Kick-Start Economic Development

Allow me to share a few numbers to illustrate how a global embrace of sustainability through collaboration will lead to marked prosperity. Consider the U.S. GDP benefits of

- **Higher recycling rates.** As we will see in Chapter Three, the U.S. recycling system is underperforming. U.S. citizens (myself included) send to landfill seven out of every ten plastic bottles we consume. By increasing our rate of recycling, new jobs would be added to the economy, and we would turn more postconsumer materials into reused materials. The additive benefit to U.S. GDP is about $20 billion annually.

- **More efficient transportation.** Still discussing the United States, traffic congestion on our roads results in 1.9 billion gallons of gas wasted per year, and costs drivers over $100 billion in wasted fuel and lost time.[4] Improvements in the quality of our roads, combined with an increased reliance on public transportation, could reduce this waste by 20 to 50 percent, yielding cost savings of between $20 to $50 billion annually.

- **Infrastructure investments.** Said simply, infrastructure investments put to work people who, as a group, suffer higher unemployment rates than the U.S. workforce as a whole. Among those who gain employment as a result of additional infrastructure investment, the unemployment rate has averaged approximately 13 percent over the past twelve months. This is more than one-and-a-half times the current national unemployment rate.[5]

- **Improved personal health.** Although the topic is not covered in this book, the issue of costs borne by individuals for obesity- and diabetes-related health care presents an additional potential boost to the economy. Analysis reveals that Americans spend roughly $170 billion on attaining such health care services. An improvement in personal health as a result of increased exercise rates and focus on nutrition, as well as a greater alignment between food and pharmaceutical companies on the topic of disease prevention, could reduce the amount spent on treatment medicines and related health care services. Lower health care expenses could increase available disposable income for individuals, leading to a consumption boost to the GDP.

- **Improved worker productivity.** Far greater than the potential addition to GDP activity through a boost to individual consumption (as a result of having more disposable income) is the benefit of a healthier population. The logic is that healthier employees would lead to a reduction in absenteeism and possibly health care costs (at least per employee), and pave the way to an even more productive workforce. Indeed, a recent Gallup poll revealed that "full-time workers in the U.S. who are overweight or obese and have other chronic health conditions miss an estimated 450 million additional days of work each year compared with healthy workers, resulting in an estimated cost of more than $153 billion in lost productivity annually."[6]

Innovation that can be commercialized will further expand when the best minds work together with the coalitions that can fund, refine, and scale best ideas quickly. Add the GDP boost from innovation to the aforementioned GDP boosts, and it becomes clear why I view cross-sector collaboration as the path to a new economic system. After all, which approach is more likely to realize these GDP boosts: a go-it-alone mentality or cross-sector collaboration?

Said simply, the Collaboration Economy will prove to be a step toward an improved global economic system. Through increased inclusion of those too small or too "out of the way," we will accelerate social development among the disaffected. Partnerships among the private, public, and social sectors will lead to improved infrastructure for energy, food, and water. Smarter recycling systems will close the loopholes in our Waste Economy, simultaneously slowing the growth rate of demand for raw materials and creating better-paying, safer jobs for our local communities.

However, we must face the fact that no silver bullet exists to cure all of the root causes of our ills. Avarice, unsustainable debt loads, distrust of potential cross-sector (and intra-industry) partners, ecological and social damage already done—all of these characteristics and impacts of the Waste Economy will continue to exist. So the Collaboration Economy will not and cannot be a panacea for all of our challenges. This said, moving toward the Collaboration Economy surely would be a significant step in the right direction.

How the Collaboration Economy Is Coming to Life

The private sector's pursuit of sustainability has served to put this evolution in motion. Over the past decade, the number of companies committing to become sustainable has significantly grown. Their intentions are noble, their actions just. Many have found ways to improve their top and bottom lines by connecting sustainability to their competitive strategies. In the process, they've reduced their environmental impacts and increased their attentiveness to issues of social equality.[7]

Although these individual companies' efforts are laudable, collectively they have not sufficiently increased our world's ability to outrace time. Huge amounts of financial capital, combined with human know-how and effective consensus-driven management practices, are required to solve our deep-seated and interconnected challenges. While the public sector debates the best road forward, time ticks away. The market plays an indispensable role in enabling the achievement of global sustainability.

Orchestrators are catalyzing two distinct changes to their industries' business models. First, these companies are setting enterprise-level strategy goals that they cannot achieve alone.

Consider this: stalwart organizations such as GE used to set stretch goals that drove their companies to new heights. Be number one or number two, or get out of the market. Although this strategy is well known, what's less well dissected is that GE and similar companies set stretch goals that did not require significant, if any, collaboration with outsiders. In other words, these companies had the internal capabilities to achieve their stretch goals. As long as they applied their core capabilities correctly and swiftly, they controlled their own growth trajectory.

The second change these companies are making to their industries' business models is to increase reliance on the civil sector as partner, to whom a greater share of prosperity must flow—not because as a global society we are choosing a hybrid form of capitalistic socialism, but because better-compensated farmers, fishers, laborers, and other workers will in turn be motivated to work harder and smarter and be capable of spending more in the open market. Prosperity breeds prosperity. Companies that equip their employees and suppliers to rise to new economic heights will in turn be lifted to greater financial performance as a result.

Consider Unilever. In 2010, the company's CEO, Paul Polman, introduced the Unilever Sustainable Living Plan (USLP), which represented a new, daring goal for his company. At its heart, the USLP aspires to decouple growth from its impact on society. This goal is a departure from the traditional business canon that suggests that growth and environmental impact move in the same direction.

Breaking away from this traditional business tenet sounds impossible, right? But Unilever knows something others don't: that relying more deeply on others, including its suppliers and smallholder farmers, is the only way to usher in its next phase of prosperity. Identifying reliance as an essential ingredient is one thing; developing the trust and resultant participation of others is another. The USLP endeavors to move from a commitment to a vision to the achievement of that vision.

Orchestrators as Landmark Leaders

Much as the Matterhorn rose out of the glaciers, orchestrators are rising from the changed SDM landscape. Orchestrators are organizations that pull together like-minded companies, social entities, and public sector agencies to achieve a vital goal that serves the common interest.

Orchestrators are bridging gaps that underinvestment, interconnectedness of interests and challenges, hyperconsumption, and a lack of thoughtful public policy have created. Although an orchestrator can be a private, public, or social sector entity, most today are companies. These companies, such as Coca-Cola, understand that their future depends on the availability of natural resources, such as water, to both their operations and their stakeholders. Coca-Cola is building a coalition of the willing because it has discovered that ensuring access to water requires a far greater set of resources (financial, technical, human) than any one company can bring to the table.

Three factors are driving the rise of the orchestrators. First is the relationship among the challenges we face. Said simply, these wicked challenges are so deeply intertwined that they elude any one entity's ability to overcome them. Second, the void in global public leadership necessitates other sectors' leadership. Third, the private sector is realizing that providing cross-sector leadership is also in its enlightened self-interest.

Intertwined Crises

In September 2012, CNN wondered whether America was in for another Dust Bowl era.[8] From 1931 to 1939, America suffered through the original Dust Bowl, an effect of a prolonged drought that covered the American Midwest. It was so severe that it forced 3.5 million residents to abandon their Great Plains homes. An infection called "dust pneumonia," caused by fast-moving dust clouds, killed thousands more.

America in September 2012 faced similar dire straits caused by volatile weather: 63 percent of the United States was in the grip of moderate to exceptional drought conditions; 80 percent of U.S. agricultural land was being affected by the drought; and the forecast number of corn bushels to be harvested was four billion less than predicted at the beginning of the year.[9]

We can draw two conclusions from the U.S. drought of 2012. First, weather has become incredibly volatile. Second, water availability and food security are inextricably linked. The drought is illustrative of the deep and intertwined environmental and social challenges we collectively face. Individually and collectively, these problems are disrupting our most basic building blocks of life: food, water, and air. Among this set of entrenched problems are

- The pace and impact of climate change
- Volatile weather evolving into the new normal weather
- A flawed global food system in need of steps to secure it
- Unreliable access to sufficient clean drinking water
- An energy system that fails to balance economic and environmental development
- Postconsumer-use materials that are all too often treated as unwanted waste instead of as imprisoned financial resources
- Societal discord with governing bodies

I could list many more "must fix" challenges, but you get the point. The breadth and depth of these problems are well covered elsewhere. Rather than recap these challenges, suffice it to say that their cumulative impact is thus far outpacing the improvements made by modified private, public, and social sector activities. We desperately need a universally agreed-on set of approaches that meet global society's needs today without comprising its ability to meet its needs tomorrow.

Two factors make this set of entrenched problems all the more vexing. The first factor is chronic underinvestment in infrastructure, one of the common elements that ties these problems together. The Organisation for Economic Co-operation and Development (OECD) has forecast that globally we need to invest at least $53 trillion in infrastructure by 2030 to continue global trade. This amount is forecast to be about 3.5 percent of aggregate global GDP between now and 2030.[10] (To put this number in perspective, consider that the United States invests about 2.4 percent of its GDP in infrastructure annually.) And the frustrating truth is that the estimates of needed investment are even higher when they factor in climate change abatement and related sustainable development technologies. The OECD estimates this additional investment at about $45 trillion.

Second is that these challenges are deeply intertwined. In addition to the U.S. drought, think about the global energy system. Electricity is generated from a range of power sources, from coal to wind. Whereas some sources are environmentally conscious (for example, renewable sources), others are inexpensive, abundant, and available (for example, hydrocarbons, such as coal). Preparing hydrocarbons for use consumes copious amounts of water. Consider natural gas accessed through hydraulic fracturing, also known as fracking. While the United States is realizing a "dream scenario"—abundant sources of natural gas and the technology to access it—fracking comes with several financial, environmental, and social costs. Chief among these costs is the method's outright reliance on water. For example, millions of gallons of water are needed to operate a single fracking well. A growing group of farmers, long counted on for agricultural output, are instead leasing their land to fracking operations for tangible returns on their sweat and investment.

To recount, the United States has an abundance of natural gas. The gas is accessible through the use of current technology. There's enough gas available both to greatly reduce the country's reliance on foreign sources of oil *and* to increase its fuel exports.

But the economic advantages come with water and food costs, among other challenges (as we will see in Chapter Two). Similar quandaries are playing out in the food, water, materials sourcing, and shipbreaking sectors, among others.

Lack of Global Public Sector Leadership

Another event in September 2012 crystallized for me why orchestrators are needed. The event, in this case a two-day meeting, was held at the Algonquin Club in Boston. The guest speaker on the second day was Ian Bremmer, president of Eurasia Group and one of the world's leading experts on political science. During his talk, Ian shared five reasons why he believes there exists a lack of leadership from the global public sector to solve vexing problems:

1. There are too many countries that matter now. Therefore, there are too many countries that can say no when specific action is needed.
2. These countries are too different. Their strong ideological differences serve as a roadblock to common views, common values, and a common way forward.
3. Countries of scale have limited capacity to provide global leadership. Consider this: New Zealand, with four million residents, has more diplomats deployed abroad than India, with a population of over one billion.
4. The United States is less interested in providing this leadership. Being the world's policeman is too costly politically and economically.
5. The key allies of the United States, such as the European Union and Japan, are much less interested, too. The EU is understandably focused on saving the EU, while Japan is working through a two-decade-long recession, among other issues.

Ian's talk put succinct words to my own view that the public sector alone is unlikely to provide (if not incapable of providing) the sustained leadership required to solve our environmental, social, financial, and infrastructure challenges.

To Ian's list I would propose two more challenges: financial constraints and time scales. Our world as a whole faces many deep-seated challenges; so do our individual countries. We're in a period of tepid economic growth globally. To pay for the items on the public agendas, our public sector representatives must deal with the harsh reality of financial constraints. At the risk of over-simplification: our public sector representatives simply do not have the financial resources needed to invest in every worthy cause. They must choose among several options, including (1) devaluing their currencies (in other words, printing more money to pay for more services), (2) attempting to borrow more money, or (3) making hard investment decisions. Choice 1 is the least attractive of the lot. Choice 2 is the most oft picked option, but it, too, is hindered by several factors, including debt ceilings, debt-to-GDP ratios of 100 percent or higher, and economic zone instability. Choice 3 is picked at least equally as often as choice 2.

So the inconvenient truth is that the public sector must make hard choices about investments. It is instructive to review the various pressures our elected officials face when making these choices. One of the most influential pressures is the specter of time scales. Simply put, elected officials want to be reelected. To earn their constituents' votes, they need to show the value they have provided while in office during their current term. As a result, shorter-term investments are often given higher priority than longer-term investments. Put yourself in the shoes of an elected official in a contested district. You have two options for investment: one that will provide immediate relief and one that will require a longer time period before paying off. Which would you choose?

For all these reasons, it's apparent that leadership must come from somewhere else.

Here we turn to private-public partnerships (PPPs) for inspiration. PPPs have been thoroughly dissected. A PPP involves a contract between a public sector authority and a private party, according to which the private party provides a public service or project and assumes substantial financial, technical, and operational risk in that project.[11]

PPPs have been an effective way to develop trust between the public and private sectors. But to this point, they have not sufficiently increased our ability to outrace time's unfailing progression.

So let's be hypothetical for a second. If PPPs provided sufficient funding to tackle not only our infrastructure investment needs but also our sustainable development needs, would we be able to outrace time?

In my humble opinion: no. Because even if financing needs were met, issues ranging from systemic effectiveness globally to best-of-breed technology must be addressed.

Interest of the Commons Now in the Common Interest

Where will global leadership on growth and sustainable development come from if not from the global public sector? There truly is only one answer: leadership must come from *all of us*—the private, public, and civil sectors. We need to throw our lots in together; otherwise we should simply give up.

As Andy, Tim Robbins's character, said to Red, Morgan Freeman's character, in *The Shawshank Redemption*, "I guess it comes down to a simple choice, really. Get busy living or get busy dying."

Same simple choice here.

Orchestrators are choosing to get busy living. They are cultivating networks of entities from the private, public, and civil sectors in order to combine the right tools and skills needed to solve specific challenges. These networks are both vital and modular; orchestrators serve as facilitators to bring together the right combination of talents to meet the unique characteristics of the problems they plan to resolve. They have to be; like snowflakes, these problems are related but greatly different. The differences are most visible along geographical, philosophical, environmental, technological, cultural, and financial lines.

For networks to form, operate, and remain aligned, each entity must perceive that it is receiving value in exchange for its contributions, especially in the absence of effective policy that in some way demands compliance in service of achieving a common goal. More and more it appears as though the interests of each sector are becoming aligned and intertwined.

As mentioned earlier, the private sector is awakening to two revelations. The first is that individual companies no longer control, but now can only influence, their own destinies. If they are to offer goods and services, they are wholly reliant on stakeholders worldwide to provide everything from supplies to local operating licenses. The second revelation is that stakeholders wield a far sharper and more powerful sword than ever before. Activists' voices are amplified by critical-mass adoption of social media; no corporate misstep goes unnoticed. Companies can no longer act like bulls in a china shop; the veiled threat of losing their right to exist is now powerful enough to influence their business behaviors.

At the same time, the civil sector is increasingly viewing corporations as potentially useful partners. This is because sophisticated members of the civil sector, mainly but not exclusively in the form of NGOs, have come to their own revelation: that they alone cannot solve the vexing local problems that hinder their development today and the prospects for their survival tomorrow. They must reach out to entities with far greater resources than their own in order to improve their current situation and ensure that they will live to see a satisfactory tomorrow. In the eyes of many among the civil sector's representatives, corporations are evolving from being the enemy to being part of the solution.

The public sector's interests are becoming aligned with private and social sector interests. As successful start-up companies emerge, innovation and economic development flourish. As larger companies become ever larger and more profitable, they are capable of hiring more citizens. And as we've already witnessed from the sixfold growth in PPPs between 1990 and 2005 in Europe, for example, governments and corporations already see common value in working together to achieve infrastructure solutions that benefit both sides.

To be clear, the private-public-social nexus enjoys neither complete agreement nor alignment. Witness the Occupy movement, for example. Many within society eye corporations with great suspicion, if not outright contempt. Surveys of society's level of trust in corporations and elected officials are documenting all-time or near all-time lows. Every batch of apples has at least one that can spoil the lot. Sadly, we regularly see new cases of corporate avarice, if not clear malfeasance.

This said, there is a growing recognition among these three sectors that we need one another. Given the depth of our interconnected challenges, I anticipate that this recognition will continue to increase over the next several years.

The Collaboration Economy Framework

Although we are in the relative early stages of trisector collaboration, my study of the orchestrators in this book reveals that they have gone through a surprisingly common set of steps to coax a result from their coalitions that is far greater than the mere sum of the parts.

As already noted, corporations are at the heart of the examples covered in this book. So in the interest of enabling other companies to answer the call for leadership, I have developed the Collaboration Economy framework (see Figure 1.1) with the assumption that a company serves as the catalyst of cross-sector

Figure 1.1. Collaboration Economy Framework

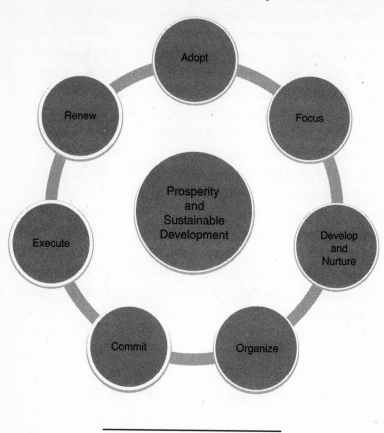

collaboration. Although I designed the framework on the basis of lessons shared from companies, I've seen both NGOs and public sector agencies use the same approach.

Adopt a Collaboration Mind-Set

The starting point of the Collaboration Economy framework is deceptively simple. All your company needs to do is understand that its future performance is dependent on the actions of an interdependent group of shareholders, stakeholders, competitors, and employees. Once you accept this perspective, your company will begin to understand that its ability to succeed is based on its ability to influence, work with, and persuade these stakeholders to work alongside one another.

This shift in mind-set will lead to a change to your corporate culture. You will want to hire and develop leaders who are adept at building relationships with a range of stakeholders. In this way, your company will begin its transition into a leadership role within the Collaboration Economy. And remember, competitive advantage in the Collaboration Economy comes not from first-mover advantage but from the elimination of most of the road-blocks in your way and the reduction of the external costs you plan to internalize.

Focus on What Matters Most

The next step in the Collaboration Economy framework is to commit to achieving one overarching goal that is in the interests of both the commons and your company—for example, water stewardship, global food security, or a healthy energy system that balances economic and environmental needs.

In this step, your company identifies at least one natural resource without which it cannot survive—food to a foods company, water to a beverage company, energy to an energy services company, and the like. Then your company considers the needs of its stakeholders, paying particular attention to the local communities in which your company operates. You will know that your company has picked the right resource on which to focus if that resource is also critical to the survival and development of these local communities.

Develop and Nurture Relationships

If your company is going to rely on stakeholders and partners, then it needs to develop a set of relationships with various entities. Orchestrators are building mutually trusting relationships with NGOs, local community activists, rivals, and government agencies. Their insight is not so much seen in their decision to build relationships as in their decision to build relationships with the *right* entities.

By "right entities," I mean organizations that are committed to ensuring the quality and quantity of the resource on which your company is focused. For this step, you are looking for entities that have talents that complement your own. You're looking for local community connections, specific expertise, access to unique technologies, and relationships with government agencies that your organization might not have. The broader the range of talents your group of relationships comprises, the more likely it is that your company will achieve its worthy goals.

One suggestion from the orchestrators I studied will help you build a set of effective relationships: face-to-face meetings remain the most effective way to build relationships. For example, one of my chapter coauthors, Petter Heier, is building a portfolio of relationships with responsible shipbreaking yards in Asia. Although he resides in Oslo, he travels to China and other parts of Asia about once every six weeks in order to build a reliable portfolio of partners.

Organize Your Coalition

To be an orchestrator, your company needs to pull together at least two types of coalitions from among their sets of relationships. The first type consists of the vast majority, if not all, of the entities with which you have relationships, formed in order to work globally to solve the resource challenge you're focused on. As with any joint effort, regularly scheduled meetings with your cross-sector partners will be vital to your organized coalition's success. For legal reasons, I encourage you to engage your company's general counsel in these meetings.

The second type of coalition is best described as "horses for courses." In other words, your company will need to organize the right group of entities from within your set of relationships to accomplish your goals at the level of the local community. As Coca-Cola works to protect the global water system, it is bringing specific entities from within its set of relationships into specific communities, depending on the needs of the local situation.

Commit to Precise Coalition Goals

A commitment to accomplishing precise goals will increase the likelihood that your coalition will succeed. It's not enough to draw up a set of commonly held interests among your coalition members. You need to get each member of your coalition to sign off on the precise goal or goals your coalition aspires to accomplish.

There's a second commitment that your company, serving as an orchestrator, must make: a commitment to operate transparently. Consider Coca-Cola. The company has dedicated itself to serving as a steward of the global water system. The company's ability to achieve its water stewardship goals is wholly dependent on the coalition it is nurturing. These partnerships require Coca-Cola to operate transparently. After all, what truly civic-minded organization would want to work with a company whose intentions and actions are not clear from the start?

Execute Through Your Coalition

Earlier I highlighted the importance of building relationships with entities that have both a common commitment to your resource goal and a complementary set of talents. Once your coalitions have precise goals, it's time to execute: your company can begin to assign specific tasks to specific coalition members to accomplish your goals.

The subject of execution ranks among the most well covered topics in the canon of business thought. There is not much new that my study of orchestrators can add, except this: the orchestra-tor's role does not end at the commitment stage. Now more than ever, orchestrators' success is wholly reliant on their ability to influence and persuade their fellow coalition members to move in a particular direction. Sometimes your company, acting as the orchestrator, will be called on to make a contribution of finan-cial or other resources that exceed the contributions of the other entities in the coalition. Remember, your role in the coalition is to ensure that the coalition jointly solves the resource challenge to which you've committed. Fairness is measured not in terms of your unique contribution to the coalition's efforts but rather in terms of the effectiveness of the coalition's efforts overall.

Renew Your Coalition's Plans

As is true of any worthwhile endeavor, rare is the effort that is perfect from the start. The most effective coalition is the one that is committed to continuous improvement. I cannot overem-phasize the importance of building a commitment to learning into your coalition's governing principles. As your group com-pletes a project, lessons learned from the experience should be documented and shared with the entire coalition. In this way, the coalition as a whole benefits by learning from the lessons identified by the few.

The orchestrators I studied use the extended capabilities they can access through their collaborative relationships to start to plan and carry out specific projects and initiatives. These com-panies use five steps to implement change at a local community level:

1. The orchestrator and its coalition develop or identify a relevant, nascent technology to pilot-test as the beginning of the technology refinement and learning process.

2. The orchestrator then builds a sense of inevitable adoption of the technology by constantly communicating both inside and outside the coalition.

3. The coalition seeks, or at least seriously considers, legislative help to overcome the limitations of voluntary action.

4. The coalition, spearheaded by the orchestrator, invests its own funds in the emerging project and related technological innovations.

5. The coalition keeps pushing for change while it both pilot-tests the technology and seeks to build political and local community consensus.

As I examined each orchestrator, I found myself wondering whether we are seeing the evolution of companies annealed by the heat of competition for fiscal performance into a softer form of corporate existence. I leave this to the wisdom of the crowd to decide. But know this: a primary driver of leading companies' orchestration efforts is enlightened self-interest. By resolving vexing issues held in common, companies can reduce their costs, increase revenue, and enhance their reputations.

There is another reason behind the private sector's voluntary leadership as orchestrators. More and more companies are waking up to an undeniable truth: without particular natural resources, they will cease to exist. For example, beverage companies like Coca-Cola rely on water; without water, they will not have beverages to sell. Their recognition of this truth has led this small but growing group of companies to readily take on the challenge of orchestration.

Unlike politicians, companies are not hindered by the need for reelection. But their executives are judged in similar fashion by the investment community. Within the private sector, too, infrastructure investments are not considered sexy, especially in comparison to investments in robust and demonstrable pipelines chock-full of disruptive technologies.

Companies such as Unilever are navigating around this pothole. The day Paul Polman, Unilever's CEO, announced that his company would no longer provide quarterly earnings guidance, two things happened. First, the company's stock price decreased by 8 percent—an indication that the investment community wanted to "price in" the uncertainty it felt due to the reduced transparency into Unilever's growth prospects. Second, the company broke the investment community's shackles, which had placed a greater emphasis on short-term results than on long-term investments. Unilever positioned itself to be a reliable, long-term partner for both the public and civil sectors.

What Will the Collaboration Economy Look Like?

The USLP provides a peek into the Collaboration Economy's shape. Paul Polman describes why and how his company is transitioning to the Collaboration Economy:

> Businesses like ours no longer have a choice. Sustainable, equitable growth is the only acceptable model of growth. It is also a very effective one. Growth and sustainability are not in conflict. There is no inherent contradiction between the two. In fact, in our experience, sustainability drives growth.
>
> That is why we are putting "sustainable living" at the heart of everything we do. We have found that once you start looking at product development, sourcing and manufacturing through a sustainability lens, it opens up great opportunities for innovation and cost reduction.[12]
>
> It is also becoming ever clearer that we cannot tackle the big issues alone: much of our progress to date has come where we have worked with others. And at the end of the day, if we achieve our own sustainability targets but no one else follows, we will not have been truly successful.

For that reason we are working with other organizations such as the Consumer Goods Forum, World Economic Forum, World Business Council for Sustainable Development, governments, NGOs and others to drive change. At Unilever we believe collaboration will become the only way of doing business in the future.[13]

Why are companies like Unilever undertaking such change, such risk, and such complexity? It's not altruism, though each company certainly is community minded. It's not a desire to do less harm to the environment, though each sees cost savings from environmental efficiencies. The reason is that each company sees a limit to its own growth under current economic, population growth, and infrastructure conditions.

In response, each of these trailblazing companies is breaking through traditional "go it alone" business practices in order to succeed. A quiver full of unusual arrows, such as hybrid financing tactics, hybrid partnerships, and cross-sector collaborations, are being employed to tackle the largest roadblocks standing in the way of renewed prosperity.

Muhtar Kent, Coca-Cola's chairman and CEO, recently crystallized the ethos of and case for the Collaboration Economy generally and water stewardship specifically when he said, "To make a difference on the challenges we all face—governments, civil society, and businesses must work together as never before. For business leaders in particular, we need to speak up, stand up, and scale up our efforts."

Part Two

BRINGING THE COLLABORATION ECONOMY TO LIFE AND SCALE

2

RENEWING THE GLOBAL ENERGY SECTOR

Eric Lowitt

Chenango County, located at the approximate center of New York State, is home to fifty thousand people. Many of the county's residents are hardworking farmers who have toiled their family-owned lands for generations. Local residents look forward with great anticipation to the seasonal opening of the Chenango County Farmer's Market to buy farm-fresh, locally grown peas, corn, cucumbers, and tomatoes, among other produce.

The county sits on top of the Marcellus Shale, a black shale bed that is estimated to contain enough natural gas to satisfy the entire demand of the United States for two years. The economic value of this natural gas is estimated to be approximately $200 billion.[1]

Farmers in Chenango County, tirelessly working to get ahead or at least to make ends meet, have begun to lease their farmland to fracking companies. Farmers who have leased five hundred or more acres of farmland have received $1 million and more in return.[2] In a county where almost 15 percent of the population resides below the poverty line, leasing farmland for fracking purposes is analogous to winning the lottery.

Proponents of fracking also view the Marcellus Shale and other similar underground shale gas fields within the country's borders as a boon for the U.S. economy. The massive flow of shale gas has led to plummeting natural gas prices, which in turn have lowered costs for both industry and consumers.[3] As reserves increase, shale gas can be exported, providing a way to further improve economic conditions in the United States.

But history instructs us that there is no free lunch. Fracking consumes an incredible amount of water. Indeed, fracking a single shale well requires millions of gallons. As we will explore in Chapter Seven, water worldwide is already dramatically stressed. Increased fracking operations would compete for water with urbanization, agriculture, and basic human consumption needs.

Additional uncertainties further complicate the fracking debate. There is limited transparency in regard to the chemicals used during fracking operations. Research into fracking's long-term effects on the Earth's underground formations, drinking water, food production, and air quality is needed for the public to have confidence in the role fracking should play in our global energy system.

The Global Energy Debate's Three Great Tensions

The aforementioned points of view show why fracking is such an incredibly polarizing economic activity. And in many ways, the fracking debate under way in the United States is a microcosm of the worldwide energy debate. In particular, there are three great tensions that form the foundation of the global energy debate. Unless we resolve these tensions, we will struggle to strengthen the global energy system.

Tension One: Economic Versus External Costs

At the risk of oversimplification, there are two dimensions to the debate over power generation sources: economic costs and external costs. As described in the Introduction, *external costs* are defined as environmental and social costs that occur as a result of an activity. In the case of power generation sources, the main external costs are environmental impacts in the form of greenhouse gas emissions and water consumption.

On one side of the debate are the pundits who believe that the Earth has a large enough stockpile of recoverable energy in the form of fossil fuels to last centuries at current consumption levels. These pundits argue that extracting this energy will not only yield predictable sources of power for generations to come but also lead to a new period of economic growth and prosperity.

On the other side of the debate are the pundits who believe that the extraction and subsequent consumption of fossil fuels will cause significant and irreversible environmental and social damage to the planet. These analysts and related observers are working to dramatically increase the percentage of our energy that is generated from renewable sources, including solar, wind, geothermal, and biomass sources, while also advocating for a significant reduction in the world's consumptive demand for energy.

What is clear is the need to further increase the available supply of energy worldwide, owing to the massive increase in consumptive demand for energy on the part of both the developing countries where disposable income is on the rise and the two-and-a-half billion citizens forecast to be born over the next forty years. And as did previous generations, our current population is demanding an improved standard of living, both for ourselves and for our children.

Tension Two: Limited Funding Availability Versus Needed Infrastructure Upgrades

Part of the method to "solve" tension one will be to upgrade the energy grid. Such a grid ideally would be capable of capturing, transmitting, and distributing ever larger amounts of renewable energy. It would also increase the efficiency of the energy that is transmitted and distributed to consumers. Despite the apparent advantages of upgrading our energy infrastructure, there are a number of roadblocks.

Chief among these roadblocks is the need for copious amounts of financial capital. Indeed, the costs of upgrading our urban energy infrastructure are a substantial part of the estimated $53 trillion that will need to be spent globally in the coming twenty years for urban infrastructure alone.

From where will this funding come? Governments' budgets have reached their borrowing limits; infrastructure upgrade needs far exceed the private sector's financial capacity, let alone appetite; and the same is true of the social sector. Clearly, no one sector is going to be the primary source of funding for necessary infrastructure upgrades.

Tension Three: Waiting for Public Sector Leadership Versus Acting Now

Judging from actions worldwide in general and the United States specifically, it is evident that the public sector is loathe to provide true leadership on the future of the energy system. This should not come as a surprise to most people, as there is a wide range of thorny issues that will ultimately require tough policy decisions.

As noted in Chapter One, elected officials operate on a notoriously short time scale. Investments that benefit their local constituents in two to three years (and then earn the votes of their local constituents) are preferable to massive initiatives that will require a decade or more to provide a combination of financial returns and behavioral change. Among these longer-term initiatives are regulations to encourage renewable energy consumption in place of fossil fuel consumption, actions to mitigate significant swings in oil prices as a result of market speculation on a massive scale, and investments to upgrade our energy infrastructure.

━━━

It is not an overstatement to say that the world's economic development over the next several decades is dependent on the direction taken by the global energy system. Energy is a sector rife with strong and dissenting opinions. Citizens, companies, and sovereign nations alike have a lot to gain—and lose—depending on the outcomes of the debates in regard to the three tensions. Perhaps the most difficult roadblock around which we'll need to navigate is the alarming lack of civil discourse among these separate but interdependent entities. The members of the Golden Triangle—the public, private, and social sectors—are at best stuck in a seemingly endless loop of analysis and debate. At worst, these three sectors are demonstrating a willingness to postpone action in the misguided hope that the energy problem will simply solve itself. In either case, we're not moving nearly fast enough.

This chapter aims to move the energy crisis conversation forward in a respectful manner. We will discuss the components of what we believe is a viable solution to the energy crisis, focusing on General Electric's decision and subsequent effort to bring to life an "ecosystem to create a lasting solution" to the energy crisis. Although GE is the sole company featured in this chapter, our belief, shared by a growing number of stakeholders, is that the platform for civil discourse and action being built by GE can serve as a model for other private, public, and civil society members to collaborate to solve our energy challenges. However, the intent of this chapter isn't to celebrate the leadership of one company but rather to highlight the leading actions a company has taken to catalyze three sectors to find the most appropriate solutions for the energy challenge.

To achieve our goal, we will cover four topics in this chapter. In order, we will explore

- The ongoing debate about hydrocarbon versus clean technology sources of power (in brief)
- The limitations and inefficiency of our current electrical grids worldwide

- An emerging ecosystem to create a lasting solution that will both facilitate and drive the energy challenge debate toward a viable solution
- A call to action for entities from the public, private, and social sectors to join this emerging ecosystem

Power Sources

There are five primary natural resources used for power: coal, natural gas, nuclear, water, and renewable sources. The sources differ in their economic and external costs. This section highlights each source's main relative advantages and disadvantages.

There is no perfect source of power. Some sources, such as coal, oil, and gas, are abundant, accessible, affordable, and distributable through the currently existing infrastructure. But use of these sources comes with a steep environmental price. Other sources, including nuclear, water, and renewable energy, are also abundant and accessible but suffer from their own drawbacks: lack of installed infrastructure, massive infrastructure installation costs, related technologies that are not yet up to the task at scale, and the roadblock of mixed perceptions among private, public, and social sector stakeholders.

The power source debate is ultimately about optimization. For economic reasons, we cannot afford to be 100 percent reliant on renewable energy. Even if we had the financial wherewithal, we just do not have the time; improving the technology and then installing copious amounts of infrastructure will likely require decades.

In the interim, we will need to rely on hydrocarbon power sources. But complete reliance on coal and natural gas yields its own set of roadblocks. At the top of the list is their impact on the environment. Even if we accepted their impact, their heavy reliance on water for operations essentially robs Peter to pay Paul.

Coal

In 2011, 42 percent of energy generated in the United States came from the burning of coal.[4] Coal is the least expensive fuel to gather, process, and burn for power, relative to all other sources. But when burned, coal emits the highest relative amount of carbon emissions. So the economic benefits of burning coal are not in balance with its environmental impacts.

There is a way to inch toward a better economic-environmental balance. It is possible to capture and store the carbon that coal emits upon burning. So-called carbon capture and storage (CCS) technology can be retrofit at coal-fired power plants. The technology would capture the carbon emissions, process them, and then store them in geologic formations.

There are three main challenges associated with CCS. First is the financial cost of retrofitting facilities to incorporate the technology. If these costs were allocated on the basis of units of coal produced, CCS technology could increase the cost of coal-sourced energy by 20 to 90 percent. Second is the need to generate 25 to 40 percent more energy to power the CCS technology. Third is the amount of space needed to install CCS technology. Many of the currently operating coal-fired power plants were built decades ago. Since then, the area around these plants has been developed, which means that the plant owners would need to buy land around the plant to install the CCS technology.

Within the Waste Economy structure, coal is the least expensive energy source. But once we add in the external costs associated with coal production and use, coal's economic (and environmental) price significantly increases.

Natural Gas

Natural gas accounted for 25 percent of generated energy in the United States in 2011.[5] We are in the midst of a natural gas boom as fracking technology has enabled recovery of natural gas stored in shale beds throughout the country. As a result, the price of natural gas has plummeted over the past few years.

Natural gas emits less carbon than coal upon burning. A recent MIT study calculated that increased utilization of existing natural gas power plants to displace coal-fired power could reduce the energy sector's carbon emissions by 22 percent in the near term.[6] Natural gas produces 43 percent fewer carbon emissions than coal for each unit of energy delivered, and 30 percent fewer emissions than oil.[7]

Although natural gas has a lower environmental cost than coal at the time it is burned, the environmental cost of extraction is proving to be substantial. In particular, the use of chemicals to fracture the Earth's plates causes considerable damage to the surrounding area's water and air supplies.[8] There is also a theory being explored that the fracturing of plates also causes a higher incidence of earthquakes in the fracking area; research into this hypothesis is ongoing.

Natural gas is abundant and accessible, and its conversion to consumable energy has a lower carbon footprint than that of coal. It would cost approximately $700 billion to convert all of our coal-fired power plants to natural gas.[9] But the need to balance the benefits of natural gas with its challenges positions natural gas as a viable transition fuel that can enable a shift from reliance on hydrocarbon fuel sources to renewable fuel sources.

Nuclear

Nuclear power accounted for 19 percent of generated energy in the United States in 2011.[10] Nuclear does not emit carbon, which—from a greenhouse gas perspective—makes it the "cleanest" of the energy sources we've explored to this point.

But nuclear has three drawbacks. First is the public perception of nuclear power plants. The unfortunate events at the Fukushima nuclear power plant in 2011 are still fresh in the public's mind. Other incidents that caused significant damage, such as Chernobyl and Three Mile Island, are recent enough to further influence public perception of the technology.

Nuclear's second drawback is the financial cost involved in building a plant. Nuclear power plants under construction in the United States range in price from roughly $4 billion to $15 billion. To convert from coal to nuclear throughout the United States would cost even more than the conversion of coal to natural gas.

Nuclear's third drawback is a lack of contemporary public sector leadership (a common theme throughout this chapter). The three U.S. nuclear power plants under construction right now suffered delays in regulatory oversight. And at least one of the power plants being built (in Tennessee) will employ analog instead of digital technology for operation and oversight. The Tennessee plant was originally cleared for construction in the 1970s; its plans called for analog technology (state-of-the-art technology at the time) to be used. Although the plant is under construction now, and digital technology is now the norm, the plant owners would need to seek federal permission to switch from its accepted plan. Such a review would be costly from a financial perspective (causing construction delays and rework) and from a political perspective, too (having to go through the plan redesign approval process).

Water

Hydropower was the source of 8 percent of the electricity generated in the United States in 2011.[11] Water-generated power has multiple advantages over the other sources covered to this point. For one, water-generated power emits only nominal amounts of greenhouse gases. Another relative advantage is that water does not require disruptive extraction techniques, which limits its economic and external costs. Finally, hydropower is widely accepted to be the most effective "load" power source (power available to meet demands for energy that exceed the "base" level of power available all the time).

As we'll see in Chapter Seven, however, water is a massively stressed resource. For now, suffice it to say that there are several external costs associated with using water for power. For one, there are other demands on bodies of water, and access to water is, at best, limited when water is dammed up for hydropower.

Nonhydro Renewable Sources of Energy

Renewable energy from nonhydro sources is on the opposite end of the economic versus external cost spectrum for energy. That is, renewable energy is the most economically expensive energy source on a per-unit basis, but also offers the lowest external cost on a per-unit basis.

The main challenges with renewable energy have to do with scaled infrastructure, investment, and perception. The reason why energy that comes from wind, sun, biomass, and geothermal sources is relatively expensive is that each source lacks installed and scaled infrastructure. The energy "sources" are theoretically free (to whom do you send a bill for the sunlight you've captured?), but the infrastructure to capture and store power from these sources has not reached economies of scale.

Billions of dollars are needed to manufacture, install, and operate windmills, solar farms, and the like. Investment dollars are limited by a combination of factors, including current economic conditions, a lack of regulatory pressure to scale renewable energy to meaningful levels, and corporate unwillingness to tie up much-needed short-term capital in long-term investments. Until local constituents agitate for renewable energy adoption en masse, their politicians are unlikely to fight hard to enact needed regulation that gives high priority to renewable energy.

▬▬▬

Although each power source has its drawbacks, we must not discount each source's strengths. The task at hand is to figure out how to use all these available resources to maximize the benefits we receive from them while being sensitive to their distinct drawbacks. So how do we begin to achieve this delicate but necessary balance?

First and most important, all sectors and stakeholders must be engaged in the discussion. Each sector is affected differently by each power source. Any overarching decision that fails to engage all three sectors will fail to gain the support necessary for all stakeholders to accept the challenges that come with bringing the decision to life.

Second, the inherent trade-offs are a reflection of our current technology. Our situation is practically begging for innovation— the type of breakthrough thinking that can completely alter the power source calculus. Perhaps there is an answer to all of the challenges described in this chapter just waiting for an innovative breakthrough.

Third, neither engagement nor innovation will happen without leadership. The time has come for the public sector worldwide to set aside differences and boldly set a global price for carbon. Then all members of the public sector, perhaps acting as one, need to go further: there must be real and fungible penalties for noncompliance with the newly agreed-on global carbon policy.

The private sector, too, must rise to the challenge. Although some companies might hesitate to get involved, we see significant benefits available to companies that provide energy sector leadership. Primary among these benefits is the high probability that new growth industries will emerge in a carbon-constrained world. The history of commerce is filled with examples of companies and entire new industries emerging at points of disruption to conventional business practices.

If the carrot is not appealing, then perhaps the specter of the stick might be more effective in sparking private sector action. That is, if the public sector sets not only a global, fungible carbon price but also fortifies this price with additional noncompliance penalties, then companies will be faced with a choice that has an obvious preferred path: either embrace change to pursue growth, or accept the consequences of inaction.

Two things are clear. First, our public sector failure to agree to global carbon standards reveals a hidden culprit—across sectors, we have not set a penalty for failing to find an appropriate economic-environmental balance among power sources. This must change. Second, our continued inaction on scaling renewable energy technology and infrastructure means that we will be in a hydrocarbon world for at least our lifetimes, if not the lifetimes of our children and grandchildren. At this point, it is extremely difficult to envision a pragmatic scenario where this is not the case.

We cannot change our immediate situation, but the time to agree on the optimal mix of power sources is now.

Energy Infrastructure

If massive change within the sphere of power generation is not likely within the foreseeable future, then we need to look to the power grid for a solution that provides sufficient power in a way that respects both economic and external costs.

There is consensus that the U.S. power grid is highly inefficient, in terms of both transmission and distribution. In particular, it is very challenging to optimize distribution to individual buildings and move excess energy capacity to where it needs to be in real time. The potential for a smart grid that is able to digitally reroute power in real time exists, but there is a great amount of work to do before there is a smart grid that covers entire regions of the world.

Waiting for utility companies and other authorities to optimize energy distribution at the consumer level is committing to a "slow go" approach. After all, what is a regulated utility company's potential benefit from making extensive investments to existing infrastructure? But time is not on our side. We owe it to ourselves and to coming generations to get on with it.

To realize the potential of an energy system renaissance is to accept a huge innovation task. Most of our existing energy infrastructure, broadly speaking, was designed and built with a different "return on environment" than is required today. And the expectations will only become more stringent over the next forty years. The changes in the energy infrastructure required to serve nine-and-a-half billion people represents a significant trial that clearly calls for innovative thinking.

———

The energy challenge is a microcosm of the need for the transition to the Collaboration Economy. The challenge itself is gigantic, multifaceted, intertwined, expensive, and rife with trade-offs. Land use, capital investments, water consumption, individuals' rights to pursue capitalistic gains, greenhouse gas emissions . . . the private, public, and social sectors' interests, motivations, and actions are continuously colliding.

There are no power generation or infrastructure solutions that are panaceas to all our energy ills. The shear enormity of the debate, the political thorniness of the issue, and the entrenched opinions about the pros and cons of power source and infrastructure options has led to a giant stalemate. It's as if there's a general consensus that no action is better than action that reflects compromises made so as not to significantly dissatisfy anyone. As a result, there is a great void in the energy field. In particular, there is a blinding need for an actor to step up and volunteer to be a leader, to build an inclusive "ecosystem" for identifying and harvesting the best ideas to move forward, to bring creative hybrid financing solutions to the table, to provide opportunities to test and refine ideas, and to provide global scale to convert ideas into viable solutions.

GE as Orchestrator of a Global Energy System Solution

Perhaps no one company has more at stake in the energy challenge than GE. Growth. Complexity. License to operate within local communities. The company understands that it cannot resolve the energy debate alone. So GE is willingly picking up the mantle of energy system leadership.

GE's intention is to use its scale to amplify best thinking: use open innovation to gather best thinking; pit most promising technologies against one another; identify likeliest winning technologies; scale these technologies rapidly; and develop consortiums to invest in the technologies that have the greatest potential to make the greatest positive contribution to solving our global energy problems.

But let's be clear. GE is not engaging in these efforts for altruistic satisfaction. The company fervently believes that there is a new era of massive prosperity to be enjoyed in return for massive efforts. The difference between other times and now is that GE is not only willing to share in the prosperity but also actively remaking itself to be positioned to work with others and cocreate this prosperity.

GE initially intended to take the path of leadership by coalition in the effort to provide certainty for utilities and other industries so that energy infrastructure planning and decisions could be made. Jeff Immelt, GE's chairman and CEO, accepted the responsibility of providing visible leadership for the United States Climate Action Partnership (USCAP). This entity, at one time comprising a veritable "Who's Who" list of corporations, came together to "call on the federal government to quickly enact strong national legislation to require significant reductions of greenhouse gas emissions." Immelt's belief was that a legislative decision could provide the desired certainty more completely and more cost effectively. Unfortunately, the U.S. government did not act (and still has not acted) on USCAP's advice and related efforts.

Jeff Immelt, USCAP, and the Birth of Ecomagination

Jeff Immelt's commitment to provide USCAP leadership was based on the belief that a consortium of energy system stakeholders that properly reflects the cost-benefit trade-offs in this broader clean-tech energy space was needed to accelerate change. Immelt and his USCAP colleagues saw that their companies did not have an adequate basis for the social and environmental analysis of investments. Said more plainly, companies are not properly pricing the total effect of operations. Ultimately, Immelt believed that science and thought alone would be the motivators pulling together the private, public, and social sectors for resolutions of the energy crisis. The thought was that with this collaborative effort, there would be a lot more focus on solving the energy problem in an accelerated way.

GE took on a prominent leadership position within USCAP at the risk of differing with customers and other partners. After all, many of GE's customers are large, coal-based utilities that could be affected by new regulation. But Immelt did what he thought was the right thing. He reached out directly to the public sector and to his peers and said, "I'm going to do this. In the long term, this is going to be good for everybody."

Unfortunately, the political will for climate change regulation did not materialize. Immelt faced a quandary: let go of the pursuit of what he believed was right for all involved, including GE, or double down on GE's investment. He decided to stay true to his vision. Spending too much time hoping for policy decisions or engaging in climate debate *delays* taking action on real change!

So Immelt increased his investment in finding and developing solutions to our global energy crisis. Specifically through ecomagination, a GE initiative that develops environmentally conscious products, GE doubled down on R&D and on related investments that can yield solutions that combine compelling economics with positive environmental performance. But there was more. GE realized that the company could not on its own bring about a solution to the energy crisis. So it set out to develop a way to look beyond its four walls for participation, for ideas, for funding, and ultimately for solutions. The thinking was, "If we can't engage politicians in the United States, then let's engage other constituents and develop partnerships." As we will see in a bit, this was the origin of the ecomagination Challenge in all its extensions.

At the time, action was clearly required. The company concluded that it needed a signal to show the market in general and its constituents specifically that it was truly committed to solving the energy crisis. So Immelt made a significant investment— he transitioned GE's sales force from internal combustion engine cars to electric vehicles (twenty-five thousand vehicles in total). Immelt looked to electric vehicles for several reasons. Chief among these was to demonstrate action and to start painting the road map to a holistic solution to the energy challenge, one that engages the whole ecosystem (public, private, and social sectors) and that would, for example, enable communities to adopt electric vehicles. The company clearly is committed to showing others that operating in the energy efficiency and optimization space is both great economic business and also great for our collective goal of resource optimization. Through such efforts as the transition to electric vehicles, GE showed that "its [energy sector] policy is action."

When far-reaching change is desired, it would be convenient if regulations were put in place so that business could get behind that tailwind. But this rarely happens. By piloting and demonstrating possible solutions, businesses help bring changes out of the world of theory and into reality by offering people examples of success. This idea of action is incredibly important.

GE and the Emerging Ecosystem to Create a Lasting Energy Solution

The GE ecomagination Challenge was GE's way of bringing together the public, private, and social sectors to catalyze energy sector innovation. The idea was straightforward: identify best ideas to help solve some of the biggest energy challenges, fund them out of a pool of $200 million, and scale winning ideas through GE's global presence. Immelt invested $100 million from the corporate budget, so GE's business units did not need to allocate investment dollars. In hindsight, this is probably the primary reason why there were only limited objections within GE to the idea of working with other constituents to bring about solutions to the energy crisis.

In addition to navigating potential internal roadblocks, the Challenge was intended to ensure the inclusion of entities GE would rarely talk to in the ecomagination universe: venture capital firms, start-ups, and individuals with new innovative ideas. In particular, GE looked to four venture capital firms to invest the other $100 million to complete the $200 million pot. The venture capital firms were very excited about the chance to participate. These firms saw both the opportunity to add to their pipeline of new investments and the ability to benefit from a scale and commercialization avenue that was unprecedented.

The other purpose in creating the ecomagination Challenge was to make sure that GE was not just reprocessing its own thinking. The company turned to the open-source innovation process richly explored by others, such as Henry Chesborough; in particular was the concept that you want competing technologies to emerge. There are many smart grid technologies out there that eventually can and will work. The problem is that no single entity alone can determine which technologies will work. By thinking through this problem, GE learned several powerful and replicable lessons that we will cover in the remainder of this chapter.

The first lesson GE learned is that if you can set up a process that takes ideas from outside your own four walls, your company gains access to a survey of technology innovations that you might otherwise miss. In some cases, this process allows the technologies to compete and allows you to place multiple bets that evolve those technologies; you can see which ones win or which are potentially complementary.

Accelerating Collaborative Change Initiatives

The second significant lesson GE learned was about the limitations of a process that merely stops at accelerating the ideas and partnerships into a funnel for action. The real magic lies in how you scale and commercialize those ideas. And that's where the ecomagination accelerator came in.

After launching the initial ecomagination Challenge, GE paused and engaged in considerable discussion with the venture capital firms and other constituents involved in the Challenge. GE realized that its partners wanted flexibility in the structure of their relationships with the company. Until this point, the most prevalent business relationship between corporations and the venture capital firms and entrepreneurs with which they worked was "Let's start negotiating how I buy your technology and brand it." GE realized that if that were the only model the company employed, it would find only a limited set of ideas. In contrast, if GE offered to work with a variety of partnership forms, then the company would access a greater range of breakthrough ideas. What GE's venture capital partners needed was the ability to reduce the technology risk associated with the solutions they were developing, use GE's customer base for pilot purposes, and gain access to GE's global distribution.

This type of relationship flexibility was relatively new to GE. To kick-start this new business philosophy, GE's ecomagination leadership put aside $20 million of the ecomagination Challenge funds and said, "Let's get these partnerships and ideas through an accelerator to scale and commercialization." Specifically, GE created an internal process whereby the venture capital businesses that partnered with these new organizations (arising from the ecomagination Challenge) had the opportunity to pitch the ecomagination leadership team to invest in the next phase of those relationships.

An energy efficiency technology company called Oblong is one example of the type of company that went through the ecomagination accelerator. Oblong has developed a proprietary technology that uses data visualization to equip energy consumers to dramatically improve their energy efficiency. GE gave the Oblong team access to the company's global research team as well as the ecomagination leadership team in order to pilot-test Oblong's technology. As a result of this accelerated investment process, GE was able to accelerate business activities that captured $350 million of revenue. Ordinarily, any large company, including GE, would have had meeting after meeting; who knows what, if anything, would have emerged from this process. Through GE's ecomagination accelerator, GE recognized that Oblong brought to the table an incredible technology that was very interesting. Then GE identified ways to get Oblong connected to the company's business and scale. The GE leadership team helped remove barriers, such as legal processes. Revenue, scale, and adoption were dramatically affected as a result.

The ecomagination Challenge and the accelerator have caused a transformation in GE's status within the entrepreneur community. In general, GE has made a very long lasting impression about its progression to being a company that is open and that stimulates innovation. GE is transforming its corporate culture to be more collaborative and entrepreneurial at the same time.

Recently, GE leadership met with Immelt on the West Coast to discuss this broad entrepreneurship idea. To continue the trend of collaboration, the leadership team brought the CEO of Oblong to the meeting. The team, alongside Oblong, was able to show Immelt that the ecomagination accelerator process is capable of truly accelerating growth for GE. The company is working with a few other companies in this process. If the Oblong success story holds for these other companies, then the ecomagination team will achieve its goal of delivering $1 billion of incremental revenue to GE.

━━━

As noted earlier, moving the private, public, and civil sectors toward a coherent and lasting solution for the energy system is difficult due to the need for alignment of incentives among the various sectors. When one looks at the global economic dynamics and the proliferation of self-interested parties, it seems obvious that global orchestration of one answer is nearly impossible. In the absence of globally organized policy, we're left with one inalienable truth, and that is the need to return to innovation. We must find a way not to force people into choosing between economics and environmental impact.

GE plans to continue to engage with all sectors in describing broad principles toward which we can all work. The company advocates setting a carbon price to spur innovation. It sees action as its best advocacy, where the company can demonstrate potential solutions through pilot tests. Vital to finding and enacting solutions will be agility—that is, a cross-sector ability to focus not on a debate about the science behind climate change but on the tangible trade-offs among our power generation, transmission, and distribution alternatives. Embracing agility will require corporations to place strategic bets, share solutions, weed out the ineffective solutions, and then scale the best ideas.

Alongside the public sector, GE has invested in research partnerships with multiple public and private sector organizations worldwide. For example, the company collaborated with the Australian business community on a prominent white paper which shows that thirty-two different countries have priced carbon and that having done so has not negatively impacted the GDP per capita as they've substantially reduced the emissions per capita.

Call to Action

One company, no matter how large or how committed, cannot reshape the energy landscape alone. If a company as large, as sophisticated, and as global as GE has decided to forge ahead, now is the time for all of us—the public, private, and social sectors—to plunge into the unknown, too. In the process we will

- Reshape our relationship with energy
- Develop and realize a portfolio of energy sources
- Save money by making an inefficient system efficient and effective

Our intent with this chapter is to convince the business community to embrace the need to change its business practices and its attitude toward collaboration. We need more companies, more public sector agencies, and more advocacy groups to serve as role models. If we could leave you with one message, it would be to say, Step out of your comfort zone and help us resolve the energy debate. Commit. Collaboration on this critical issue will make you more relevant in the global market and thus will be great for your business.

3

TURNING PACKAGING MATERIALS INTO CAPITAL

Kim Jeffery, Michael Washburn, Robert F. Kennedy Jr., Chris Bartle, and Eric Lowitt

The Collaboration Economy will lead to growth that accelerates sustainable development. At the center of this economic system is the belief that used resources—what many consider waste with limited intrinsic value—are actually imprisoned resources waiting to be unlocked as products once more.

Consider this: we could add well over $20 billion to U.S. GDP *annually* by resetting our recycling system. Indeed, the combination of the avoided costs of cleanup and the market value of the materials is well above $20 billion annually by itself—and that's before adding the value of the additional economic activity and environmental benefits of recycling.

Sadly, the current U.S. recycling system is sending that $20 billion to landfills. Waste is at the heart of our current economic system. We buy stuff with nary a thought about what to do with it once we're done using it. When we do think about the role waste plays in our lives, it's usually a variant of this type of thought: "My house, my car, my office—cleanliness is next to godliness—and throwing away the stuff I've used is the quickest, least expensive way to make me feel better about my surroundings." Throwing away the stuff we no longer want is easy; without a second thought, we can toss it into a convenient bin, or, if it's too big, we can hire someone to haul it away for us. And then we move on to the next thing on our to-do list.

Every time we simply throw something away, we throw money away. It's that simple. Packages, bottles, cans, that toy your child no longer wants—money, money, money. With an economy as fragile as ours, why do we tolerate throwing money away? Because we currently don't have an immediately available system for recovering value. But we also aren't aware or educated enough about how and why freely discarding stuff is analogous to freely discarding money.

Our current system of recycling packaging materials is not doing its job. Regrettably, copious amounts of fungible resources—postconsumer-use materials—are sent to landfills daily.

Every ounce of material that goes into landfill is a missed opportunity for a job and for a greenhouse gas savings (because it takes less energy to reprocess material than it takes to extract it). That's true of glass, plastic, metal, paper, and other materials. Indeed, a study by the Tellus Institute on behalf of the Blue-Green Alliance demonstrated that *1.5 million jobs* would be added in the United States if the national recycling rate were to reach 75 percent. A 75 percent packaging recycling rate would reduce carbon dioxide emissions by 276 million metric tons by 2030—equivalent to closing seventy-two coal-fired power plants or taking fifty million cars off the road.[1]

We propose adopting a better system, one that will yield economic development and reduce environmental degradation. The system we propose is popularly called *extended producer responsibility* (EPR), which places responsibility for recycling postconsumer-use material on the shoulders of the brand owners who manufacture and bottle beverages. EPR represents the future of recycling in the United States. The system makes companies accountable for the externalities of their business activities, and it aligns economic development with environmental stewardship.

The Current U.S. Recycling System Is Not Sufficient

Virtually every person in the United States has consumed a beverage from a plastic bottle or aluminum can. Over the years, we have learned to value the convenience of beverage containers for milk, juice, water, soda, beer, and so on. It's easier and often more sanitary to grab a prefilled bottle on the go rather than finding a container from our house and filling it with our preferred drink.

However, U.S. citizens have not yet learned to responsibly dispose of these bottles. Indeed, the United States suffers from *the lowest packaging recycling rate of **almost every** developed country on Earth.* To illustrate, let's look at plastic bottles. Whereas only approximately 30 percent of postconsumer-use plastic bottles are recycled in the United States, nearly 98 percent of the same types of bottles are recycled in developed countries like Finland. Glass, paper, and aluminum recycling rates are in roughly the same proportion.

In the United States, the vast majority of this wasted packaging material ends up in landfill. By *packaging materials*, we mean not only plastic bottles but also printed paper; paper in the form of cardboard, fiberboard, and the like; and glass, steel, and aluminum packaging. A recent study by As You Sow estimated the value of discarded packaging material to be about $11.4 billion per year in the United States, an important factor in economic calculations pertaining to packaging, as packaging is the main component of litter.[2] Thus, the U.S. packaging materials disposal system serves as exhibit A of the Waste Economy in action.

Why do we waste so much packaging material in the United States? As we suggested earlier, consumers do not find recycling easy or worth their time. For instance, every time we consume the contents of a plastic bottle, each one of us makes an implicit decision; we ask ourselves, *Which is a better use of my time?*

1. Do I drive to a supermarket to reclaim my five- or ten-cent deposit, maybe with other bottles I've collected over time in a less than completely sanitary container? (This option assumes that you live in one of the ten states with a bottle bill that requires deposits.)

2. Do I just throw away my bottle and go about my day?

Given this mental calculus, it is no wonder that recycling rates are so low. Notwithstanding the commitment of the few to recycle, the facts show that the many view the effort as not worth their investment. After all, they have to consider the cost of gas to go to the store or recycling center *plus* the cost of their time. And in some places, consumers go even further in their thinking to wonder about whether the entity that collects the deposits is in fact using the deposits as it promised or whether the bottle collection entity is actually recycling the collected bottles.

Consumer resistance to continuously recycling packaging materials results in economic, environmental, and social development waste. We can do better . . . and we must if we are committed to growth as a path to sustainable development.

We believe that the packaging materials disposal system of the Waste Economy can and should be turned into the "materials recovery and remanufacturing" sector of the Collaboration Economy. As we noted, there is considerable value being lost and considerably more to be saved and gained—at least $20 billion in annual GDP contributions.

Reinventing the U.S. packaging recycling system requires two ingredients. First is a new model, one that is more effective, more efficient, and more capable of processing all kinds of packaging material. Second is active collaboration among the private, public, and social sectors to shape this new recycling model and bring it to life. As we will discuss in this chapter, not only do both ingredients exist, but there are replicable lessons that companies can learn from one leading company's efforts to build a cross-sector coalition to effectuate this reinvention.

Bottle Bills and Packaging Recycling—Why Do We Need a New Solution?

Let's trace the steps in the current U.S. model of packaging recycling to see why a new solution is so desperately needed.

First, brand owners like Poland Springs (owned by Nestlé Waters North America) sell packaged drinks to retailers throughout the country. The retailer then sells the product to a consumer at a price that may or may not include a "deposit." (As noted, whether there is a deposit depends on whether the retailer's store is in one of the ten states with bottle-bill legislation in place. In the case of all other packaged goods, the consumer does not make a deposit.)

In bottle-bill states, not only are the bottles returned (at rates that vary from approximately 60 to 95 percent), but recycling rates of other consumer packaging, such as nondeposit glass and plastic containers, cardboard paper, and the like, are higher than those in non-bottle-bill states. This strongly suggests that consumers want to recycle used packaging, given the opportunity. Nevertheless, as we mentioned, overall recycling rates even in bottle-bill states pale in comparison to rates in nearly all other developed countries.

Bottle-bill states use only some of the collected deposits (which become the property of the state) to administer and nurture an intrastate packaging recycling system (in the form of bottle-bill funds). This system includes agreeing to contracts with haulers—companies that pick up trash at residences, at recycling centers, and from municipal landfills or transfer stations. In addition, these states build and staff recycling agencies to oversee the system. For example, California's e-waste recycling agency employs about eighty professionals. The system also purchases and distributes recycling receptacles that consumers can use to separate postconsumer-use materials to be recycled from those that cannot be recycled (refer to Figure 3.1).

But bottle-bill funds are not accountable to overall recycling, nor are they generated by deposits on any other kinds of products—indeed, beverage types that are actually covered by bottle bills are even inconsistent across the states and subject to much lobbying. Thus state-level bottle bills, while considerably enhancing recovery of the bottles subject to deposit and slightly

Figure 3.1. How Funding Works Within the Current U.S. Packaging Recycling System

How We Currently Pay

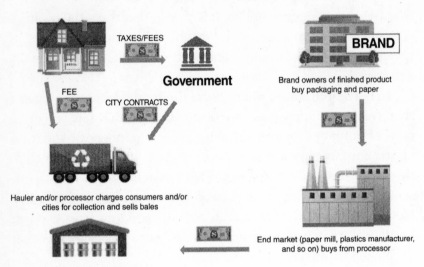

Source: Recycling Reinvented

increasing recovery rates for other packaging materials, also introduce a giant flaw in a recycling system that should cover all kinds of packaging materials, and amount to a separate tax on the beverage industry.

Non-bottle-bill states (and some bottle-bill states) fund recycling at the state and local level in a variety of ways—sometimes through a separate line item on a tax bill, sometimes with a budgeted appropriation, and sometimes with a fee payable directly to a hauler.

The potential to nationalize the bottle-bill philosophy is limited by the fact that bottle bills are not feasible for all states; enacting a bottle bill requires the state to have available financial resources, land, haulers, political will, and myriad other ingredients. Even if a bottle bill were feasible for every state, most states would be hampered by current economic conditions—they simply don't have the money needed to improve recycling.

Collaboration and the Elements Needed to Turn Waste into Resource

Not surprisingly, the key to improving packaging materials recycling in the United States is cross-sector collaboration. Members of the civil sector have to want to recycle more. Government needs to provide the legislative prompt. And the private sector must take life-cycle responsibility for the resources it consumes.

Consumer Willingness to Adapt to a New System

Consumers resist change when they believe that current conditions are ideal. This phenomenon holds true in the United States for the packaging recycling system. After all, people see a current recycling system that is reliant on deposits and believe they have a good deal. They get to decide if they want to recycle their bottles and other packaging materials. They know the cost involved—typically five cents per bottle. They know they can get that deposit back if they return the container. Governments have a good estimate of the amount of revenue that unclaimed deposits will produce, and consumers are content to let the state use their deposits.

But the system is more costly and provides far less transparency than we all think. In reality, consumers pay more than the five-cent deposit per container. To see how, let's look at two familiar moments in the consumer's experience with his or her favorite beverage: the point of purchase and the point of return.

Retailers strive to devote as much floor space as possible to selling groceries—not accepting containers. Predictably, they wanted compensation in return for accepting the containers. So legislators created one- to four-cent "handling fees" as compensation. "Pickup agents," the haulers who pick up the returns from retailers, also collect a fee for their services. The addition of reverse vending machines (the machines that "eat" and then convert containers into shredded materials for reuse) to retail stores was seen as an effective way to improve the system, as they make collection and sorting easier. Nearly everyone who touches a returned bottle or can collects a fee, and together, these fees—which can pile five cents or more on top of the nickel deposit—find their way into higher shelf prices. In total, consumers who live in bottle-bill states pay rather significantly for the invisible fees required to run most take-back systems.

If they understood these hidden costs, consumers would be likely to welcome a new system that provided convenient access to recycling facilities, operated with full transparency, and placed a similar or even smaller cost on consumers to participate.

Access and Trust

Roughly 50 percent of U.S. households are in municipalities that do not provide curbside trash (or recyclables) pickup. Access to packaging recycling facilities then is particularly critical to enable one-half of U.S. households to recycle if they choose to do so. Unfortunately, outside of reverse vending machines in grocery stores, access to recycling facilities when consumption occurs outside the home (called "away from home" in the food and beverage industries) is at best very limited. For example, if you are reading this in America, think about the last time you noticed a PET plastic recycling bin at your local gas station. It's unlikely that you can think of the last time, because access to such bins is very limited.

Another crucial differentiator is civil sector trust—trust in the system to invest its collected funds in its prescribed manner. The current U.S. bottle-bill or tax-driven packaging recycling system fails this test, too. By and large, government-run bottle deposit jurisdictions break a basic trust with the consumer, who has paid an environmental tax that is not geared to the cost of recycling but instead is arbitrarily set—but the consumer is not receiving the full environmental benefit. The handling fees paid by industry and the unredeemed deposits paid by consumers simply do not wholly go toward enhancing a state's environmental infrastructure, despite what many idealistic consumers might think and bottle-bill advocates might hope.

Increased Scope in Packaging Material Recycling

A final element in enacting the ideal packaging recycling system is ensuring that the scope of recycling systems is supported by holistic public policy. As we will see in Chapter Six, the EU Parliament, among other political bodies, is actively considering legislation that would enact a so-called lease society—consumers and manufacturers would find incentives to work together to return and process postconsumer waste of all kinds. By comparison, bottle-bill-style recycling is not expandable to other packaging, paper, or compostable waste because bottle bills rely on getting all of the "empties" back to the store ("retailer take-back"). It's easy to see why this system is flawed: food stores simply should not be the place we bring our garbage. They do not have the physical space to play this role, nor should they—as opposed to other possible receiving locations (such as purpose-designed recycling transfer stations)—bear the costs. In fact, retailers of any kind are ill equipped for this job and cannot, for instance, provide the infrastructure for paper recycling, which accounts for 40 percent of landfill waste.

It is time for a new legislative approach in the United States that reimagines the gathering and handling of postconsumer-use packaging materials as a materials management strategy and seeks economic growth and sustainability.

We propose three goals for the new recycling system:

1. Dramatically increase the amounts of postconsumer recyclable material available for domestic manufacturing of

new packaging and paper, thereby making higher levels of recycled material in new products economically attractive compared with virgin materials.

2. Rationalize the current decentralized, undercapitalized, and municipally administered household recycling system with efficiency that increases recycling tonnage while reducing overall costs per household.

3. Maximize environmental benefits from recycling compared with other disposal options.

The new approach we propose already exists and has been adopted in much of Europe, certain provinces in Canada, and elsewhere. As we noted earlier, the system is called extended producer responsibility, or EPR. All it will take to bring EPR to life in the United States is collaboration across the private, public, and social sectors. Before we explain why, let's first explore EPR in more detail.

Extended Producer Responsibility

EPR for packaging and printed paper requires brand owners to assume the cost of collecting and sorting household recyclables. Producers, not government, will be at the heart of the new packaging recycling system. Under EPR, the brand owners for each type of packaging material will collaborate to create a separate nonprofit organization—known as a *producer responsibility organization* (PRO)—to set fees to collect and redirect packaging, to educate consumers, and to calculate how to allocate the overall cost of recycling paid by each brand owner. Government's role will be to set targets and monitor performance—to referee the system, not to administer it. (Please refer to Figure 3.2.)

Let's see an example of EPR in action by reviewing how the system would handle a PET plastic bottle. First, the PRO determines the cost of fulfilling its obligations under the legislation

Figure 3.2. How Funding Works Within an Extended Producer Responsibility Recycling System

How Dollars Would Flow Under EPR

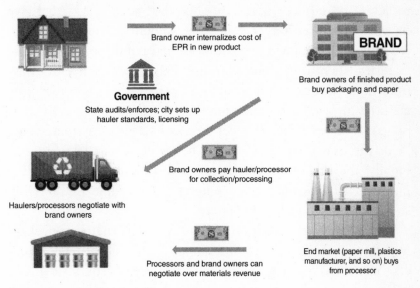

Source: Recycling Reinvented

and fairly distributes the cost among brand owners. Each brand owner—note that retailers count as brand owners for their private-label products—would remit directly to the PRO without the necessity of involvement or separate accounting by retailers, consumers, or government, and each brand owner would set the cost of its own products, determining how much to include of the amounts paid to the PRO. This results in far more efficiency than the system under a bottle deposit regime, where deposits must be separately accounted for and tracked by producers, distributors, retailers, and the state.

Next, the PRO contracts with waste haulers, recycling facilities, and municipalities for packaging materials collection at negotiated rates. (Public sector facilities would be eligible to be utilized [and compensated] by the PRO.) The PRO is both well positioned and strongly incented to identify opportunities for efficiency in the recycling system to reduce costs and increase recycling rates. EPR requires that in order for the PRO to achieve its state-mandated target collection amounts, it must invest in building curbside pickup capabilities and public-space recycling facilities where they don't currently exist (particularly in away-from-home locations); it would also perhaps invest in recycling facilities for separation and bundling, as well as public education programs. Over time, the per-unit costs of this system would be driven down, we believe, well below current bottle deposits. Finally, the PRO would be required to report on the recycling rates for each type of recycled material (for example, PET, HDPE, steel, newsprint, and cardboard).

In two ways, the creation of PROs will lead to higher packaging material recycling rates by equipping and educating consumers to be active participants in the recycling system. First, PROs will fundamentally change consumers' access to recycling. For example, we don't know about you, but in the United States when we clean out our cars, we're usually at a gas station. But there's nowhere to put the bottles. So we semiconsciously look both ways to make sure no one is watching us and then toss our plastic bottles into the regular trash bin. PROs would change this by paying for and providing packaging material recycling bins away from home, in locations such as gas stations and stadiums. PROs would also provide recycling bins to residences that currently do not have such bins (let alone recycling systems). If you live in a rural area, maybe you have to go to some kind of drop-off center. There might not be one there today, but the PRO would create one.

Second, PROs would heighten society's awareness of the importance of recycling packaging materials. Specifically, PROs would provide money for consumer education so that people can learn about the various recycling options available to them.

So how do we know an EPR system can be successful in the United States? We've studied and learned from the success of similar EPR systems that are widespread in Europe and spreading throughout Canada. Of note, countries with EPR systems in place tend to recycle affected materials at rates higher than 70 percent.

EPR Adoption

Up to this point, we have looked at the private and social sector roles in nurturing higher rates of recycling. Active public sector participation will be essential to bringing EPR to life. Said simply, without legislation, EPR cannot exist.

But EPR in the United States must fit the nation's unique political, economic, and social character. Therefore, we believe that simply adopting an existing program from outside the United States is neither operationally nor politically feasible. For example, Western Europe and Canada have a higher tolerance for government intervention in the marketplace. The United States operates as a federal system in which states have taken the lead in recycling, followed by counties and municipalities. Many states do not lack for landfill space. The U.S. EPA, unlike the European Union with its EU Packaging Directive, does not currently have the authority to set up EPR for packaging, and Congress is unlikely to take any action nationally in the near term.

Yet EPR for some materials has already been enacted in thirty-two U.S. states. For example, twenty-three states have enacted laws addressing electronic recycling, fifteen states cover the safe disposal of automobile switches containing mercury, ten states require beverage container recycling, nine cover the handling of lead batteries, and nine address collection of used mercury thermostats. These laws are providing cost savings for the states. For example, an electronics take-back EPR program enacted by the state of Maine is saving the state about $3 million annually. So precedent exists in the United States for the enactment of an EPR law, with cost savings following in lockstep.

Leadership Needed: Nestlé Waters North America Builds an EPR Coalition

Packaging recycling is obviously an enormous and complicated issue, and leadership is needed to bring any worthwhile endeavor to life. The private sector has a stake in bringing about a more effective system, such as EPR. But as we have seen, nurturing such change requires a leader that operates through coalition. In the U.S. packaging recycling system, that leader is Nestlé Waters North America (NWNA).

NWNA, a wholly owned subsidiary of Nestlé, wanted to take first things first, tackling the materials making up 70 percent of the waste stream by volume—that is, consumer packaging and printed paper. NWNA consumes four hundred million pounds of PET plastic annually. The company has set a stated goal of achieving a 60 percent recycling rate for all PET plastic beverage containers in America by 2018. NWNA has experience in environmentally conscious packaging reduction, most notably having led the industry in reducing the weight of its water bottles.

For NWNA, the starting point to forever changing the beverage industry's business model was to build partnerships with other brand owners, including retailers with private-label brands. The company quickly realized that the change it wants to effect is far larger than it alone can achieve. Perhaps far more important was the further realization that recycling affects everyone— private, public, and social sector members alike. Therefore, a new system would need to be built through cross-sector collaboration if it were to be accepted and ultimately effective.

The development of a cross-sector coalition has proven essential to NWNA's broad change imperative. After all, the shift to an EPR system will affect all three sectors. EPR's coalition includes local governments, state legislators, commodity associations, haulers, NGOs, and, of course, rivals. The coalition includes organizations that operate in all facets of packaging recycling, including brand owners who want the material; end-use markets, such as high-tech electronics manufacturers that use recycled plastic in their ink cartridges; and retailers who want more post-consumer recycled paper content for their packaging. NWNA's most important insight was the recognition that companies outside the bottled water market also have an interest in increasing the volume of recycled materials available to make new products.

One essential step in building the coalition was to show potential partners and detractors alike that the shift to EPR is inevitable. The company created a constant drumbeat among stakeholders in support of change to EPR. This drumbeat included direct statements from NWNA, interviews and speaking engagements including people from NWNA, newspaper and trade journal articles about EPR, and participation in highly visible business forums.

Through its coalition, NWNA designed draft legislation enacting EPR on a state-by-state basis for the public sector to consider. The coalition and subsequent draft legislation were designed with a specific purpose in mind: to ensure that when the coalition discusses EPR with a state legislator who asks, "Who supports this?" the coalition can point to a multitiered group of stakeholders.

To bring this coalition to life, NWNA entered into dialogue with customers and strange bedfellows alike, including Alcoa, Walmart, Target, and Coca-Cola, as well as labor representation, NGOs such as the National Resource Defense Council, and several county commissioners. In total, NWNA has engaged more than five hundred stakeholders in order to test, refine, and bring EPR to life in the United States.

No matter how large the coalition becomes, NWNA and its collaborators cannot simply start to set up EPR systems across the country without legislation. So NWNA and its coalition are working with state legislators to best evaluate the effectiveness of the current situation and to understand how EPR will help their states become more environmentally conscious and fiscally responsible in the process.

Keeper Springs Involvement in EPR

NWNA is not the only bottled water company seeking change to the current system. Smaller bottled water companies are, too. For example, Robert F. Kennedy Jr. and Chris Bartle, Keeper Springs's owners, are actively collaborating with NWNA in the effort to bring EPR to the United States.

Keeper Springs is a bottled water brand that gives 100 percent of its profits to the environment. Modeled after Newman's Own, Keeper Springs has for twelve years advocated for change in the bottled water industry, particularly with respect to packaging, as its core consumers—environmentalists—increasingly criticized bottled water companies for not taking responsibility for packaging. From Keeper Springs's point of view, EPR represents a pathway to preventing plastic pollution, to developing sustainable packaging, and to putting environmentalists on a friendlier footing with our consumer-oriented free-market economy, which has brought so much wealth to the country.

Lessons NWNA Has Learned Along the Way

NWNA's experience bringing EPR to the United States can serve as a roadmap to the construction of the Collaboration Economy and shed light on the private sector benefits of such an economy. In particular, NWNA's experience yields several lessons that can enable others to nurture effective cross-sector partnerships.

Shield Ideas from Poorly Informed Arrows

Numerous organizations have a history of shooting down new ideas before the ideas are brought to life and scaled—and it's much easier to kill an idea than to enact it, no matter how sound. These folks dispatch their government relations team to convince legislators to vote against new bills. NWNA studied the past to develop an effective plan to enact EPR systems at the state level. To counter the inevitable attacks from parties who want to resist change for the better, the company has made itself the focus of EPR opponents' consternation, thus shielding EPR from efforts to block its adoption.

Be Transparent to Develop Trust Among Skeptical Competitors

NWNA has been thoughtful about ensuring the transparency of its intentions and actions as it crafted its EPR campaign. Indeed, its frank transparency is taking hard-nosed competitors by very pleasant surprise. Consumer packaged goods companies, the beverage industry in particular, are fiercely competitive with each other. As NWNA discovered, when you bring together a group of rivals, inevitably the competitive juices flow. These competitive feelings fuel disruptive distrust, which then drives people into a psychology where they expect to engage in a cloak-and-dagger fishing exercise.

NWNA has learned to immediately take the air out of this game. The company enters meetings by asking (potential) coalition members questions like "Guys, what do you want to know? You want to see the draft EPR legislation? Here it is. You want to see the transcripts of the meetings and the notes and who was in the room? Great! Here it is."

Pilot Tests Are Good Investments

NWNA is working with a range of organizations, including Greenopolis (a packaging recycling company) and Keep America Beautiful (an NGO perhaps best known for its iconic public service announcements showing a crying Native American, which aired in the United States in the 1970s), on a number of pilot programs to help encourage recycling where the company can measure results. These are essentially research programs for NWNA. The company hopes to figure out, at the local level, what specific packaging material recycling tactics are most effective and efficient to implement. Such insight will enable companies in its coalition to be more agile if and when EPR legislation is enacted.

Put Your Money on the Line

In order to source recycled PET plastic, NWNA is building a $30 million PET recycling plant that will produce forty million pounds of recycled PET annually. Nestlé is building the plant because there is a real business opportunity in the long term. The price of (recycled) PET today is 20 percent more than virgin, and there's something wrong with that. If you've already expended the energy to make the bottle once, why would it cost 20 percent more the second time around?

If NWNA is going to be successful in making recycled PET plastic a viable business, it needs to be getting back as much material as possible. It is not going to be a viable business long term if recycled PET continues to be priced 20 percent higher than virgin. The company is investing so that it can look at the economics of using recycled packaging materials. NWNA and its coalition of partners want to understand how to make the cost of using recycled packaging materials competitive with using virgin materials. Collectively, industry needs better recycling rates—not just for beverages, but also across the board for all PET containers.

Call to Action

The call to action for all companies is to join the large and growing coalition NWNA is building. EPR is happening all around the world. In some instances, other parts of your company have engaged these systems elsewhere in the world. This should tell you that EPR is a reality, and there should be some lessons from those systems that inform how we craft a solution for the United States, state by state, and eventually at the federal level.

And instead of having a visceral, instinctive negative reaction to collaboration with peers, let's actually have a sophisticated, fact-rich discussion about what works and what doesn't, because none of us has the option to hide anymore.

NWNA has committed to making great and lasting change, but it's going to need a lot of help. So the company is trying to drive a dialogue across civil society, and it needs people to participate in that dialogue. If you can't participate in a constructive fashion, you have no legitimate right to claim that you're a good corporate citizen, because this is one of the biggest things happening in the consumer products sustainability arena. And in our view, being absent from the conversation is ducking your public obligation.

4

RENEWING THE GLOBAL FOOD SYSTEM

Jan Kees Vis, Hal Hamilton, and Eric Lowitt

In November 2010, Unilever announced that it would endeavor to decouple growth from its environmental impact. By 2020, Unilever aims to halve the environmental footprint of its products and to improve the lives of a substantial number of smallholder farmers. Unilever's ambitious goals are illustrative of the Collaboration Economy in action. Growth can be achieved in a way that *supports, not inhibits,* positive environmental and social development.

Unilever plans to accomplish these goals while continuing to grow. Up until this point, growing while also reducing one's footprint has been a feat rarely accomplished. So when you peel away the onion, you see something rather remarkable. Instead of setting goals that a company could achieve alone, Unilever has set goals that can only be achieved through collaboration. Another peel closer to the center of the onion, and you realize that Unilever has rooted the success of its business goals in the success of its sustainability goals.

If we take a broad view of Unilever's landscape, we can see why the company chose this path. After all, at the center of this calculated risk resides a nearly incomprehensible fact: to feed our burgeoning global population in the next forty years, we need to produce as much food as we produced in the past eight thousand years combined! While the population expands, the amount of land that can yield food is fixed. As we will shortly see, a confluence of factors has created a perfect storm that threatens the sustainability of the world's food system. Not only must food production be doubled while use of resources is cut in half, but the producers of food must escape poverty. This chapter will show how the transformation to the Collaboration Economy presents a way to shore up global food security.

Unilever's business growth depends on increasing the value of brands like Hellman's, Knorr, and Lipton, all of which have taken on attributes of quality and naturalness connected to sustainability. The success of these brands now depends on the capacity of Unilever's web of suppliers and partners to deliver environmental as well as business performance.

Performance requires collaboration along three dimensions:

- Internally across procurement, R&D, marketing, and with sustainability experts

- In value chains with strategic suppliers who share R&D as well as codevelopment of new ways to reduce the environmental footprint and improve social conditions

- Among competitors to develop farmer training, industry-wide standards, and measurement tools

Our Stressed Global Food System

Food and beverage companies are facing a rapidly changing world. Global demand is rising as the world's population grows. Yet the planet's ability to meet this demand is threatened. Soils are degraded by decades of exploitation. Water sources for irrigation dry up as glaciers melt and aquifers are pumped deeper and deeper. Volatile weather increases droughts and temperature swings. The International Food Policy Research Institute predicts that climate change will reduce global agricultural productivity by 10 to 25 percent by 2080.[1] In the past, food and drink manufacturers and retailers have generally benefited from low prices of agricultural commodities due to oversupply in agricultural markets, and they therefore divested out of primary production. Now the world is shifting into greater volatility, and both global and domestic companies face supply risks.

By 2050, the world's population will exceed nine billion, a third higher than today. Nearly all of this population increase will occur in developing countries. The 2011 McKinsey & Company report *Resource Revolution: Meeting the World's Energy, Materials, Food, and Water Needs* predicts that "a combination of rising demand for agricultural products and slowing agricultural productivity growth . . . could mean that there is a need for an additional 175 million to 220 million hectares of cropland from 2010 to 2030—an increase of 10 to 15 percent from today's levels."[2] If current consumption trends continue, food demand is projected to increase by 70 percent in this time.[3] This alone represents a daunting challenge to overcome. The frustrating truth is that our ability to meet this challenge faces several formidable headwinds.

Rising demand for biofuels is further exacerbating the pressures on land. The UN's Food and Agriculture Organization recently issued a report titled *The State of Food and Agriculture*. The report explores the implications of the recent rapid growth in the production of biofuels. It concludes that "the rapidly growing demand for biofuel has contributed to higher food prices, threatening the food security of poor food buyers in both urban and rural areas."[4]

The long-term resilience and ability of food systems to respond sustainably to the world's needs are under pressure. Our current global food system does not have a bright future. The calculus of production and consumption must change.

Achieving Global Food Security

A straightforward vision can inform and shape our collective food security actions over the next forty-plus years. The vision is to have a global food system that nutritiously feeds more than nine billion people in perpetuity. Included in this vision are three necessary accomplishments. First, the system must feed these people well by providing quantity without sacrificing quality. Second, the system must produce and harvest food with environmentally sustainable methods. In order to ensure that the system will work in perpetuity, it is requisite that our soil, forests, and oceans are healthy. Third, poverty among people in the system must end. Tragically, about two-thirds of the world's desperately poor and hungry people are farmers or farm workers.

The vision isn't new, but what is new is the means of bringing the solution to life. The ethos of the emerging Collaboration Economy provides the foundation for securing the world's food supply. Many of the building blocks of this foundation require partnering among organizations—suppliers, rival firms, nonprofits, universities, and government agencies.

Governments are needed to invest in agricultural infrastructure, extension services, and community development. NGOs help ensure good trading relationships by managing pilot projects that enable farmers and buyers to codesign improvements in the environmental and social performance of supply chains. NGOs, universities, and consortia of companies can also support metrics and tools for continuously improving impacts at the field, farm, and landscape levels.

Collaboration is never easy. Institutional memory alone prevents rivals from partnering because they have been competing for market share for so long. Supply chain relationships are usually top down, but accomplishing sustainable sourcing requires partnerships among suppliers and buyers. The public sector is frequently viewed as the "enemy state," and public affairs departments are primarily mandated with defending the business against regulation. Some of the NGOs with expertise are also critics, and collaborating with your critics requires a tolerance for risk.

Smallholder inclusivity is particularly challenging. Decades of underinvestment mean that small-scale producers in developing countries often operate in areas with inadequate infrastructure (roads, electricity, and irrigation). They lack access to skills and services (training, credit, inputs) and are highly dependent on favorable weather. Their lack of uniformity and scattered locations require creative solutions to aggregating production.

Low incomes mean that many smallholders lack education, have poor health, and have limited capacity to deal with shocks, such as sickness or extreme weather events. If contracts are not adaptable to changing market conditions, offer less than adequate returns, or don't work within farmers' income needs at key times, problems of "side selling"—selling contracted crops to a third party—may arise.

Specific barriers for women, together with on-farm issues such as management of waste, safe use and storage of chemicals, water quality, soil management, and the treatment of farm labor, often need to be addressed to make supply chains socially and environmentally responsible. Without investment to overcome common barriers, supply problems may arise, reinforcing the impression that smallholder involvement inevitably raises costs and leads to variations in product quality and problems with integrity and traceability.

Intermediary organizations between farmers and buyers are required not only to aggregate production but also to provide support and services to ensure the quality and consistency of production. Lead firms need to recognize and support these services.

It is clear that linking smallholders with well-functioning local or global markets—ranging from local street markets to formal global value chains—plays a critical part in long-term strategies to reduce rural poverty and hunger.

Inclusivity is also essential to be able to provide food for nine billion people by 2050. Smallholder farmers make up 85 percent of the world's farmers. We need to work with every farmer and every piece of land being cultivated in order to meet the food consumption needs of our growing population. To achieve this, government and business alike will need to find new models of growth that are in both environmental and economic balance.

Unilever Changes Its Business Model

In 2011, Unilever publicly acknowledged that growth at any cost was not viable. Given the dynamics that are challenging the global food system, combined with the fact that Unilever is a for-profit company, not growing is not an option. Unilever therefore set out to tackle a vexing question: *How can consumption become sustainable?*

As Unilever wrestled with the question of how growth could accelerate the path to sustainable development, the company reached several conclusions. The main decision it made was that the only way to achieve growth aligned with sustainability was to take responsibility for impacts of products, including water consumption, greenhouse gas emissions, and waste. Unilever began to integrate business strategy with sustainability strategy.

A second, perhaps more revolutionary, conclusion was that the company could no longer control its own destiny: it could only influence the likelihood that it would achieve its strategy. Indeed, if one looks at the environmental impacts of Unilever's products, it's clear that a substantial part of Unilever's greenhouse gas footprint comes from upstream in its supply chains, primarily from farming. To solidify and build on its influence over its own destiny, Unilever took a dramatic step. It accepted responsibility for the *entire* greenhouse gas footprint of its products across the entire value chain. This encompasses everything from the base ingredients of its products all the way through the use of energy and water by consumers of its products and the disposal of waste after consumer use. The company is taking a gamble, in that it knows how limited its influence over consumer behavior is. So among other steps, it is working to educate consumers about the fact that their behaviors have a definite and measureable impact on the world.

Unilever began its sustainability journey with sourcing policy. Because half the raw materials the company buys are from farms and forestry, a secure supply of these materials is a core business need. Unsustainable farming practices will have serious repercussions on the environment and in grower communities. Unilever concluded that this presents an operational and reputational risk to its business. After all, the company's business is dependent on a complex network of thousands of farmers: smallholders as well as large agribusinesses and third-party suppliers.

As we will see throughout this chapter, Unilever's policy of sustainable sourcing is critical to its growth plan. Sustainable sourcing not only enables the company to manage a key business risk but also presents an opportunity for growth in a way that accelerates the journey toward sustainable development.

The Unilever Sustainable Living Plan Changes the Game

As noted earlier in this book, Unilever's plan to decouple growth from its impact on society is called the Unilever Sustainable Living Plan (USLP). The USLP is a reflection of a deeply held belief. The company appears to sincerely believe that for a business to have a license to operate, a license to sell, and most particularly, a license to grow, it has to adapt its business model to its supply chain's needs in order to collectively generate positive economic, social, and environmental outcomes.

Sustainable sourcing became a pillar of the USLP as a result of Unilever's fifteen-year-long (and counting) quest to understand and then achieve a sustainable agriculture program. This program began as an attempt to evaluate the best approach for Unilever to make a meaningful difference. It was fueled not by an arrogant belief that Unilever had all the answers but rather by an understanding that the company has access to more knowledge than the average farmer. Its network of university and government affiliations provides a steady flow of insight. In this sense, Unilever can serve as connector and agent of change, either directly or indirectly to farmers, usually through the company's suppliers.

Collaboration: The Key Ingredient

Unilever's focus on sustainable sourcing began with ingredients for which it had direct relationships with farmers—for example, tomatoes, peas, and tea. With the USLP commitment to 100 percent sustainable sourcing by 2020, Unilever now also needs to influence complex long-distance supply of bulk commodities like soy and corn. It needs to be able to verify that these commodities are produced with attention to environmental and social impacts, and it also needs to take account of food security where these products are grown. It can't do these things alone.

Unilever therefore collaborates with other food companies to create standards and verification tools. Some collaborations enable Unilever to innovate with ingredients and adapt to changing markets. For example, in Ghana, Unilever buys fruit from the Allanblackia tree for oil production, but the length of time needed for the seeds to germinate was causing supply constraints. By listening to farmers, Unilever's supplier, Novel Corporation, has discovered a couple of innovations that have been combined to reduce germination times.

Collaboration with both the public and civil sectors enables issues that companies are less well equipped to deal with—such as access to shared resources (for example, land) between households, opportunities for women, issues of education and health (such as HIV)—to be addressed through co-investment. A third-party "facilitator" who understands the separate worlds of commerce and development can often support the creation of new trade relationships, reducing risks for all parties and gradually building up mutual trust between them.

Collaborating with the public and civil sectors are one thing; working with intra-industry rivals is something entirely different. Yet there is a realization among consumer goods companies that there is a shared interest in securing the future supply of raw materials. One shared aim of food companies is to raise the skills and productivity of smallholders so that they increase their income while buyers benefit from sustainably sourced crops and security of supply.

What Is "Sustainable Sourcing"?

Each of Unilever's agricultural raw materials, whether tea, tomatoes, or soy, has a different growing method. When Unilever began working on this issue, there were no agreed-on definitions of what sustainable farming meant for these and other crops.

Over the past fifteen years, the company has developed detailed guidelines on what sustainable agriculture means for its key crops. Unilever defines sustainable sourcing according to eleven social, economic, and environmental indicators:

- *Soil health:* improving the quality of soil and its ability to support plant and animal life
- *Soil loss:* reducing soil erosion that can lead to loss of nutrients
- *Nutrients:* reducing the loss of nutrients through harvesting, leaching, erosion, and emissions to air
- *Pest management:* reducing the use of pesticides
- *Biodiversity:* helping improve biodiversity
- *Farm economics:* improving the product quality and yield
- *Energy:* reducing the greenhouse gas emissions associated with farming
- *Water:* reducing the loss and contamination of water supplies from agriculture
- *Social and human capital:* ensuring the capacity of people to earn and sustain their livelihoods as well as enhancing farmers' knowledge, training, and confidence
- *Local economy:* helping sustain local communities
- *Animal welfare:* ensuring animal standards are based on the "five freedoms" defined by the Farm Animal Welfare Council

These eleven indicators are now formalized in the Unilever Sustainable Agriculture Code—detailed guidelines for agricultural best practice. The code applies to all Unilever suppliers of agricultural goods, the farmers producing them, and contractors working on farms. The code is incorporated into the company's contracts with its own growers.

The USLP, above all else, is a public commitment to the Collaboration Economy. Unilever has gambled on, or invested significantly in (take your pick), the likelihood that it can nurture numerous partnerships across the triumvirate of sectors to achieve its goals. Within the USLP, Unilever has set three objectives it plans to achieve by 2020. It will

- Help more than a billion people take action to improve their health and well-being.

- Decouple its growth from its environmental impact, achieving absolute reductions across the product life cycle. Its goal is to halve the environmental footprint of the production and use of its products.

- Source 100 percent of its agricultural raw materials sustainably and enhance the livelihoods of hundreds of thousands of people in its supply chain.

With the USLP squarely in mind, Unilever committed to improve the livelihoods of more than five hundred thousand smallholder farmers and small-scale distributors in its supply chain. General consensus throughout the global food system is that the largest untapped potential in agriculture resides with small farmers. A characteristic that illustrates the ethos of the Collaboration Economy is that Unilever has publicly committed to help these smallholders improve their agricultural practices and thus enable them to become more competitive. By doing so, Unilever plans on improving smallholders' livelihoods.

But make no mistake, Unilever's smallholder efforts are not simply altruistic. Rather, its strategy to improve the lives of smallholder farmers is driven by the need to be a good citizen in growing market areas and is informed by the belief that more affluent farmers can lead to bigger markets for Unilever products. Indeed, small-scale farming is the dominant model of farming in the regions in the world where Unilever intends to grow its business, including Asia, Africa, and Latin America.

Unilever must achieve an impressive twofold goal in order to complete the USLP's mission. First, given the sheer number of farmers to reach, Unilever must devise an effective outreach campaign. Second, to improve farmers' livelihoods, Unilever must provide tangible value to the smallholders it plans to engage.

Unilever's approach is to work closely with its suppliers to help them improve their farming practices and minimize their environmental impacts. Such adjustments incur costs and investments; some of the top suppliers might balk at taking on these extra efforts.

Unilever has to offer mutual benefits to its suppliers. So if suppliers successfully embrace sustainability, the payoff to supply chain partners is that they will be able to exploit Unilever's global scale, growth potential, and brands. Unilever has had to develop a new procurement culture, employing a lighter touch and working more transparently, and has had to offer longer-term commitments to its key partners.

Unilever's efforts are intended to gradually change the way the company interacts with its suppliers. One change: the company is engaged in many more conversations with its suppliers now than at any other time in its history. Unilever has a group of between 150 and 200 suppliers that it considers to be strategic. It has instituted supplier summits as a way both to communicate about the USLP with its suppliers and to enable its suppliers to further develop their own businesses. As an example of these "Partner to Win" events, Unilever and its suppliers jointly looked at three issues: sustainability, innovation, and talent management. Specifically, the company first presented an update on USLP. Then it showed suppliers where Unilever's pain points exist. Unilever asked its suppliers for help: the company presented its suppliers with a series of questions, and they, in turn, told Unilever what they think they can contribute in terms of one of these three issues.

At the same time, the company has dedicated considerable resources to building a portfolio of partnerships with its suppliers in the form of joint business development plans. The arrangements are fairly simple. If Unilever can grow its sales as a result of a supplier's efforts, then it can give more business to the supplier. The company is finding that addressing the topic of sustainability results in very different conversations with suppliers accustomed to talking with Unilever solely about price, volume, and technical specifications.

Similar to partnerships with large suppliers, Unilever's smallholder inclusion efforts must find ways to provide smallholders with mutual value. So Unilever has focused on providing smallholders with incentives, training, and tools to help improve their production and raise their standard of living. In the process of working with smallholders, Unilever also plans on improving environmental conditions in the global food system, sharing best practices intended to maintain and improve soil fertility, enhance water quality and availability, and protect biodiversity.

Incentives for Farmers

One of the biggest challenges Unilever has had with showing farmers ways to improve their methods is the need to overturn the assumption that sustainability efforts increase costs. Unilever's experience has been that as a rule, implementing sustainability practices at the farm level improves overall management and also leads to better yields and lower costs. Much of sustainable agriculture is all about employing the best technology available and ensuring that the best agricultural practices are applied consistently.

More often than not, sustainable sourcing programs in the past helped farmers reach a point where they could get certified against a sustainability standard. But support dwindled or disappeared once that point was reached. And often, only part of the produce could be sold as certified in a premium market, whereas the rest had to be sold as conventional. This demotivated farmers. The benefit of applying sustainable practices in farming (codified in a standard or not) should lie in the fact that farmers can improve the quality of their soil, the quality of their produce, their yield levels, and their livelihoods. The benefit for the farmer should therefore take center stage in any approach to sustainable sourcing.

Training

Working with others, Unilever had provided training on better agricultural practices to over three hundred thousand smallholders as of the end of 2011. The training is structured to equip farmers to improve practices, increase yields, and earn higher margins—all of which lead to improved livelihoods. Together with Rainforest Alliance, the Kenya Tea Development Agency, and the Sustainable Trade Initiative, Unilever's Lipton tea brand supports farmer field schools in Kenya. As a result, 250,000 farmers in Kenya have now undertaken training. Nearly forty-five thousand more have also been trained in Rwanda, Sri Lanka, and Indonesia; and in a separate initiative in Turkey, Lipton reached another five thousand smallholders. Unilever is now working to establish whether this has increased these smallholders' income and improved their livelihoods.

Tools and Resources

In 2010, Unilever launched the Cool Farm Tool, a calculator to help farmers reduce carbon emissions on their farms. In addition to raising awareness of the impact of their actions on the climate, the tool prompts farmers to make improvements that often cut bills as well as benefit the planet. It is designed to be simple and practical to use, allowing farmers to identify the changes that will have an impact on reducing emissions. It also allows farmers to prioritize options by running different scenarios to see how much of an impact they make. The calculator takes account of a wide variety of factors, such as soil, climate, livestock, land use, and input intensities, then presents the user with measures that can be implemented at the field and farm levels.

In the spirit of collaboration, Unilever has made the Cool Farm Tool available for other companies to use free of charge. Nearly twenty companies are using the tool, and now Unilever has ceded its intellectual property to a broadly owned Cool Farm Institute.

Example of the USLP in Action

Unilever's future success is dependent on its brands' adoption of the USLP and related activities.

Knorr is one of Unilever's biggest brands, present in over eighty countries with such products as soups, bouillon cubes, and seasonings. The Knorr brand team worked with Unilever's sustainable sourcing team to understand sustainability broadly and the Sustainable Agriculture Code specifically. They saw an opportunity to differentiate the brand from competitors based not on the sustainability story but on the documentable sustainability efforts under way throughout Unilever as a result of the USLP. The Knorr team figured that its suppliers would play a critical role in Knorr's ability to pursue sustainability; the question was how to get suppliers on board with needed changes and expected behaviors.

For suppliers to prove that they are in compliance with the Sustainable Agriculture Code, they need to buy and use a particular brand of environmental impact measurement software. This involves, first of all, an economic engagement from them (buying the software). It also involves a change in how they work, because now Knorr requests that suppliers monitor these different environmental indicators. So the economic and change factors were significant to Knorr's suppliers and the farmers that supply the suppliers. Knorr decided to support its suppliers to make these and other additive changes to their operations.

Knorr set up a €1 million partnership fund to help suppliers improve their sustainability practices. The fund provides 50 percent of the investment needed for suppliers and farmers to adopt technologies and practices that put them in compliance with Unilever's Sustainable Agriculture Code. In 2011, the fund set up twenty-eight projects with suppliers in ten countries. To make suppliers aware of the Sustainable Agriculture Code and the Knorr Sustainability Partnership Fund, Knorr held its first sustainable agriculture summit in November 2010. Through events such as this summit, the company has shared best practices with its suppliers and upstream farmers. For example, through the fund, two grants were awarded to Spanish tomato grower Agraz. As well as cutting water use, Agraz has supported biodiversity by creating an environment in which such birds as white storks and black-shouldered kites can thrive. Agraz's farm has now been designated a Knorr "Landmark Farm." This is a win-win situation because Agraz is showcased as one of the best tomato suppliers, and Knorr in turn references Agraz as an example of best practices in sustainable farming.

These supplier summits equip Knorr to build deeper relationships with its suppliers. During the summits, the company emphasizes the impact its suppliers have on Knorr's ability to differentiate from its peers. In particular, Knorr highlights not only its suppliers' efforts but also the ultimate impact of these efforts on Knorr's ability to achieve sustainability. This little extra context goes a long way toward transforming vendors into loyal partners.

Suppliers' Response

Initially, Knorr was uncertain how its suppliers would react to the Sustainable Agriculture Code. After all, the company was asking for extra efforts from its suppliers: to transform themselves into sustainable sources and to invest time, know-how, and scarce capital into their operations. However, the majority of suppliers viewed the requirement to become sustainable as a natural extension of working with Unilever; as one supplier put it, "We understand this is a continuous improvement journey; we can improve so Unilever can ultimately improve too. Nobody can stand still in this situation."

Deciding in Whom to Invest

The Knorr Sustainability Partnership Fund relies on the eleven indicators from the Unilever Sustainable Agriculture Code to evaluate projects for which suppliers are requesting funding. The company considers only those proposals that clearly help suppliers improve in any of these metrics.

A multidisciplinary team of Knorr and Unilever executives was created to determine which projects receive funding. Members of the Sustainable Sourcing Working Group come from marketing, supply chain, procurement, R&D, and the sustainable sourcing team. The group evaluates proposals monthly.

Internal Unilever Changes

Clearly, several internal changes are needed for a global company like Unilever to carry out its USLP and collaboration efforts. The company has made three internal adjustments: one change signals to the market how long-term-focused Unilever truly is; the second change was the creation of new groups within procurement; the third change is the development and subsequent adoption of a certain type of software.

Long-Term Focus

Paul Polman, Unilever's CEO, is convinced that Unilever must not waver from its long-term perspective. As part of his commitment to this view, he spearheaded a change in the company's quarterly communications with the investment community. Specifically, Unilever no longer provides corporate forecast updates every quarter.

Organizational Changes

The company's sustainable sourcing development group is responsible for establishing all the sustainability standards that Unilever uses in procurement and has developed the model for how to engage with suppliers on sustainability. There is also a procurement operations sustainable sourcing group. This team coordinates the implementation of Unilever's sustainable sourcing policy. Questions this team considers include *Where are the big volumes? Where do they come from?* and *Who are the big suppliers in each commodity group that the company sources?* Unilever has delivered face-to-face training sessions, blogs, e-modules, and other training materials in order to prepare the procurement function to source materials sustainably.

Procurement- and Collaboration-Enabling Software

Unilever relies on its Web-based tool called EIGER to inform procurement and supplier decisions. EIGER specifically provides maps giving detailed information about agricultural raw materials, biodiversity, water, GDP, and population. The software, the database of which was compiled from a range of R&D organizations and institutes, helps Unilever identify new supply chains and new supply routes to ensure a secure supply of raw materials over the long term. It identifies opportunities and risks posed by global environmental and social trends that the company needs to consider when making sourcing decisions. These include

- *New sourcing countries:* Where do crops grow best? Where will they grow best in the future?

- *Water vulnerability:* Which areas suffer water scarcity? Which will in the future? What is the irrigation water demand for an area's crops?

- *Biodiversity impacts:* Are existing or new sites and supply chains close to or inside biodiversity conservation areas?

Challenges to Unilever's Approach

As we've seen, sustainable sourcing is at the heart of the USLP. But how can Unilever, or any company, *know* that it is receiving sustainably sourced goods? This is a challenge for Unilever, as only a third of Unilever's agricultural raw materials can be sourced against current certification standards like Rainforest Alliance and Fair Trade or through roundtables like the Forest Steward-ship Council and the Roundtable on Sustainable Palm Oil.

In regions where there is no global or national standard, Unilever has to work with industry bodies and roundtables to develop standards and ensure that primary producers apply them. For raw materials without a formal certification standard, Unilever asks its suppliers to assess their farmers against the eleven key indicators described earlier in this chapter and to use software to track their progress and identify opportunities for continuous improvement.

Call to Action

Our call to action for other companies is to participate in the reframing of the food sector's business model. Heed the lessons Unilever is learning to fast-track your company's learning process.

In some ways, collaboration with rivals and suppliers is the only way certain necessary investments can be made. Together with retailers, food manufacturers, including Unilever, are closest to consumers. We need to translate consumer needs into goals for our suppliers; in turn, these suppliers must work with their suppliers and ultimately the farmers to ensure that these values are incorporated. Our aim is to ensure continued access to our key agricultural raw materials and ultimately to develop market mechanisms that allow consumers and retailers to influence the sourcing of raw materials through their buying habits.

As executives even within Unilever have discovered, companies only make changes that are cost-neutral or that gain consumer support. They cannot add costs, in isolation, that make them less competitive. They would not survive. Some of the costs of sustainability require co-investment by other sectors.

The limits to change within individual value chains or competitive markets will frame the next frontier of large-scale business transformation. Some of the most experienced leaders are describing these limits to one another, articulating that they see the limitations of acting alone, particularly where they run into costs that can't be borne by the supply chain in the current competitive structure, or where the competitive structure itself includes perverse incentives. These frustrations lead either to backsliding or to a willingness to collaborate across the sector and with unlikely allies, such as NGOs that have previously been critical.

The most important collaborative initiatives will marshal the best competencies of business, NGOs, and the public sector. The fertile ground of systemic change is in this partnership arena; one outcome will be the creation of new organizational forms that enable practical management of the environmental commons as well as coordinated investments in opportunities for the poor. Unilever is showing how to execute as well as dream.

5

RESPONSIBILITY AS PROFITABILITY: TOWARD RESPONSIBLE SHIPBREAKING

Petter Heier and Eric Lowitt

The following are some recent headlines:

- Nigeria, May 2, 2012: Abandoned Ships a Rusting Hazard in Nigeria Waters[1]
- Pakistan, March 3, 2012: Gaddani Shipbreakers Defy Death Everyday[2]
- Brussels, February 23, 2012: Asbestos Still a Threat to Thousands of Workers in the Shipbreaking Industry[3]
- Bangladesh, January 13, 2012: Supreme Court Asks High Court to Examine Shipbreaking Rules[4]
- Bangladesh, October 17, 2011: Bangladesh Ship Breaking Workers Die After Inhaling Gas[5]

The maritime shipping industry is schizophrenic. There is no other way to describe an industry that both embodies meticulous care *and* abhors responsibility at the end of its vessels' useful lives. For an industry that has literally been around since the dawn of time (see Noah's Ark) and thus has had ample time to operate idyllically, it is inexcusable that the industry's actions continue to inspire headlines like the aforementioned five.

Commercial shipowners are finally working on making ship dismantling safe and environmentally conscious. In the process, these companies, led by Grieg Shipping Group, are shepherding the emergence of a new business model for the industry, one that holds the promise of ensuring that those headlines become at worst outliers and at best obsolete. The new business model can best be described as *responsibility as profitability*. To see why this business model is a critical change of pace for the industry, let's first look at the current state of the shipping industry.

Overview of the Maritime Shipping Industry

The maritime shipping industry has been a vital part of global commerce for centuries, perhaps millennia. Indeed, until the mid-twentieth century, shipping was the only way to move products (and people) across bodies of water. Today's shipping industry is regarded as one of the most efficient modes of transportation in terms of both cost and environmental footprint.

Vessels go through three phases in their life cycle: birth, use, and dismantling. The arrival of a new vessel to a shipowner is cause for celebration. How often have we seen new vessels "christened" by smashing a bottle of bubbly against the hull?

Shipping vessels receive meticulous attention during their useful lives. The vessel is under the care of an entire organization, ashore and on board; each individual has his own responsibilities. A superintendent is responsible for overseeing these efforts. One important part of the superintendent's role is to inspect the vessel frequently in order to ensure that the standards on board are as expected by the owners and also to coordinate and cooperate with the management on board for the daily operations for the next months. The maintenance on board is crucial in order to keeping the vessel in top condition. Along with safety issues, there is also an economic factor to proper maintenance. For instance, a poorly maintained vessel will often require more frequent replacement of steel because it has corroded faster than on a vessel that is in good condition.

The public sector is involved during a vessel's life, too. Indeed, regulatory inspectors go on board every vessel once a year to conduct a survey; every fifth year, there is a special survey that is much more in depth. They check everything from the condition of the machinery and the steel to the condition of the paint on the ballast tanks.

Considering that the useful life of shipping vessels is between twenty to thirty-five years, it's easy to understand why they are maintained to quite demanding standards. The end of that period, however, marks the end of that caring approach.

A vessel that has reached the end of its life is not very easy to dispose of, and doing so in a sustainable way is even more difficult. In the old days, it was quite easy to dispose of a vessel: the old wooden frigates would sail until they sank. Today few shipowners and other involved parties are thinking about the end of a vessel's life, and many should be.

The ship recycling industry is infamous—mostly due to an almost total lack of safety and environmental standards. Traditionally, vessels have been sold, often through middlemen, to the highest bidders—normally the yards (or plots) that have invested the least in training, equipment, and facilities.

It's not uncommon for a vessel to first be stripped of any physical ties (for example, logos) to its owner. Once devoid of such identifying markings, the vessel is then sold through one or more middlemen to a shipbreaking yard. The vast majority of these shipbreaking yards are in various parts of Asia. All too often, the rusting, stark hulls of once proud vessels, having been stripped of valuable steel, are left to rot on beaches in Bangladesh and other developing countries.

In the Waste Economy, the process through which these abandoned vessels are "dismantled" yields an astronomical collective economic cost. The environmental damage caused by this accepted process is almost incalculably high. But these incredibly severe costs pale in comparison to the widespread loss of health, limbs, and human lives (as noted in the chapter-opening headlines).

Oil can be spotted just offshore from where these vessels are dismantled. Workers from all age groups, in and of itself disconcerting, use anything they can find to take the ship apart—blowtorches, axes, hammers, and so on. It has been reported that eight people die each month at these sites. It is an understatement merely to say that numerous environmental and social challenges arise as a result of these companies' dismantling efforts.

There are about three hundred demolition plots worldwide serving international shipping clients. Less than 10 percent of these yards are of a standard considered acceptable according to modern safety and environmental regulations. There are vast differences among the recycling yards in the most active countries. Companies in India, Pakistan, and Bangladesh dismantle vessels through the beaching method, consisting of running the vessel aground on the beach (a plot), where the vessel is dismantled. A correspondent with the *Asahi Shimbun* newspaper in Japan recently described the beaching method like this: "Decommissioned ships are run aground and then hauled to the beach with ropes, much as slaves in ancient Egypt moved huge stone blocks to build the pyramids."[6]

How can an industry almost as old as time itself be both lauded for its meticulous care shown toward cargo and vessels *and* called out for its lack of care at the end of ships' lives? Can solving this riddle offer a path to greater prosperity for shipbuilders, shipowners, and ship breakers while also improving both the environmental impact of shipbreaking and the lives of workers who depend on the industry for jobs? And what type of collaboration among these disparate entities is needed to do so?

In the Collaboration Economy, the shipbreaking business model will be transformed into an engine of economic prosperity, stable employment, and reduced dependence on the environment for natural materials and energy sources. This chapter shows how, and discusses what a leading company is doing to shepherd this change and what your company can learn from this company's experience.

The Current Model of Ship Dismantling

The current model of ship dismantling consists of this chain of steps:

- Using a broker, the shipowner first sells the vessel to a middleman.
- The middleman or cash buyer then sells the vessel to a dismantling yard in a developing country, such as India, Pakistan, or Bangladesh. Alternatively, the middleman trades the vessel to another broker if it makes economical sense for him; this may occur against the original shipowner's will. In the process, all links between the vessel and the shipowner are removed.
- The vessel is dismantled by workers who have few acknowledged rights or safety measures to protect them from their risky activities.

It bears repeating that the external costs of these activities are severe. First consider the environmental impact of dismantling a massive ship consisting of steel and many hazardous materials (such as asbestos, freon, oils, and other chemicals), which are spilled into the shallow waters of ecologically fragile beaches. The vessel's cables are often burned right on the beach. There is mounting evidence that, for example, several critical species of fish are rapidly disappearing from countries that dismantle vessels in an irresponsible manner.

Far worse, however, is the incalculable human cost to the workers. If a worker is moderately lucky, he will *only* be blinded or develop an illness as a result of prolonged exposure to toxic materials. Less lucky are the workers who lose a limb or, even worse, their lives.

Why would a shipowner accept these adverse outcomes? There are at least two reasons. First is that among vessel disposal options, the beaching method of ship dismantling pays the highest available price to the shipowner. Shipyards that use the beaching method are able to offer the highest prices for used vessels as a result of their chronic underinvestment in both their facilities and their workers. The resultant operational decisions cause numerous negative environmental and social impacts. Examples of these operational decisions include the low wages they pay their workers, the employment of a workforce that is primarily composed of nonorganized migrant workers, an appalling lack of safety measures and equipment to ensure worker safety, underreliance on proper methods to dispose of hazardous materials encountered during the dismantling process, and chronic underinvestment in proper tools and technologies. The shipyards recoup their investment in the vessel by reselling the steel they strip from it.

The second reason shipowners choose to accept the significant downsides to the beach method is that they have not been forced to internalize the external costs of using this method.

Currently, shipowners choose one of two options to dispose of vessels that have reached the end of their useful lives. So far in this chapter, we have discussed only one option, the more lucrative beaching method. The second is the less lucrative, more responsible quayside dismantling method. Government-approved yards in China, for example, use quayside demolition methods combined with the use of heavy cranes and floating or dry docks.

The majority of shipowners prefer the profitability that comes from selling their used vessels to beaching-method shipyards to the positive reputation effects that come as a result of perceived altruistic behavior—to the tune of four to one. That is, of the approximately eight hundred vessels that are dismantled each year, 80 percent are dismantled via the beaching method.[7]

Given the unacceptable environmental and social costs of irresponsible ship-dismantling activities, the question becomes, *How do we get the shipping industry en masse to embrace responsibility?* The key is that companies must internalize the externalities of their actions. These external costs are of such a magnitude that only collective action among the Golden Triangle of sectors can bring them down.

This process is now under way, though it is off to a rocky start. Indeed, the journey toward internalization began in earnest in 1998. The International Maritime Organization (IMO), a UN agency charged with developing a regulatory framework for shipping, began operations in the 1950s. The Basel Convention, covering the trade of hazardous materials (including end-of-life ships), was entered into force in 1992. In 1998, the IMO's Marine Environment Protection Committee began to consider the need for responsible shipbreaking policies. These deliberations bore fruit in 2002 when it was determined that the IMO should develop regulatory guidelines to be adopted by the UN Assembly. In 2009, the IMO adopted the Hong Kong Convention (HKC), a legally binding instrument that aims to raise shipbreaking to responsible standards. However, the HKC has still not entered into force because an insufficient number of countries have ratified it. It is anticipated that the HKC will not be entered into force until 2020 at the earliest.

Perhaps the most significant contribution the HKC will make is the enactment of a requirement that all shipowners develop and maintain an inventory of hazardous materials for each of their ships. But no matter how thoughtful, the HKC moves neither fast enough nor far enough to promote responsible ship recycling worldwide. For one thing, as noted, the HKC will not go into effect for several years. Perhaps more important, the HKC neither directly nor publicly bans the beaching method. Although such a ban was seriously considered, it was determined that beaching-method shipyards would prevent the adoption of the HKC, delaying the adoption of other useful changes to ship recycling policy. So the HKC will eventually lead to improvements, but will not force companies to be accountable for internalizing the externalities of their actions.

Toward a New and Responsible Method of Ship Recycling

In place of the current outdated and flawed ship recycling model, shipping companies such as Grieg Green are adopting a new, more responsible approach.

The story of Grieg Green's origin is not extraordinary. The fact that it isn't suggests that almost any company can follow in Grieg's footprints. One of this chapter's authors, Petter Heier, has long worked with Grieg Shipping Group, including among his roles the responsibility of vessel superintendent, as described earlier in this chapter. As a graduate-level business student, he developed a business plan for Grieg Shipping Group to create a for-profit company to promote responsible ship recycling methods. Essentially Petter presented his plan to Grieg Shipping Group's senior leadership team, which approved the plan. They then installed Petter as CEO of this new company, provided him with investment capital, and charged him with responsibility for bringing the vision to life. In late 2010, Grieg Green was launched.

Grieg Green is setting about to change the way ship recycling occurs. Simply put, the company is building a portfolio of ship recycling yards to which it can send ships for responsible dismantling. Grieg Green works only with quayside ship recycling companies, as it has found the quayside method of ship dismantling to be both more environmentally friendly than the beaching method and compliant with international safety standards.

Equipped with this portfolio of relationships with independent quayside ship recycling yards, Grieg Green then seeks to buy end-of-life vessels from shipowners, including competitors of its parent company, once these shipowners request bids for their vessels. If Grieg Green wins the bidding process, it then transfers the vessel to be dismantled to one of the responsible shipyards in its relationship portfolio. Grieg Green will sell the newly purchased vessel to a responsible ship plot at exactly the same price that it paid for it.

When it prepares to purchase a vessel, Grieg Green enters into two simultaneous negotiations: purchase with the shipowner (occasionally through a broker) and sale of the vessel to a quayside yard. The company's profit comes from earning what's known as an "address commission" of between 2 and 4 percent (dependent on a variety of factors) from the shipowner. The address commission is a commission paid by the shipowner to Grieg Green in return for Grieg Green's addressing (and then solving) the problem of responsible ship disposal by the shipowner.

One would correctly wonder how a new company is able to earn the trust of its rivals, especially in this hardscrabble market. Here is where we can learn a lesson from Grieg Green's experience. The company positions itself as an intermediary counterparty for both parties of the transaction, the shipowner and the recycling yard.

Indeed, most shipowners have limited knowledge of the ship recycling yards in China. To these owners, Grieg Green provides security for the financial transaction but also a hedge against the shipyard's potential default and possible lawsuits. After all, many companies in the shipping industry have experienced extremely complex defaults and lawsuits in China. Such experiences can be traced back to a lack of a deep relationship between the shipowner and the ship recycling yard. Grieg Green has built these kinds of relationships not only with the yards but also with governmental representatives. The company has earned trust within China; such trust is a competitive advantage, as it takes a considerable investment of time to develop these relationships.

Grieg Green's acting as an intermediary also provides value to the recycling yards, particularly in the form of trust. There are thousands of owners in the process of selling their ships; conducting detailed due diligence on each of these shipowners represents a significant cost (and associated risk) for the recycling yards.

In this way, Grieg Green is setting about a chain of events that will ultimately reshape how the shipping sector operates and how shipowners selectively collaborate with otherwise fierce rivals.

━━━

Here is what we believe needs to happen in order for this new model of ship recycling to become the standard approach. Shipowners must be held responsible for the end of the lives of their vessels. Ideally the same owner would own the vessel—and responsibility for its impacts—throughout its entire life, including its disassembly. This is challenging for many reasons. One issue has to do with the state of maritime legislation. The industry needs legislation that governs the practices for ship recycling that apply to the entire value chain (from new building to downstream waste management) of a vessel. This legislation has to be as "waterproof" as possible, taking into consideration the challenges of the global shipping industry with flag issues. (Any owner can register its vessel in any flag state in the world for which those rules will apply.) It is also crucial that this legislation ensure fair competition in the market.

Bringing the Responsible
Ship Recycling System to Life

We've seen throughout *The Collaboration Economy* how trailblazing companies collaborate with rivals to address vexing and significant problems held in common. The shipping industry's recent history further underscores the value of such collaboration. Peers in the shipping industry do have a history of working together when solving an issue serves their common interest.

Witness the maritime shipping industry's Energy Management in Practice (EMIP) initiative, for example. The EMIP started in March 2010 with the intention of reducing harmful emissions through improvement of the efficiency of ships. The project is a result of cooperation among several leading shipping companies. An important ambition for the project is to increase knowledge of energy management within the shipping community in Norway. The importance to Grieg Shipping Group of participating alongside rivals during the EMIP project can be explained thusly:

> Grieg Shipping Group has a strong belief in this project for several reasons. One vital reason is the acknowledgment that the probability of success related to improving energy efficiency on ships is substantially increased by cooperation between serious shipowning companies that want to "make a difference." Another reason is the fact that this project will encompass, in a structured way, integration of all earlier and current efforts done related to improving energy efficiency in the Grieg Fleet. The same is the case for the other companies. The end product of this is expected to yield positive effect both financially and environmentally. The positive effect will hopefully contribute to improving the shipping community's environmental reputation in society.

Industry associations have their place. But for broad and lasting change to occur, intra-industry collaboration needs to address ever more vital business activities held in common among peers.

Grieg Green: Responsible Shipbreaking as Competitive Strategy

Grieg Green is proving prophetic by building this offering now. The European Union, in an effort to take the HKC further, announced new rules in March 2012 that will take the form of a regulation that proposes a system of surveys, certification and authorization for the large, commercial vessels that fly the flag of an EU member state, covering their whole life cycle from construction to operation and recycling. The system builds upon the Hong Kong Convention for the safe environmentally sound recycling of ships, which was adopted in 2009. Today's proposal aims to implement the convention quickly, without waiting for its ratification. Under the new system, European ships will have to draw up an inventory of the hazardous materials and apply for an inventory certificate. Ship recycling facilities will have to meet a set of environmental and safety regulations.[8]

But regulation enacted by the EU faces strong opposition in the developing world, especially from the beaching method ship-dismantling yards. These companies argue that the ratification and subsequent enforcement of the HKC and the EU's follow-on regulation will force them to incur significant expenses, potentially high enough to shut down many of these companies. If this were to happen, their argument continues, then the economies of the countries in which they operate would suffer. Jobs would be lost. Corporate tax revenues would decrease. And access to steel would be compromised.

Countries including Bangladesh are actively mulling over both sides of the argument about shipbreaking methods. Although the outcome is in doubt, one thing is clear: Grieg Green is not waiting on legislation in order to act. The company has developed a service to provide an attractive alternative to shipowners considering the beaching method to dispose of their vessels. In so doing, Grieg Green is emphasizing the "responsible" (and cost-neutral) choice to the shipowners' aforementioned disposal deliberations: responsible recycling at rates competitive with beaching method prices.

Ingvild Jenssen, director of the NGO Shipbreaking Platform, a coalition of human and labor rights and environmental organizations focused on the prevention of the beaching of toxic end-of-life ships in developing countries, sees that legislation alone will not move the industry to universally adopt responsible means of shipbreaking. Society must work with private sector companies to ensure that the market plays its role in promoting responsible shipbreaking. This is why, she said, her NGO is also looking to the corporate sector for willing partners to join the struggle toward change:

> Most recently, we've realized that simply focusing on legislative solutions or political solutions is probably not enough. So we've initiated a corporate campaign, where we will be trying to work more actively with the progressive shipowners.
>
> So we're pressuring the industry with market solutions, not just legislative and political solutions. That's something we're looking forward to working on and which will be coming up in parallel with our continuing to conduct advocacy, especially here at the European level and in the courts in Bangladesh.

Despite the inherent strategic and economic logic of the Grieg Green model, the company cannot just sit back and wait for business to come to it. Working without the support of immediate and binding global regulation, Grieg Green faces very strong headwinds. One of the difficulties has to do with the set of relationships with the middlemen who broker deals between shipowners and the beaching method shipyards. Shipowners are understandably loath to take on potential new headaches; their business activities are complex enough now. So why should these companies choose to form new relationships with companies such as Grieg Green and develop new processes to administer these relationships? After all, the revenue shipowners receive from the brokers for their vessels is dwarfed by the revenue earned from the shipowners' ongoing activities.

Compounding this rationale for the status quo is the one-two punch of institutional memory and traditionally accepted rules of engagement with the competition. Said plainly, installed in the brains of senior executives in the shipping industry is a now-outdated belief that rivals are rivals, not collaborators. So why would a shipowner buy ship-dismantling services from the competition?

Here's where Grieg Green is actively working to counteract inertia with action. The most important part of the company's development was that it had to build a portfolio of responsible ship recycling yards. Grieg Green handpicks from what it considers to be among the world's top recycling yards, using a proprietary "scorecard" rating method. The company follows up and obtains reports from regular inspections. It monitors its portfolio of yards regularly to offer clients the most competitive and environmentally friendly yards in the market at any given time.

Grieg Green has invested a lot of time, not only conducting audits of the yards to ensure that they are meeting the company's standards but also building relationships with the shipyards. As mentioned earlier, most of these responsible shipyards are based in China, where relationships are essential.

The next challenge was to reach out to Grieg Shipping Group's rival shipowners. There are a very large number of shipowners worldwide, and Grieg Green is a small organization. Grieg Green used a variety of methods to amplify its reach. For example, the company took out advertising in newspapers based on the thought that "responsible shipbreaking really could work."

But the company learned a powerful lesson in China: non-Chinese companies' senior executives really have to meet the people behind the companies. So Grieg Green set a strategy to connect with all these shipowners by working through the ship disposal brokers. After all, the brokers are always involved in the transaction when the ship is sold or bought. Grieg Green has built relationships with these brokers, collaborating with potential rivals in order to extend Grieg Green's reach while bringing to scale this new responsible shipbreaking model. Brokers are motivated to participate because they can possibly earn additional business. Today Grieg Green knows and is in contact with almost all of the world's top brokers.

In addition to its broker outreach strategy, Grieg Green also identified the truly "green" shipowners, given that these owners are more likely to be early adopters of this new collaborative dismantling model. The company realized that working with its parent company's competitors is wrought with difficulty, but decided to pursue this approach to get closer to its target end customers. Basically Grieg Green took this approach in order to sell its products in a better way, because the brokers are not really selling all its services. However, identifying all these owners and visiting with them takes a tremendous amount of time.

Despite the difficulties, this approach is paying dividends. Consider one recent experience with a shipowner in Europe that competes with Grieg Shipping Group. Grieg Green bid for one of this company's end-of-life vessels but lost, despite offering a very competitive price. The company had told Grieg Green early in its development that it would never use Grieg Green services. But then there was a management change that led the company to make a 180-degree turn on its stance on working with competitors. The new management team at the competing company said, "Well, maybe now we can consider Grieg Green services."

After Grieg Green lost the first project on which it bid, the company sent a representative to the shipowner's office to learn more about why it lost and what it could do better next time. Shortly thereafter, the competing shipowner had another project. Grieg Green bid on and won the project. If the Grieg Green representative hadn't visited this customer, it was likely that the company would not have won that project either. This exemplifies why, when you are initiating great change, it is very important to meet the people involved throughout the industry. One needs to explain the process—in Grieg Green's case, why responsible ship recycling is good business all around.

The end result of Grieg Green's efforts to rebuild the shipping industry's business model for responsible ship recycling is that it is contributing positive free cash flow to its parent company. Scale effects of buying ships and facilitating responsible ship recycling will likely yield even higher incremental profitability.

So it is clear that Grieg Green's efforts are not altruistic but profit driven in nature.

Challenges

There are several challenges that stand in Grieg Green's way of effecting great and lasting change. For example, only a handful of owners are willing to be responsible. This is where legislation is critical. Unfortunately, until binding legislation with teeth is enacted, money talks. Rules and regulations need to be enforced, not just enacted. Few owners today are willing to bear the cost of sustainable recycling. When a shipowner is in a financially difficult situation, the first function he will pull resources from is the sustainability function. So ideally we would have a common standard worldwide for recycling at the same price.

But the biggest issue we must resolve is how to engage the companies in Bangladesh, India, Pakistan, and the like, where the beaching method is most prevalent. After all, this industry is very important to these countries' economies. So how will we then fund those countries in order to improve their practices to meet proper recycling standards? Because many of the shipbreaking yard owners in South Asia are making large profits, it will be difficult to motivate these companies to change their shipbreaking cultures, employee conditions, tools, processes, and activities on a massive scale. Should a global fund paid into by countries based on their fleet volume be established to bring beaching-method shipyards up to acceptable standards? These kinds of issues remain outstanding. Grieg Green plans on addressing these issues with the help of its peers, the public sector, and society itself.

Call to Action

Standards for ship dismantling likely will require standards for ship design and construction down the road. Most likely to be affected is the treatment of hazardous materials. This shift is already under way. For example, asbestos was forbidden in ship construction some years back. Other hazardous materials are increasingly being banned from use in vessels. A future challenge is the use of materials that only become hazardous in the recycling process (such as paint that might not be toxic as it is but becomes toxic when burned, which is almost an inevitable practice when the vessel has to be cut in many small pieces).

Shipowners' ability to customize the inner functions of their vessels currently serves as a viable source of competitive advantage. It is possible that the uniqueness derived from the physical infrastructure of vessels will become less distinctive in the wake of ship design standardization. This will leave other services offered by the shipowners as the primary means of gaining competitive advantage. Grieg Green and others like it are truly changing how the shipping industry operates today and tomorrow. Companies in this industry have two choices: get on board or get left behind on shore.

6

RENEWING CONSUMERISM

Judith Merkies MEP, Roope Mokka, and Eric Lowitt

It has always seemed as though a car manufacturer could make a car that is capable of lasting multiple decades. One might replace a battery here, a component there, but otherwise the car could be shared across generations. Of course, "planned multigenerational sharing" of cars would cripple car companies' business models. For one thing, how many people are willing to spend the equivalent of the purchase price of a small house to buy a car?

Yet in Livermore, California, is evidence that this scenario was played out at least once, granted for a less expensive product. In 1901, a lightbulb made by the Shelby Electric Company was installed in a local firehouse. Seventy-five years later, a full police and fire truck escort accompanied the same lightbulb, still capable of shining, to its current firehouse location. Now called the Centennial Light Bulb, this handblown bulb is still burning.

Nearly twenty years after the Centennial Light Bulb was installed, lightbulb manufacturers realized that their very existence would be threatened if they went on making lightbulbs that burned on forever. Together they embraced a guideline that lightbulbs could burn one thousand to fifteen hundred hours at most, thus protecting their business models. Today we are accustomed to frequently replacing our lightbulbs, casually discarding the burned-out bulbs in the process.

━━━

We are adrift in stuff. Politicians reinforce this buy-and-discard dynamic, calling on consumption for growth. This illustrates one way that the interests of the public and private sectors (and, through conspicuous consumption, society as a whole) have diverged from the interest of the environment. It is apparent that we need a coalition of all involved parties if we are going to change the situation.

Throughout *The Collaboration Economy*, we've visited global economic powers in the process of transforming their strategies, their operations, and their corporate cultures. This could give the impression that we're trading off one sector of last hope to cure all our ills (the public sector) for another (the private sector). But a basic tenet of the Collaboration Economy is that all sectors need to pull their weight equally.

So what about the public sector? Rio+20 (the June 2012 UN-convened gathering of countries to pursue a global agreement for climate change policy) and the subsequent UN climate change meeting in Qatar in fall 2012 were the latest disappointments in a string of abject failures by our governing structures to set a course for collaborative change. In the United States, carbon regulation is as likely to pass these days as a return to Prohibition. This story is repeated throughout the world.

Well, surely the civil sector is making great strides, right? Witness the Occupy movement and Arab Spring demonstrations. But is this collection of well-intended and successful efforts sufficient to right the planet's wrongs in a way that drives a new era of prosperity? Not alone.

The market cannot do this alone, either. That's why we've dedicated this chapter to exploring two intriguing efforts initiated separately by the civil and public sectors. Both initiatives think in terms of performance instead of property, and both foster a society in which green choices are more evident for each stakeholder. And most important of all: both have the potential to align growth with sustainable development.

The first section explores the *gatekeepers* concept, which is a hub-and-spoke approach to reach, engage, and influence all citizens in the Collaboration Economy by activating the desires of their combined roles as consumers, citizens, employees, and so on. New approaches to business can also serve to bridge the interests of stakeholders. The second section, therefore, will look into the creation of what's known as a *lease society*. This cross-sector effort to dematerialize—that is, to provide desired services without permanently losing the materials needed for the physical products—is poised to yield tangible results.

Gatekeepers, Prosperity, and Sustainable Development

We all play multiple roles in life, and these roles influence our daily behaviors. At any given time, we are spouses, partners, children, voters, employees, activists, friends, consumers, and influencers. Sometimes these roles lead to conflicting desires. As a homeowner, for example, you might be apt to vote in favor of higher local real estate taxes to invest in better schools for your children. But as a consumer, paying higher real estate taxes reduces your disposable income, pushing off that compelling luxury purchase you have longed to make.

The role of the consumer is the primary role that pundits tend to consider when reviewing society's current contribution to the global economy. In good and bad economic times alike, sovereign nations (and companies) are loath to discourage growth in consumption, for self-evident reasons. Taxes are lowered, stimulus packages are passed, tax-free holiday weekends are cause for celebrations—all in the name of driving the consumption portion of the economy. This makes sense; individual consumptive demand accounts for the majority of global GDP.

Our collective hyperfocus on the consumer role in society has shaped how we view society's influence over the path toward sustainable development. For example, we fixate on consumer surveys about buying preferences related to so-called green products. We applaud surveys which reveal that 90 percent of consumers positively value the sustainable characteristics of products.

We fret when only 20 percent of these same consumers report *actually buying* a green product. Companies that cater to the individual consumer market point to this paradox as an excuse (or reason) for not investing in or offering green products to consumers.

The Collaboration Economy's viability rests upon society's members weaving sustainability behaviors into all their multiple roles. This is not to say that the activist role in particular is not well played. In fact, we believe the opposite: the activist role has played a more positive, change-inducing role in the path toward the Collaboration Economy than has the consumer role. Without activists, there would be no NGOs, for example.

Never before have so many people had so many choices to make with so little time to make each one. We are an instant-gratification society, oftentimes valuing "getting it done" over "doing it right." In our quest to immediately get "the answer," we're not afraid to look to others for advice. Critical-mass adoption of social media has turned anybody with an Internet connection into a potential influencer.

Sadly, the civil sector as a whole hasn't flexed the muscles of its "influencer" role to achieve the Collaboration Economy's goals. But Finnish think tank Demos Helsinki, with initial gravitas and funding provided by SITRA (an influential innovation fund supported by and reporting to Finnish Parliament), is actively working to change this. Over the past four years, Demos Helsinki has researched the question of how to influence the largest possible group of citizens in terms of their relationship with energy. Its core finding is the existence of "gatekeepers" who can (and do) successfully wield influence over citizens' energy use.

The gatekeeper model can be an effective tool for the public and private sectors to effect measured change. By "gatekeepers," we mean individuals and organizations that stand at the intersection of individual consumers and the products and services that consumers desire. Gatekeepers are professionals and industries that are present in people's consumer behavior decisions, such as big energy decisions (that is, decisions that lock our energy use to a certain level for a long time). Gatekeepers include banks that negotiate loans for property; restaurants and grocery stores that define our diets; lifestyle media that create the idea of "normal" homes and diets; hardware stores that sell materials for home renovators; and so forth.

At the center of the gatekeeper model is the Decision Tree. This is a tool that shows all the places where a consumer interacts with a resource. As illustrated in Figure 6.1, the Decision Tree breaks down consumer energy use into everyday decisions. Each decision identifies a place for new business. For example, freeing the individual from car use is rich in new business opportunities—not just rental cars, carpools, taxis, public transport,

Figure 6.1. Decision Tree of Energy Consumption

Energy Gatekeepers in the Decision Tree

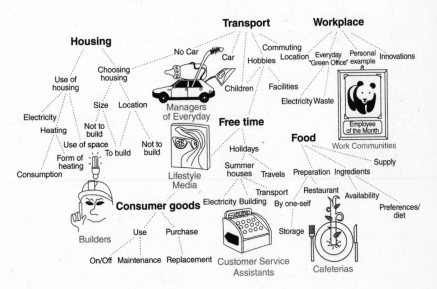

Source: Demos Helsinki

and so forth, but also in the services that enable children's hobbies and shopping for groceries to take place without the need for a car. The key is that any business seeking to deploy the gatekeeper model should look at what decisions affect its customers' footprints and look at ways to offer alternatives to these decisions.

Demos Helsinki has worked with hundreds of professionals from over thirty leading Finnish companies to test a new approach to combining business and social dimensions for financial success. It calls its approach the Peloton strategy. (A peloton is the group that rides together to save energy during a bicycle race; it also means "fearless" in Finnish.) Peloton aims to change consumer behavior: to create new choices, new products and services, new alternatives that are not based on efficiency and niches.

The real opportunity is found in the ability to create new markets by changing people's behavior. Most of the companies with which Demos Helsinki has worked have managed to shift attention from the environmental impact of their enterprise to how all stakeholders can benefit from the behavioral change of customers.

Let's take an example from Demos Helsinki's practical work with chains of hardware stores. Homeowners go to their local hardware stores to buy tools, hardware, and other durable goods to improve their homes. Time has shown that the most effective way for homeowners to cut their level of emissions in the home is through energy refurbishments. Despite their reliance on local hardware stores for home improvement tools, homeowners rarely turn to their preferred hardware store to help them do the refurbishment in an energy-conscious way.

Enter the hardware store. In one of Demos Helsinki's recent Peloton "concept creation" workshops, participating retailers discovered two things about their business when trying to grasp this market opportunity. First, their hardware stores can and should access this market—doing so leads to higher levels of customer retention and value. Second, if they wish to access it, they need to understand customer needs much better in order to become more service oriented.

The core idea of Peloton strategy is that the wicked problems (climate change, food and energy security, among the most vexing) are here to stay worldwide. Therefore, a company that succeeds at creating products and services aimed at solving these challenges will experience nearly unlimited demand in the global marketplace. Freeing people from the need for energy is one of the most probable future services that can be a source of growth for businesses. By learning to use the gatekeeper model, companies can begin to integrate social dimensions into their business activities and offerings.

For those who read strategy literature, this idea must sound familiar. W. Chan Kim and Renée Mauborgne call this kind of market creation "blue ocean strategy."[1] According to Kim and Mauborgne, there are two ways for companies to create new products and services: competing to meet current demand (red oceans) and creating new demand (blue oceans). In the red ocean modus operandi, the company looks at the product offerings of its competitors and takes action in an effort to differentiate from its competitors. The characteristics of red oceans include fast commoditization and "bloody competition." Most, if not all, companies aiming to enter environmentally and socially conscious (that is, "sustainable" products) markets deploy red ocean strategies.

Blue ocean strategies do not look at competition but rather at alternative approaches to reaching new consumer groups. In a famous example, Yellow Tail wine was aimed at changing the behavior of non-wine drinkers. Launched in 2001, it became the most popular wine imported to the United States and accounts for nearly half of all Australian wine purchased. In blue oceans, demand is created rather than fought over. Competition is irrelevant because the rules of the game have been changed.

Similarly, we should not ask how we can make our current products greener and therefore attract ecologically motivated consumers. *Instead, we should be thinking of ways to replace the most resource-heavy forms of consumption.*

This represents a fundamental shift in perspective. It's a shift that makes sense from both the business perspective and the natural resources perspective. For example, instead of asking how to make cars more efficient, we're asking what kinds of services would free people from the daily need for cars; instead of looking at the technical aspects of insulation and heating, we're asking what kind of services would free consumers from the need for extra space for infrequent guests and storage of temporarily unused stuff.

The main criticism of blue ocean strategy has been that it requires leaders of corporations to make a leap well beyond their companies' comfort zones. Most organizations and employees are here to maintain the status quo, no matter how bloody the competition. When a company deploys the Peloton strategy, the push comes from employee emancipation: employees who previously worried about their professions' contribution to climate change and other ecological ills are deeply motivated when they can turn the table around and start working for the common good.

The Peloton strategy has an additional outcome that other bold strategic moves often lack: it resonates with employees' values and taps into professional pride. When working with gatekeepers involved in consumers' energy purchase decisions, Demos Helsinki has found that the Peloton strategy motivates gatekeepers by transforming their professional role: formerly sinners, they become heroes. Specifically, the Peloton strategy transforms these professionals into people who can create new business, succeed in their work, and help curb their customers' emissions at the same time. Understanding this, Demos Helsinki has stressed the importance of personal and even ethical engagement to the Peloton strategy.

In its series of Peloton workshops with key gatekeeper industries (hardware stores, grocery stores, and so on), Demos Helsinki has looked at how to create blue oceans of sustainable consumption. Demos Helsinki's findings demonstrate that studying the needs, perspectives, and motivations of people during their big resource and energy flow decisions yields four insights for smart companies:

1. *Opening gates via gatekeepers drives personal engagement and strategy deployment.* People who are gatekeepers by profession are emancipated by the knowledge that by doing their job well, they can help people live according to their values and save the planet. In other words, the cognitive dissonance caused by ever-increasing ecological consciousness in relation to people's day-to-day jobs can be turned into an asset. There is reason to believe that this cognitive dissonance can have a serious impact on the productivity and innovativeness of the workforce. A growing mountain of studies shows that being able to express one's values at work (or at least not being forced to work against them) is increasingly important for the workforce at large—especially in workplaces that already recognize themselves as "values driven" and "human-centric."

2. *Understanding energy is understanding people.* Energy has a special nature—it can be used as labor almost anywhere. Therefore, the consumption of energy on an individual and household level tells an interesting story about a person's lifestyle. A recent Finnish study discovered eleven-fold differences in the environmental footprints of households.[2] Demos Helsinki has seen that in practice this means that analysis of the use of resources can yield a great "map" for understanding people, as powerful as the analysis of the use of time or money. In practice, understanding the reasons behind people's use of energy and other natural resources provides a way for companies to become customer-centric— something that has been very hard for most gatekeeper industries, such as food and construction. Becoming a gate *opener*—changing consumer behavior with new services and

products—can help a company tremendously in becoming human-centric.

3. *Concept is king.* Products and services that change customer behavior need to be communicated by strong concepts. Concepts are business offerings that you and your customers understand; rather than aiming to differentiate based on price, brand, or other traditional marketing factors, successful concepts offer people a new way of doing things. Kim and Mauborgne call concepts "taglines": "Tagline is a phrase that captures the essence of the 'to be' strategy in a way that speaks forcefully to both a company's employees and the target mass of buyers. A blue ocean strategy has a clear-cut and compelling tagline. A compelling tagline ensures that the strategy makes sense. It helps customers identify immediately what is offered, and it helps employees identify what they should concentrate on, thereby, bringing focus to the execution of the strategy."[3] The classic example of a concept is a fast-food restaurant. People order, pay for, and receive their food at the counter. The concept's success means that people using the restaurant understand how it is supposed to work.

4. *Governments can't do it alone.* Curbing emissions by law has been difficult for governments all over the world. In our experience, Peloton companies have been proud to recognize that they have an important role in cutting emissions. Politicians need to reshape their idea of sustainability away from only suppressing emissions toward also creating markets and changing behaviors. Businesses not only do business but also affect people's everyday lives.

———

Up to this point in *The Collaboration Economy*, we've explored cross-sector change that has been reliant on voluntary effort. But what if not enough participants take these necessary actions voluntarily? The public sector will also need to act. The follow-ing section explores one such (potential) public sector action: enacting legislation to bring a lease society to life. In the lease society, consumers lease instead of own the products they choose to consume. The consumer returns the product to the manufac-turer or a middleman for recycling at the end of the product's useful life. Here's how the lease society, an illustrative compo-nent of the Collaboration Economy, might operate.

The Lease Society

As we saw demonstrated by the lightbulb industry in response to the Centennial Light Bulb, planned obsolescence is an essential pillar of the Waste Economy. Moreover, the relentless produc-tion associated with planned obsolescence pits economic growth against the health of the planet. But the realization is hitting us that the road of a fully deregulated Waste Economy will not lead to bliss, any more than will the complete subversion of the capi-talist money and job allocation mechanism. Moreover, history shows that a planned economy model knows even grimmer downsides. The public sector's remit, therefore, is to let markets do their work in a way that serves mankind.

Our best option is to improve on the capitalistic model that has provided centuries of economic development. In particular, we need to find a way that aligns economic with social devel-opment. A society in which consumption of services and the continuous return of postconsumer-use materials are encouraged provides the framework for such an improvement on today's economic model. This is the heart of the Collaboration Economy: consumers and companies working in a "cradle-to-cradle" loop so that each benefits from the experience—in a way that signifi-cantly reduces ecological damage.

There is growing sentiment within the European Union's Par-liament in favor of passing legislation that paves the way for a lease society model. In a lease society, the underlying assumption is that consumers want the service offered by a product and not the physical material of the product itself. Simply put, in this model, consumers lease instead of buying a product outright. In this way, consumers and corporations, at the urging of the public sector, work together to solve the "prisoner's dilemma" of product consumption: getting companies to make more durable products without destroying their businesses in the process.

The manufacturer in a lease society would retain responsibility for its product throughout the product's entire life span, including its use and removal. Embracing this model would bring us closer to a circular economy. Consumers would not be allowed to discard the products they have fully consumed, because the physical materials that make up the product would not be their property. Companies would have to consider the entire life cycle of the product. In this way, they would be motivated to pay more attention to the recyclability of the materials they choose in manufacturing their products.

A range of major political groups is advocating the creation of a lease society. For example, the EU Parliament enacted a range of extended producer responsibility directives, including the Waste Electrical and Electronic Equipment (WEEE) directive and the Restriction of Hazardous Substances (RoHS) directive. These and other directives, both those enacted and those currently being drafted, are signaling to manufacturers operating within the EU's boundaries that they must be prepared to account for the external costs that come from their business activities.

Such directives would impress upon manufacturers the benefits of designing and manufacturing products with as small an environmental footprint as possible. This approach could also set off a chain of events in the private sector. For example, companies would likely work more closely with local municipalities, gatekeepers, and citizens themselves to reclaim postconsumer-use materials. Best practices in product design would be shared among rivals (to solve vexing environmental problems larger than any one company alone could tackle), or those companies with products that have a superior environmental footprint could find themselves in possession of new, defensible competitive advantages in the form of lower external costs.

We could also see the dawn of new corporate procurement policies, whereby companies use their purchasing power to influence suppliers to produce only sustainable goods. For example, Vodafone worked with Samsung to create an energy-efficient mobile phone (the Samsung Blue Earth) designed to be environmentally friendly throughout its product life cycle.

There is a way for the public sector to bring a lease society to life. It could enact a policy similar to the EU Emissions Trading Scheme to motivate households to modify their consumption behaviors. Households could find themselves with a choice: they could purchase products outright and be responsible for the product's environmental impacts annually; or they could lease products, deciding instead to enjoy the benefits of the product while "parking" financial responsibility for the product's environmental costs on the manufacturer.

Inverting the Economic Rationale

Whether you lease a carpet or a telephone, the costs on the producer's side will be lowest when the product lasts for its entire leasing period. Conversely, the replacement of a product would be entirely on the producer's account. Companies would thus want to extend their products' life span and have no incentive to launch, say, a new version of their tablet computer every few months. Instead, a company will outpace its competitors only if it develops a single durable device that can be employed, enjoyed, and, as necessary, virtually updated and that lasts the entire leasing period.

The consumer would benefit, too. Instead of worrying needlessly about an unsalable electronic device that is outdated (even those purchased recently that are outdated as a result of a product line upgrade), customers would lease a super-durable life-span-lasting tablet (or laptop or smartphone) on which upgrades to versions 2.0, 3.0, and so forth would be rendered as a service.

Innovation would play a critical role in the lease society. Sticking with the example of the tablet computer for a moment, one would see innovation in its software. Products would be most likely to last through the entire leasing period if the parts of the device that are most exposed to tangible innovation or damage (for example, the screen and the battery) could be detached and upgraded easily.

A lease society model would handsomely reward those companies that employ systems thinking. That is, the high-performance producer would also consider the moment when the product comes back in the door. This would seem to favor companies that design products that are durable and easy to reuse or disassemble (or both).

The reason that such super-durable devices are not yet sold on a large scale is that such a strategy could hasten the bankruptcy of a company. But if the manufacturer were to embrace a model whereby the consumer pays monthly fees (in part because the consumer is incentivized to do so), the manufacturer would eventually prefer the development of such durability and a small environmental footprint.

Inspirations for the Lease Society

You may be noting similarities between the concept of the lease society and ideas in earlier works by prominent thought leaders. Indeed, the lease society concept has drawn inspiration from several well-respected thinkers. In his book *The Ecology of Commerce: A Declaration of Sustainability*, Paul Hawken imagines a society in which "When you bought a refrigerator, a television, or a car, you would buy the license to use and operate it. The license would be transferable so that you could give or sell it to a friend if you wanted to. But the product could not be disposed of or thrown away. It would have to be returned by the final user . . . [to] the manufacturer or retailer. Retailers of consumer products would become 'de-shopping' centers where customers would drop off the products no longer needed and obtain newer ones."[4]

William McDonough and Michael Braungart herald an era of "eco-leasing" in their universally well-known and critically acclaimed book, *Cradle to Cradle*. They describe their experiences with a "rent-a-solvent" concept, the service of renting chemicals used to remove grease from machine parts: "The idea behind rent-a-solvent," they elaborate, "was to provide a degreasing service using high-quality solvents available to customers without selling the solvent itself; the provider would recapture the emissions and separate the solvent from the grease so that it would be available for continuous reuse. Under these circumstances, the company had incentive to use high-quality solvents (how else to retain customers?) and to reuse it, with the important side effect of keeping toxic materials out of waste."[5]

A 2012 Ellen MacArthur Foundation paper suggested that high-end washing machines would be accessible for most households if they were leased instead of sold; customers would save roughly one-third per wash cycle, and the manufacturer would earn roughly one-third more in profits. Over a twenty-year period, replacing the purchase of five 2,000-cycle machines with leases of one 10,000-cycle machine would also yield almost 180 kg (or about four hundred pounds) of steel savings and nearly three tons of CO_2 equivalent savings.[6]

Chemical Leasing: The Lease Society in a Business-to-Business Setting

Opportunities to apply the lease society model are not found only in the consumer electronics market. A plethora of sectors—including chemicals, carpet manufacturers, and tire vendors—has already espoused the environmental and financial benefits yielded by the lease society business model.

(Continued)

Industry pundits view chemical leasing as a very promising solution for handling hazardous substances with the required prudence and keeping hazardous materials out of the waste stream. Again, performance—rather than ownership—is central. SAFECHEM, a subsidiary of the Dow Chemical Company, has conceived a business model that sells surface cleaning solutions instead of just chemicals. This paradigm shift renders a reduction of the environmental impact of the chemical processes.

For instance, only twenty years ago, 754 kg of solvents were required to remove 100 kg of oil from metal surfaces. Then regulations were enforced that prompted companies to shift to closed cleaning machines, which resulted in a reduction of almost 600 kg of solvents. SAFECHEM took this a step further by introducing a chemical leasing model, reducing the consumption to less than 10 kg.

Of course, the sales of chemicals decrease in this model, but selling solutions enables SAFECHEM to capture the value of delivered services instead of relying on the volume of chemicals sold. Charging a fee per cleaned part or per defined time period, the model also offers a high degree of cost transparency for the customer.

Chemical leasing is also ramping up in other industries, such as the textile industry. Here the leasing model engenders the reduction and reuse of process water and helps avoid the release of micropollutants and nitrogen compounds.

But scaling the SAFECHEM success story to a broader range of chemical practices will not happen overnight. The process requires a high degree of alignment among all business partners along the supply chain and also demands a relatively high degree of awareness and confidence on the side of the customer. But SAFECHEM is working continuously to optimize the business model.

Private Sector Concerns About the Lease Society

Clearly much thinking remains to be done before we decide to adopt a lease society model. Steps needed range from building the civil sector's level of fluency, let alone familiarity, with such a model, to attuning the necessary legal frameworks, such as easing restrictions on waste flows (that are tantamount to material flows in a circular model). A recent article by B.P.A. Vander Velpen et al. highlights other areas in need of careful consideration, such as proprietorship, legislative streamlining, quality assurance, and allocation of risk demand.[7] These steps are vital to attaining a fully circular and generic leasing model, but early results from areas ranging from chemical leasing to car sharing (think Zipcar in the United States) are striking and promising.

Call to Action

The Collaboration Economy aligns economic and social development. Balanced participation of the Golden Triangle of sectors is essential to bringing the Collaboration Economy to life. The public and social sectors are active participants, but room for improved activity remains. The gatekeeper and lease society models provide frameworks to enable both sectors to play an even more active role in shaping the world today and well into the future.

There are few who would dispute the need to improve on our current global economic model. With change comes sacrifice, be it in the form of higher prices, constrained choices, or something as yet unforeseen. But, paradoxically, in order to function optimally, the free market has to be subject to a number of rules. Citizens who reside in the democratic regions of our world have not only the right but, frankly, the obligation to speak up in order to influence the shape of change. If you choose not to participate, your decision is akin to not living up to your responsibilities.

The public sector can and should be held equally accountable for inaction. Many within the private sector are visibly signaling the need for change; but without legislation, the private sector will be left to act only on a voluntary basis. The trailblazing companies highlighted in *The Collaboration Economy* need the public sector to act as partner in the effort to align economic and social development.

7

CONNECTING THE WATER DROPS

Bea Perez and Eric Lowitt

Dammed for hydropower, flood control, and commerce reasons in the 1950s, Lake Lanier has long been at the center of a water quarrel among the U.S. states of Georgia, Florida, and Alabama. Varying demands on the lake are at the core of a contentious and ongoing legal, governmental, and commercial dispute.

The city of Atlanta, Georgia, is quite passionate, if not emotional, about the lake because it's a critical source of drinking water and holds the key to the further economic development of the city. Go downstream about fifty miles, and you encounter Alabama Power, a power plant that is rather concerned about the temperature of the water because the lake serves as cooling water for the company's coal-fired plant. Farther south, in Florida, oyster fishermen in Apalachicola Bay in the Gulf of Mexico are equally passionate about how the lake is used, as their livelihoods depend on the amount of freshwater and nutrients flowing into the bay.

———

Water is stressed by a perfect storm of interrelated factors. As the Lake Lanier example shows, people's need to pursue their livelihoods, the need to ensure food availability, society's energy needs, imperfect regulations, and the desire for economic development are in conflict over water. Add increased urbanization, water consumption by agriculture, the advance of climate change, chronic underinvestment, and uneven pricing structures, and a picture of a truly stressed natural resource emerges.

Water brings the Collaboration Economy together. Energy, food, recycling, shipping, consumer behavior—sustainability in regard to each of these themes relies on water. We drink it, we cook with it, we bathe in it, we use it during religious ceremonies, we manufacture with it, and we rely on it for our livelihoods. When we look for life, we crash a satellite into planetary bodies to see if ice emerges. Water is the source of life as we know it.

Because water is so prevalent in *everybody's* daily lives, it makes sense that *everyone* should have a seat at the table when it comes to making decisions about it. Unilateral action is woefully insufficient—too much is at stake, and too many factors and perspectives must be considered. Only by bringing the private, public, and social sectors together can we de-stress water and ensure the sustainability of the world's most precious resource. The questions we need to resolve include *How to get everyone involved? Where will leadership come from? And can cross-sector collaboration successfully play an essential role in de-stressing water?*

Our Current Water System

More than 70 percent of our planet is covered by water. The vast majority of it—97 percent—is seawater and undrinkable in its natural state. Of the remaining 3 percent, 2.5 percent is inaccessible—locked in Antarctica, the Arctic, and glaciers. So only 0.5 percent of the water available worldwide is readily accessible.[1]

The water we rely on comes from a variety of sources. Among the natural water sources are surface waters (lakes, rivers) and groundwater (accessed through springs and boreholes). Both sources are supplied through the hydrological cycle as rain, snow, and ice. Water made potable through desalination—a series of processes that remove salt and other minerals from seawater (as well as from some high-mineral-content groundwater)—is an additional source. Desalination provides drinking water for about 230 million people daily.[2]

Globally, we have enough water to meet our needs. The global water issue is about *when* and *where* we have water interests, the quality of that water, and the choices we make in those *times* and *places* for the best use of that water.

We're collectively failing. Today one out of every seven people worldwide is without safe drinking water. Every day, six thousand children die from diseases associated with a lack of access to safe drinking water.[3] Many rivers no longer reach the sea due to overuse upstream, and pollution adds to the challenge.

Water is moved from its local source to where people who wish to use it are—homes, workplaces, water fountains, and so on. Water infrastructure—the water storage (reservoirs), treatment, and distribution systems (pipes and pumps crisscrossing underground) to connect source with place of use—was installed by massive public investments made decades, if not centuries, ago.

It's possible for water to be highly stressed in places where it is abundant. It's also possible for water to be under low stress in places where water is not abundant. An example of the former: let's say you're on the banks of the Amazon, the world's largest river by volume. There is no water stress in terms of its amount or its availability. But let's say you want to drink it or build a city next to it or use it on a farm; you can't because there is no infrastructure. So you can have stress in terms of a lack of safe water access or, as in the case of the Amazon, a lack of means to move the water to where it is wanted.

An example of the latter: the deserts of northern Chile are among the driest places on Earth. Yet Coca-Cola has three bottling plants there—in Irique, Aquiqe, and Antofagasta. Why does Coca-Cola operate in places that rarely see a drop of rain? Because each of these three cities is a properly planned community that gets water from both a reliable snowmelt (from the Andes to their east) and desalinization technology. These three communities use water conservation techniques that the citizens and businesses adopt and accept because they have decided to properly value water and water services.

What Is Stressing Water?

Given our daily reliance on water, one would rightly assume that communities have been developed with water quantity, quality, and availability in mind. If we have enough water to meet our needs, then what is behind water's rise to the top of our global concerns?

Population Growth

Simply put, more people mean more demand for water, and not just for daily drinking consumption. More people also mean more demand for products (that use water for manufacture and cleaning), for food (agriculture consumes 70 percent of the world's freshwater annually), for energy production, and for livelihoods.

Urbanization

People move to cities for jobs and for opportunities to build better lives. As the population increases, urbanization places significant additional stress on the surrounding water supplies and support infrastructure. As new cities emerge, local water quality and quantity can likewise be massively stressed.

Economic Development

More people also will lead to more jobs, more products, and more consumption, all of which increase the demand for water. Water quantity will be affected as water is consumed directly in manufacturing processes; water quality will be affected by several events, including discharge from manufacturing and from cities with inadequate treatment, and runoff from farms, carrying fertilizers and pesticides.

Climate Change

Climate change is altering Earth's water system in numerous ways. Sea levels are rising due to the warming of oceans (which leads to expansion) and the melting of ice caps and glaciers. Significant changes in precipitation patterns are leading to severe droughts in certain areas and historic floods in other areas. In the summer of 2012, nearly 60 percent of the United States was experiencing drought or severe drought conditions. At the same time, other parts of the world, including Bangkok, were suffering from tragic floods. The water cycle is rerouting water from places that need it to places without the infrastructure to handle it. Weather has always been difficult to forecast consistently, but climate change is adding considerable uncertainty.

The impact of climate change on water is challenging both society and nature's ability to adapt to these changes.

Policy and Investment

Water isn't a challenge solely for the developing world. Indeed, the developed world also suffers from chronic underinvestment in water and sanitation infrastructure. Considerable funding is needed to maintain aging systems, deal with emerging pollutants, and handle growing demand. Water policy may also add stress: competing and conflicting policies can result in overallocation of available water.

When we add in all of the global activities that rely on water, the current system reveals itself to be wholly insufficient to meet our needs today without adversely compromising tomorrow's ability to do the same. Water issues are so intertwined that one cannot simply say, "This is about policy" or "This is about science" or "This is about hydraulics . . . agriculture . . . recreation . . . drinking water . . ." It's about all these things and more.

Toward a Solution That De-Stresses Water

Given the current and soon-to-come pressures we've just outlined, the global water system as it is will fail more people going forward. Change is needed.

There are many reasons to encourage the private, public, and civil sectors to work together to de-stress water: renewed local licenses to operate, access to much-needed technology and expertise, conservation of water needed in nature, and entrée to water that in turn will fuel economic development. But much needs to be done in order to align economic, conservation, and social interests in the water arena.

Collectively, we have to have smart and integrated water regulation. The rules of water consumption, management, and stewardship must be set, clear, and consistent. We also need to spark a newfound respect for water across all sectors and age brackets. At the heart of this effort should be a multidisciplinary campaign that is clear in message and visceral in image.

Increased respect for water will lead to more efficient water usage, conservation of aquatic ecosystems, a greater willingness to reinvest in water infrastructure, and a more pronounced effort to do what we can to reduce the impact on water quality caused by our daily choices. As we will see, at the heart of these efforts should, can, and will be collaboration across sectors to initiate a global movement to de-stress water for today, tomorrow, and well into the future.

Smart and Integrated Water Regulation

Because water is the ultimate common good, it is the ultimate responsibility of government. Most governments, in both the developed and the developing worlds, have either a paucity of water regulations, inadequate regulation, or more than adequate but overly complicated and conflicting regulation in terms of the various entities that manage it.

Coca-Cola's experience serves as an example of the latter problem. Since 2005, the company has conducted more than 386 community water projects in ninety-four countries, including one in the Rio Grande with World Wildlife Fund for Nature (WWF). Along one stretch of Mexico's side of the river, Coca-Cola works with a state and a federal Mexican regulatory authority. On the U.S. side, the company works with the Fish and Wildlife Service, the Department of the Interior, the State of Texas, and various other public sector agencies. Each entity has a say in management of the river. Predictably, these entities' points of view and requirements differ, creating confusion, slowing work, and placing a roadblock in the path to an ideal solution.

There is no doubt that the government must be water's ultimate protector. Integrated thinking about and implementation of water policies that respond to the current stresses would greatly increase the likelihood of effective short-term actions and long-term investments made by all.

Education to Inspire a Newfound Respect for Water and Water Services

Kids who grew up in the United States in the 1970s learned the importance of not littering through one particularly moving set of public service announcements (PSAs). Recall the iconic crying Native American in Keep America Beautiful's PSA about litter and pollution prevention. The series aired on TV during the 1970s . . . and we can instantly recall these ads almost forty years later. Why was this series so powerful and so memorable? Because it made a visceral and visible connection between our daily decisions (conscious or otherwise) and their impact on the environment.

Worldwide, we need to develop a newfound respect for water and water services. The private and public sectors should stand shoulder to shoulder to coshape and co-invest in a campaign to spark and nurture this respect.

Our history instills confidence that we can once again catalyze a new movement in part through a PSA campaign. And we must. Society has just as large a stake in the health and future of the global water system as the private and public sectors. What would make these proposed new educational spots just as moving and powerful as the Keep America Beautiful spots would be visceral and visible connections among the actions of the private, public, and civil sectors and the subsequent impact on our lives today and tomorrow.

The campaign would be most effective if it

- Helped people understand the difference between what water does for us and how reliant we are on it
- Showed how interconnected water is with food and energy
- Illustrated the myriad stresses that water is under
- Explained clearly and simply the need for water quality and infrastructure investment
- Explained the need for adequate water to remain in nature, allowing ecosystems to function properly
- Targeted every age bracket

Altering Our Relationship with Water

A greater respect for water would lead us all to make three essential behavioral changes. First, we would use water more efficiently. Second, we would be more willing to invest in de-stressing water, in both the developed environment and in nature. Third, we would steward water quality.

The first ideal behavioral change is more efficient consumption of water. History shows that when people have a healthier respect for water, they use it more efficiently. For instance, in the southeastern United States, there was a historic three-year drought that ended in 2009. At the time, the government called for a 10 percent reduction in water use. It was really applicable just to water extractors, meaning those people who take freshwater resources directly from surface water or groundwater. But all local citizens chipped in and responded, and water use did go down and has historically stayed down.

The second change is that people will be more receptive to paying for water services. The campaign should show how citizens who are charged a municipal water bill are not actually paying for the water per se, but rather the infrastructure to bring the water to their home. Then, when a significant upgrade or new system is needed, the public would be more receptive to helping fund the upgrade. Similarly, people will better understand nature's role in regulating water flows and quality and, therefore, be more willing to support conservation measures.

The third area of change has to do with water quality impact. When people understand and respect water, they also start to consider the impact of their water consumption—for example, runoff from parking lots and roads, roofs, farming areas, factories, and so on. There are numerous actions people can take right now to reduce their impact on water quality. For example, citizens can keep their cars maintained, watch excess fertilizer and pesticide use, and support government action on industrial wastewater limits, treatment of municipal sewage, and control of nonpoint source runoff from agriculture.

Engaging the Private, Public, and Social Sectors in Local and Global Stewardship

The water system has become so stressed that no one entity alone can ensure the system's long-term success. One would like to say, "It's government's job. Business just creates business. NGOs serve as a watchdog while governments control and manage the water system." But we can't sit around and say, "I'll wait on government to fix this," because governments either are unaware of the problem or just don't have the capacity—or the problems are just too big.

Simply put, all three sectors must act as stewards of the global water system. Within this context, leadership from the private sector is an essential ingredient to the collective effort of de-stressing water. The private sector can accomplish a great deal in the water system for the common good (including its enlightened self-interest) by stewarding the specific resources that are essential to the industries in which they operate. Coca-Cola is serving as an orchestrator in order to help nurse the global water system back to health and to fortify it.

Coca-Cola: Water Stewardship Is Business Strategy

Muhtar Kent, Coca-Cola's chairman and CEO, believes that the time is now for the three sectors to work together in the journey toward water stewardship and sustainable development: "Until now, governments and NGOs have been doing the heavy lifting when it comes to sustainability, with business playing more of a supporting role. For the future, we need to bring the three together in what I like to call the Golden Triangle. Business, government and civil society, each doing what it does best, all working as one. Creating through collaboration and cooperation what none could achieve alone."[4]

Water means everything to Coca-Cola. Said simply, without water, Coca-Cola could not exist. All of its beverages contain water. The company also uses water in its bottling plants to keep things clean, and many of its ingredients are agricultural products that rely on water (for example, sweeteners, juices, and teas). Coca-Cola understands water's criticality. It also understands that only by working with its public and civil sector partners can it effect a great and lasting change.

The vast majority of Coca-Cola's business is conducted locally. The company sees itself as a nonexport company wholly reliant on the local communities in which it operates. And as a consumer goods company, Coca-Cola realizes that it has to prove its value daily to these local communities.

Coca-Cola is dedicated to maintaining its license to operate on a community-by-community basis. To do so means that it must serve as a reliable partner to these communities. A precondition for consistently serving in this capacity is for Coca-Cola to listen to both the local communities and the public sector agencies that are affected in some way by Coca-Cola's operations. At the heart of local communities' concerns is the state of their water: its quality, its quantity, its infrastructure, and its future.

Connecting Water and Competitive Strategy

It is possible to de-stress water—for example, there exist technologies that can assist in solving core water issues. However, although technology is incredibly useful, it is not a panacea. Other considerations must be a part of the solution to de-stressing water. Coca-Cola plans to be an active part of this solution. To this end, the company has developed and committed to a global water stewardship strategy that encompasses the short, middle, and long term.

As noted, water is essential to Coca-Cola's existence. If water is at risk, then the company is at risk. This enlightened self-interest is a main reason why Coca-Cola values, respects, and stewards that resource. The company has realized that it has to say, "Wait a minute. Our plants are in the same communities where both our employees and the people to whom we're selling products live. If the community does not have enough water, and the ecosystem, the watershed that we share with them and others, isn't sustainable, then we don't have a sustainable business." So the company has to get it right in communities and watersheds, in policy as well as in its operations and supply chain.

The company's water story is not just about water efficiency but also about water stewardship. At Coca-Cola, the lightbulb of clarity began to shine when the company shifted from thinking about water in its products and plants (for example, efficiency, wastewater treatment, storm-water management, and water quality—all still vitally important) to the water in communities and watersheds Coca-Cola shares.

This shift began to occur in the early 2000s. Myriad events— the focus of the UN's Millennium Development Goals, public perception of the company's water use (particularly in India), and its growth in the bottled water market—made it apparent to Coca-Cola that it needed to better understand and respond to water issues.

The water stress that the company saw was not limited to the developing world. Water quality, aging water and sewage systems, and storm-water management are real problems throughout the developed world. Even at home in Atlanta, as the American Southeast experienced a severe and prolonged drought, Coca-Cola saw the topic of water supply come to the forefront of public concern and debate, and certainly to the top of its own concerns. Flooding was occurring in Pakistan but also Nashville. Severe water contamination was an issue in Hungary as well as in China. Groundwater reserves were becoming depleted in India but also in the U.S. Midwest. No place, no person, no government, and no business is immune to challenges to and limitations of the water system.

In 2004, Coca-Cola developed a water risk assessment process to obtain plant-level information across its global operations. It developed and deployed a survey to capture information across six main areas of potential risk:

1. Efficiency of water use
2. Compliance with wastewater standards
3. Watershed sustainability
4. Water supply reliability
5. Social and competitive context
6. Supply economics

In 2005, the company combined results from this survey with comprehensive water and related datasets using geographical information systems and spatial analytics to develop a complex water risk assessment model that enabled the company to better understand risk exposure. This risk assessment was fundamental in developing a water stewardship strategy focusing on plant performance, watershed protection, sustainable communities, and raising awareness of global water challenges to inspire action.

Coca-Cola's successful evolution of its stance on water stewardship across the Coca-Cola system (the company and its nearly three hundred bottling partners) rests on two concepts: codiscovery and collaboration. From the beginning, the company involved its operations, globally and at all levels of management, in building its global water stewardship strategy. This codiscovery process began with hundreds of interviews conducted with people throughout the system to gain insight into their thoughts and experiences with water as it pertains to the company's business. Coca-Cola then compiled this information and reported back to employees in order to ensure that associates could "hear" each other and understand the issues and concerns being faced in diverse parts of the world. The company figured that it was better to hear this information straight from each other than through academic studies or NGO reports. Needless to say, this level of involvement helped engage its system.

As Coca-Cola refined the qualitative risk assessment into a comprehensive and quantitative one, it again went back to its global system and asked colleagues to provide the real "meat" of the data that would form the risk equations. Leadership compiled a thirty-page survey with about three hundred questions, translated into seven languages, and asked a cross-functional team at each plant to complete the survey. Because the team members had been sensitized to the issue by the codiscovery process, Coca-Cola received a 94 percent response rate to this voluntary survey.

The company used the global risk assessment to develop its strategy to focus on plant performance, watershed protection, sustainable communities (starting with water), education, awareness, and water policy. Over time, as the company's water stewardship thinking continued to evolve, it developed pilot programs, tools, and partnerships. This collaboration continues to enable Coca-Cola's continued progress toward its water stewardship goals.

Coca-Cola's Water Stewardship Goals

Coca-Cola embraces its water stewardship strategy with an overall goal, to be met by 2020, of ensuring that there is an amount of water equivalent to what the company and its bottling partners use in all of its products and production. To achieve this water stewardship goal, the entire Coca-Cola system is focused on the following three areas:

- Improving water use efficiency by 20 percent by 2012 compared with a 2004 baseline (a goal that Coca-Cola has met)
- Treating all wastewater from its manufacturing processes
- Replenishing water in communities and nature through the support of healthy watersheds and community water programs

As a consumer of water and as a company with a presence that is simultaneously global and local, the Coca-Cola system recognizes a particular obligation—and a unique opportunity—to be a responsible steward of this most precious of resources.

Earning Three Water Licenses

The most important thing the company has learned through its ongoing water stewardship learning process is that it requires three types of licenses to water, everywhere it does business:

1. The physical license (that is, sustainable quantity and quality of water resources)

2. The regulatory license
3. The social license encompassing the social and political acceptance of its water use

In times when water is plentiful and water stress is low, social concerns relating to water resources naturally wane. During these times, businesses tend to focus more on technical licenses (for example, hydrogeology, abstraction wells, and treatment systems) and legal licenses (fees, contracts, regulatory approvals, and permits).

But when a resource like water is stressed, it is imperative to move beyond those first two licenses and into the social, or emotional, license. People everywhere have some degree of cultural, spiritual, or personal connection with water. Therefore, societal acceptance of Coca-Cola's water use in the time and place Coca-Cola uses it, along with the political will to support that acceptance, is essential. For a global brand like Coca-Cola's, that emotional acceptance is not just for communities surrounding its plants but also for its consumers worldwide.

Cross-Sector Collaboration

Equipped with this local community insight, the company is working to nurture and engage its partnerships to participate in solving local, vexing issues within its bailiwick. This is where Coca-Cola serves as an orchestrator within the Collaboration Economy. The company views the resolution of local community challenges as strategic, not purely philanthropic or being a good corporate neighbor. Among other things, this means that the company must continue to be a reliable partner for the long haul.

Partnerships Are Essential

Coca-Cola has recognized that it needs to partner with a range of organizations to marshal best-in-class expertise, credibility, leverage, and local networks to serve as a global water steward.

To this end, the company formed three large global partnerships that its system selectively leverages on a case-by-case basis. At Coca-Cola, these three global relationships build on hundreds of local partnerships.

Coca-Cola's three global partnerships are with USAID, WWF, and the United Nations Development Program (UNDP). The company started with these three big, global, corporation-led partnerships to prove that collaboration among the private, public, and civil sectors on a water solution is feasible and legal, should regularly occur, yields substantial mutual benefits, and can be built upon.

Coca-Cola initially governed, funded, and managed all of these partnerships through a limited group of central water champions. Over time, the Coca-Cola system of business units and bottling partners has taken increasing responsibility for the growth of these partnerships. Another mark of success is that the company has managed to balance its resource commitments with its partners' contributions. These partnerships are designed to succeed because they emphasize the achievement of mutual objectives on whatever the topic may be, such as capacity building, safe water access, watersheds, and the like.

The partnerships also provide the type of local gravitas that can lead to access to greater resources and therefore greater impact. For instance, Coca-Cola, in partnership with UNDP, recruited the Chinese government to participate in a local community water partnership project. What started out as a $150,000 investment pool grew into $7,000,000 as a result of this partnership.

Thinking and Acting "Glocally"

Community Water Partnership projects (CWPs) are the heart and soul of Coca-Cola's work to de-stress water worldwide. The sheer breadth of the challenge to de-stress water requires a mobilization of partnership and collaboration at the local community level at a massive scale. CWPs are Coca-Cola's way to orchestrate this effort to overcome the scale of water issues; they are showing real results. In some countries, CWPs are carried out by means of the company's partnership with WWF; in others it's USAID or UNDP. Coca-Cola is committed to nurturing and maintaining a highly complex and interdependent business model to de-stress water at the local level for the benefit of all. In this way, CWPs are helping bring the Collaboration Economy to life.

Much has been made of the "think globally, act locally" approach to global strategic management. Coca-Cola is flexing its "glocal" muscles, realizing that no two local communities are exactly alike; a one-size-fits-all solution cannot and will not succeed. Therefore, part of its global water stewardship strategy is not only to understand the unique set of issues faced by the local communities in which it operates but also to determine which partners Coca-Cola can work with in the area. For example, consider the company's global partnership with WWF. When Coca-Cola wanted to make a strategic investment and difference along the banks of the Yangtze River in China, it turned to WWF for local insight and support in addressing water challenges.

The Yangtze River project's success rested on the ways and means of local agriculture; Coca-Cola and its partners realized that it made sense to offer access to best-in-class irrigation techniques (including instruction in those techniques) to reduce water pollution. In this way, the Yangtze River CWP wasn't just about the water and the river basin; it was about everything surrounding the river. More than three thousand people have directly benefited from this project. Further analysis reveals that the project has also helped protect the drinking water of more than four million citizens in the surrounding areas. Although Coca-Cola can benefit from the improved health of the Yangtze River and its surrounding region, the project is about bringing value to the community that will last much longer than the original work Coca-Cola and WWF started.

This kind of significant impact cannot be achieved alone. There are just too many layers, too many interdependencies, and too many constituents with which to work. The only way to complete these vital projects is in collaboration with others, where each partner provides access to its unique skills, knowledge, resources, and technology.

Coca-Cola: Innovation and Ambidexterity as Means of Fortifying the Global Water System

Coca-Cola's water stewardship strategy also equips the company to take an active role in advancing innovation that conserves and manages water resources to benefit all communities, nature, and business. This focus on innovation is an irreplaceable arrow in the quiver of the company's competitive strategy. After all, each local community situation is unique. The technology that worked in one place might not work in every area around the world. Hence the need for innovation.

Here, too, is another replicable insight for other companies to follow: Coca-Cola's water stewardship and competitive strategies exhibit a certain ambidexterity. That is, although the company has stringent procedures and policies, it encourages flexibility, too. There are times when the company has to think, OK, *is there a different path, a better path? And how can we consistently innovate? And who are the partners with whom we would need to work?*

At Coca-Cola, this focus on innovation is beginning to yield significant benefits. In some communities, the problem is water quality, not quantity. This abundant water is unfit for human consumption; it's beyond dirty, as it serves as a receptacle for animal and human waste. The company recently set up a partnership with Dean Kamen, the inventor who created the Segway as well as numerous medical devices. Kamen has developed a device to purify the dirtiest, most undrinkable water.

Coca-Cola had a choice to make when Kamen brought his invention to the company. Some companies would have dismissed the technology outright, falling prey to the "not invented here" syndrome. But Coca-Cola enthusiastically agreed to explore the technology. In this way, the company signaled its belief that it's preferable to have the *right* solution than to have *created* the solution. This attitude is consistent with the role of orchestrators in the Collaboration Economy. As a group, these entities eschew the temptation to believe only in their own creations. Instead, they actively seek the best solutions, even if those solutions come from outside their four walls.

In the Kamen technology case, Coca-Cola decided that its global reach and network of partners would be its best contribution to a collaborative approach that could further its stewardship efforts. Indeed, Kamen's device could be a disruptive technology that could unlock and ultimately restore this water for local communities' use.

As it would with any potentially disruptive innovation, Coca-Cola decided to first pilot-test this device. On the basis of encouraging results from the pilot test, which it conducted in Ghana, the company agreed to expand the test to more than fifty different water-stressed communities. This innovation experience is in itself leading to other innovative efforts. Indeed, Coca-Cola is now looking to the future to ask, *As we learn more about innovation, how can we partner with others to identify and amplify the key lessons learned by the entities with which we partner?*

Replicable Lessons Learned and Capabilities Developed

As we've seen, Coca-Cola's water stewardship efforts are beginning to yield benefits to local stakeholders, to the company's partners, and to Coca-Cola itself. But water stewardship is not a short-term initiative; it's a long-term imperative, the scale of which far exceeds any one company's leadership and network efforts, and which is rife with local roadblocks and challenges yet to be discovered. Companies across every industry—food, energy, water, shipping, consumer goods, financial services, natural resources, and the like—are affected by the pursuit of a global water stewardship campaign.

This section outlines some of the lessons Coca-Cola has learned during its journey. Our fervent hope is that other companies and organizations will seek to replicate these lessons and best practices in order to join Coca-Cola and its partners in the pursuit of a de-stressed global water system.

Codiscover to Develop Broad and Valuable Support

Codiscovery is manifest throughout the efforts to develop and refresh the company's water stewardship strategy. The risk assessment at the beginning of Coca-Cola's initial water strategy development work was carried out by engaging its system down to the plant level in gathering the information, reporting it back, and validating it with these same participants, and then achieving alignment on the strategy. On the basis of this collection of local information, the company then set its water goals.

Early, widespread engagement equipped Coca-Cola to begin to collaborate across the Golden Triangle. The creation and subsequent reliance on an internal stakeholder engagement guide became a vital part of Coca-Cola's efforts to engage myriad stakeholders in collective water stewardship endeavors.

Undertaking codiscovery was a necessary challenge; this approach took a lot longer, a lot more money, and a lot more people to set the company's water stewardship strategy as compared to a top-down executive mandate. Once the strategy was launched, it had an enhanced probability of success because it was already vetted throughout Coca-Cola's global system of local plants. Codiscovery continues to pay dividends.

Understand That Your Organization Can Only Influence, Not Control, Its Destiny

In the private sector, control of one's destiny has long been an illusion; more organizations need to recognize this truth. (We will discuss this topic further in Part Three.) For Coca-Cola, this lesson was learned in the 1980s when it launched New Coke. The consumer response was tepid at best; the market strongly wanted the traditional Coke product back.

Your company's ability to earn margins is intimately connected to your stakeholders; you must listen to them, even when they are angry. Achieving success in the Collaboration Economy requires the participation of the entire team. All companies would do well to remain mindful of what their local communities, as well as their employees and consumers, want.

Perhaps the most salient part of this realization is the recognition of the need to ask yourself a couple of probing questions: *How do we actually create awareness of the real issue that exists and get people to join the journey if they're not aware?* and *How do we leverage momentum, drive action, and get everyone to work together?*

Employ Partnership Best Practices

It's only natural that as Coca-Cola operates more and more through partnerships, it continues to identify lessons learned from its experiences. These lessons include the importance of being clear about the objectives of each partnership up front, then being brutally honest in evaluating the abilities potential partners can bring to the table—truly sitting down and spending time in advance to map out *What problem are we trying to solve?* and *Whom do we need to bring to the table?*

Working alongside peers has been instrumental in moving local community water projects forward. As noted earlier, local situations call for local solutions. Sometimes your company will not have the right set of capabilities to solve a local issue. For example, Coca-Cola has a program in Ghana in partnership with Diageo. Although they are not direct competitors, both companies rely on water sourced locally, so from that point of view, these companies can be viewed as competitors. The idea of collaboration with peer organizations would scare off some companies, but

Coca-Cola and Diageo have a common set of goals for local communities in Africa. Coca-Cola found that working with a peer in that local marketplace actually helped further a project that benefited the community. Companies that compete in the marketplace need to see collective action on wider challenges (such as water) as *precompetitive*.

The lesson here is that there is value in becoming willing to work with nontraditional partners or people you've not worked with before or folks with whom you might compete in certain areas. The subtle essential ingredient to these partnerships with strange bedfellows is an honest commitment on all sides to put aside individual agendas and understand that everyone is working toward a common goal, a common vision for a common solution.

Stay the Course During Pilot Tests

Let's return to the Dean Kamen water purification device example. Coca-Cola ran a test of the invention in Ghana. What's the objective of any test? To learn. Predictably, the test did not go off without a hitch. For example, the device was originally too big to go on Coca-Cola's trucks.

There are some other companies or individuals who might have looked at the results and said, "OK. We didn't like how it all turned out, so we're not going to do anything—we're just not going to move forward."

Coca-Cola's reaction to the bumps in the road was different: "OK, how do we work together to solve them? What engineers do you have? What people do we have on the ground? How do we involve maybe another person who can help us solve this one issue with the technology? And now we're progressing. Will we actually learn more in the next phase of the test?" The value of pilot tests can only be unlocked when your organization commits time to really work through the kinks and learn from the experience.

Focus on Employee Skills Development

Throughout Coca-Cola's water stewardship journey, the company's water experts have noted that they have become much better listeners. Of equal importance is their embrace of systems thinking, looking for connections that go beyond just the obvious aspects of a problem in order to see how the problem is interconnected with other challenges and conditions.

Nurture Cross-Functional Collaboration

Change within and outside Coca-Cola's bottling plant system has been reliant on cross-functional engagement. Adjustments within plants can be mapped out by engineers and environmental experts; but Coca-Cola realized that as soon as the scope of change expands beyond a plant's four walls, it needs to engage its public and community affairs teams and to work alongside the plant's general manager. This cross-functional team ensures that Coca-Cola is capable of talking not only to peers in other industries but also to local government and community organizations. Going outside the walls of Coca-Cola's plants has led its employees to think cross-functionally and to develop skills to be successful in informing and maintaining successful partnerships with governments, NGOs, other businesses, and other stakeholders.

Integrate Global Partnerships to Extend Your Core Capabilities

The company views its global and local partnerships as mutually beneficial assets. When thinking through a local CWP project or similar endeavor, Coca-Cola's employees have access to a distinctive quiver filled with the arrows of partners' unique capabilities. So employees know that they can directly engage with partners like WWF on a case-by-case basis. They are equipped to choose somebody else if they require a more rare and specialized skill set to solve a local community issue.

Challenges to Coca-Cola's
Water De-Stressing Efforts

Well-designed and well-intended legislation, such as antitrust regulation, can serve as a roadblock to Coca-Cola and its partners' water stewardship efforts. Although industry rivals can and do work together on certain issues through their industry trade associations, there is value in working shoulder to shoulder with one's largest and fiercest rivals to solve problems faced in common.

Other barriers exist around which Coca-Cola must navigate. There is a pervasive mind-set within the Golden Triangle that if an idea has already been tried once and failed, the idea then has a high likelihood of failing in other circumstances. Said differently, institutional memory can and often does block ideas from transitioning into live pilot tests. The culprit is the assumption that the ideas failed due to a lack of proper thought or design. The ethos of the Collaboration Economy—collective thinking and action—can enable a high-potential idea to succeed. Maybe the time wasn't right, and now the time is here, so we just have to work harder as a collective group to solve the issue. It's not just new ideas that have the potential to lead to positive disruption. Previous ideas tried differently hold a similar promise.

Call to Action

There is no company, no public agency, and no member of society exempt from the ills of the global water system. We're all affected by and involved with water in some way. As citizens, we have an obligation to our neighbors (in a global sense) and our descendants to invest in and protect the global water system. To those in the public sector, you have significant regulatory work ahead of you—enacting new regulation, enforcing current regulations, reshaping regulations outdated by the march of time.

If you are a leader in your corporation, you know that water, like energy and raw materials, can either accelerate or erode your company's performance. We offer three pieces of advice. First, gain a thorough understanding of your company's water relationship: consumption within the four walls of your business, your water inefficiencies, and your value chain's reliance on water as a resource. One tool that can help is the Aqua Gauge, jointly developed by Ceres and a number of corporations, including Coca-Cola   (http://www.ceres.org/issues/water/aqua-gauge/aqua -gauge).

Second, understand your relationship with water in specific locations relative to the stresses water faces in those locations. For example, do you have a manufacturing plant in a rural part of a developing country where water is scarce?

Third, develop a strategic response to your findings. One such response could be to set a water replacement goal, similar to Coca-Cola's. As you craft your strategic response, think about specific initiatives to achieve your goals. For example, you might commit to ensuring access to clean drinking water in five local communities clearly under water stress that are also most critical to your performance.

Above all else, recognize and accept that you can't do this alone. Reach out to global and local NGOs, local communities, industry trade groups, and even rivals and critics to align and amplify your efforts. We can all benefit from your collaborative efforts.

Part Three

PUTTING IT ALL TOGETHER TO MOVE FORWARD

8

BECOMING A
COLLABORATIVE LEADER

Our current version of capitalism has reached its sell-by date.

—Paul Polman, CEO of Unilever

Do you think that the leadership skills and traits needed to succeed in the Collaboration Economy are the same as those proving useful in the Waste Economy? Think again, because central to the shift in ethos behind this evolution is this fact: companies can no longer control, but now only influence, their own destinies. As we know, the skill set for command-and-control situations is vastly different from the skill set for influence-and-persuasion situations.

This chapter discusses the leadership traits CEOs and soon-to-be CEOs need if they are to succeed in the Collaboration Economy. Interviews with several prominent CEOs—leaders representing Coca-Cola, Grieg Shipping Group, Whole Foods, and Seventh Generation, among others—bring these traits to life.

Few would disagree that history is our best teacher. So to confirm these CEOs' advice and lessons learned, I studied the insights that can be gleaned from the actions of another charismatic and transcendent leader—President John F. Kennedy—during a similar "crisis": the Cold War. Not surprisingly, the advice from today's CEOs closely resembles the lessons from Kennedy's leadership.

I want to make one final note before we examine the essential leadership traits required for the Collaboration Economy. Each

CEO was at first reluctant to talk about himself. Not because these individuals do not believe in the Collaboration Economy (quite the opposite, as we'll soon see), but rather because they did not believe that they were worthy of providing advice to their peers. Illustrative of this feeling was this verbatim exchange I had with one interviewee:

Me: Now that I've described the leadership chapter to you, can I count on your support and participation?

CEO: Support, yes. But what right do I have to advise my peers? We're equals.

This exchange brings to light the first CEO leadership trait essential for success in the Collaboration Economy: *humility*. Humility as a trait can be described as having an unwavering and wholly authentic belief that one is not above anyone else. "Why are you asking *me* to advise others? What have I done to stand out from the crowd?"

To be clear, a deep-seated confidence in one's ability is a basic building block of success in any walk of life, and especially if your role is to be the chief determiner of the "whats" and "hows" of your company's journey. So let's not mistake humility for lack of confidence. The difference between the two is that the most humble CEOs do not have the need to outwardly demonstrate just how good they are. Their internal confidence does not require external validation. Instead, they prefer to place the spotlight on their colleagues, their companies, and their partners.

Welcome to leadership in the Collaboration Economy.

The Essential Skills and Traits of Leaders Operating in the Collaboration Economy

In any organization, success is determined by the tone and tenor set by its most senior group of leaders. Often employees are either inspired or demotivated by the actions and dictates of the leader. The health of a company's innovation pipeline is reliant on the leader's level of dissatisfaction with the status quo. The vibrancy of an organization's supply chain is dependent on the leader's view of whether suppliers are vendors or partners.

In the Collaboration Economy, the importance of having the right kind of leader is amplified. As we've explored, companies are no longer capable of solely determining their destiny; now they can only influence it. Even as the need for operating in concert with stakeholders is becoming more apparent, the vast majority of corporate leaders remain dedicated to the twentieth-century mandate to maximize shareholder value.

This view is decidedly myopic on two fronts. First, as we know, shareholder value is measured on a quarterly basis. Whether CEOs acknowledge it or not, they are quite aware that their employment is dependent on outperforming both their peers and their shareholders' expectations continuously in the short term. This awareness shapes and colors their investment and strategic decisions. But if we have learned anything from the classic tale of the hare and the tortoise, we know that slow and steady movements, not intermittent bursts of speed, win the race.

The second limitation arising from twentieth-century leadership practice is the belief that stakeholders neither provide value to nor expect to be provided value by corporations. Corporations adhering to this view both strangle their growth prospects and narrow their range of potential partners, to the detriment of their shareholders.

Leaders and aspiring leaders alike can do better—for themselves, their shareholders, and their stakeholders. With this in mind, I interviewed CEOs of Collaboration Economy–minded small, midsize, and large corporations. They described a number of the leadership traits they both live by and expect from their direct reports—future CEOs among them. Not surprisingly, the traits these CEOs cited are quite similar. In addition to humility, mentioned earlier, these traits include

- Seeing your leadership position as a privilege, not a right
- Nurturing an unwavering commitment to a true purpose
- Serving as activist-in-chief for your constituents
- Operating in a time frame longer than tenure
- Believing in and relying on partnerships
- Acting with integrity, guided by an ethical compass
- Having an iron stomach . . . and patience
- Feeding constructive discontent

Seeing Your Leadership Position as a Privilege, Not a Right

A trend in U.S. presidential debates is forming: the opponent outshined three out of the most recent four incumbent presidents during the first debate between the two candidates. In 1984, Walter Mondale outshone President Reagan. In 2004, Al Gore outdid President Bush. And in 2012, Mitt Romney outperformed President Obama. The one exception was President Clinton, who outdebated Bob Dole in 1996.

Several theories attempt to explain why this trend is forming. One is this: that incumbent presidents come to expect deference, based on their experience in office. So the idea that they would have to engage in an open and contentious debate with someone else is not consistent with their mind-set, given their four years in the Oval Office, and thus their initial debate performance is impaired.

Presidents Reagan, Bush, and Obama won both their subsequent debates and reelection. One reason why each president rallied after his initial stumble is that he was reminded that his position is one of privilege, not of right. These leaders had to fight to keep their position. Once they remembered this axiom, they changed both their stance on debate and their tone during the debates.

Twenty-first-century CEOs are keenly aware that their role comes with great responsibility. Rather than view their remit as "maximize shareholder value," they realize that it is to serve their stakeholders' best interests. As John Replogle, CEO of consumer goods company Seventh Generation, explained,

> The difference [between CEOs operating with twentieth- versus twenty-first-century mind-sets] starts with how we view our position. Understanding how you view your position as CEO informs where you put your emphasis. I approach my role as CEO as one of privilege, responsibility, and stewardship.
>
> While some CEOs emphasize the creation of shareholder value, my view leads me to emphasize actions and investments that further Seventh Generation's mission.

Petter Heier, CEO of Grieg Green and coauthor of Chapter Five, echoed Replogle's view, noting that "Grieg Green is more important than me. I would happily leave the company if my departure was for the best of the company. The CEO role is about the company, not about me." Here's acid test number one to assess your (or your CEO's) alignment with twenty-first-century leadership traits: In an honest moment, would you (or your company's CEO) say the same thing?

Nurturing an Unwavering Commitment to a True Purpose

Every company has a mission. "Be the world's best quick service restaurant." "Provide solutions to meet our customers' needs." "Continuously achieve superior financial and operational results." These three mission statements are real examples of Fortune 500 companies' current missions. They are simultaneously meaningful and meaningless. Managers can look to them for general guidance, but these statements do not provide specific goals to strive for in day-to-day operations.

Most mission statements fail an additional test: the purpose test. What is the purpose of the company? Each of the examples here talks about financial goals achieved through meeting customers' needs. But as we know and explored in Chapter Six, customers embody only one of society's myriad roles. Where does intent to provide value to stakeholders reside in "Continuously achieve superior financial and operational results"? Moreover, how are employees supposed to know that their company *wants* them to work with local communities for the benefit of all?

We've reached a point where having a purpose beyond creation of shareholder value is vital to a company's long-term success. John Replogle understands this. He leads by this mantra: "Without mission there is no margin." The company's mission—reduce and remove toxins from our world—informs competitive strategy, product development, and positioning decisions.

The CEO of a much larger consumer products company shares the same view. Paul Polman, CEO of Unilever, believes that his company must "play our part in improving lives, enabling a more sustainable way of living by consumers, and provide shareholder growth. This is our purpose."[1]

Unilever's purpose informed one of Polman's most well known and progressive decisions:

> The opportunity to connect with employees around a shared purpose is hugely powerful and more needed than ever . . .
>
> One of the most dangerous trends in our modern capitalist society has been the tendency towards short term thinking. For us, feeding an investor community that wants quarterly guidance is not conducive to effective business management.
>
> That's why we have abandoned guidance and moved away from quarterly profit reporting. We don't run the business on 90 day horizons, so why report on that basis? We have also restructured our compensation arrangements to put more emphasis on rewarding performance over the longer term.[2]

Here's acid test number two: If your company succeeds beyond your wildest dreams, what vexing environmental or social challenges will you have solved?

Serving as Activist-In-Chief for Your Constituents

Soon after the U.S. Congress temporarily rose above its partisan bickering and increased the U.S. debt ceiling, Howard Schultz, CEO of Starbucks, decided not to make additional political campaign contributions until lawmakers "stop the partisan gridlock in Washington, D.C."[3]

Less than one month later, over one hundred CEOs signed a pledge to follow suit. One month after that, Schultz, *Fortune* magazine's 2011 Businessperson of the Year, had a half-hour conversation with President Obama, at the president's behest.[4]

CEOs have a platform that few others can access. An aspect of this platform comes in the form of gravitas. Consider Karl-Johan Persson, CEO of H&M. His company buys nearly $1.5 billion of ready-made garment products from Bangladesh.[5] Given the company's reliance on Bangladesh for garment products, it is in H&M's best interest to ensure that local workers are treated with dignity and respect and are paid fair wages. In addition, further investment in Bangladesh's garment industry can ensure that the industry continues to mature as a reliable source of economic development for the country.

Rare is the CEO whose company does not have similar interests. The difference is that Persson, driven by a sense of social responsibility, *acted* on this mutual interest. He traveled from Sweden to Dhaka, Bangladesh, in September 2012 to meet with Bangladesh's prime minister, Sheikh Hasina, and leaders of the Bangladesh Garment Manufacturers and Exporters Association to make the case for increasing worker wages.[6] Time will tell what effect Persson's visit and plea will have. But one thing is clear: Persson understands that his platform brings with it responsibility for furthering stakeholders' interests.

Schultz and Persson espouse the view that business is about more than making money: it's about acting in the best interests of all stakeholders. Walter Robb, co-CEO of Whole Foods, explained this view to me:

Sustainability is about fundamentally rethinking how to make your business endure. For example, consider employees. Sustainability forces you to reevaluate how you treat employees. You cannot endure as a company if you run your business by myopically thinking about employees as P&L pawns. Instead, the twenty-first-century leader thinks of employees as stakeholders in your business.

Then treat them as such—as colleagues who can thrive within your organization, enabling your company to thrive as a result. My job is to find the spirit and creativity in someone and help draw this out. Employees need to feel that they are truly part of the mission—they are a part of the decision process. Collaboration is not just with other entities but also with the individuals in your company.

Robb's view is echoed by Miles White, CEO of Abbott Laboratories. In a recent interview with *Barron's,* White talked about the importance of striking a balance that serves his company's myriad stakeholders: "I don't think you can just take the position that you solely exist to make money for shareholders. You have got to find a balance, and I can tell you that no one ever thinks you are in balance or that you have it right. But that's one of the challenges—to have a balance where the company is doing the right thing for its owners, its shareholders, [and] its employees. But also for the people you exist for."[7]

The twenty-first-century leader is one who understands that his or her leadership position includes responsibility for serving stakeholders' interests, not merely shareholders' interests. Often this means taking an activist stance on an issue that connects to your organization's core mission.

Here is acid test number three: Can you articulate which issues are most meaningful to your stakeholders? If so, when was the last time you served as an activist for change on behalf of your stakeholders?

Operating in a Time Frame Longer Than Tenure

The CEOs I interviewed emphasized the importance of operating both in the here and now and in the long term. Eager to probe what sounded like a platitude, I asked: "Which would you prefer, a boost to your ego or to your legacy?" I wanted to test whether they think and act more in the short term or in the long term. The entire group of interviewees placed legacy above ego, though there was not a strong outward desire for either.

I was intrigued. And I found myself thinking about a similar insight I had when I researched President Kennedy's leadership of the space race during the 1960s.

Central to Kennedy's goal to land a man on the moon by the end of 1969 was his belief that the goal was about more than him. He knew that he would not be president when the goal was achieved; he would not directly reap the benefits of his vision and leadership. After all, his second (and final, per U.S. law) term in the Oval Office would end in 1968. Kennedy epitomized the leadership trait of thinking and acting in a time frame that will outdate you.

Solving our vexing challenges requires leaders to set goals that in all likelihood will postdate their time in their leadership position. We will not solve our global water, energy, or food challenges in the next three to five years. Leaders need the courage to look beyond any innate desire for personal glory. Otherwise their resolve to start in motion the wheels of long-term progress might be choked off. The twenty-first-century leader understands that accomplishing goals is a team effort.

Here's acid test number four: Are you actively investing in and championing goals that will in all likelihood be achieved after you are no longer CEO?

Believing in and Relying on Partnerships

Perhaps one less well known fact about the space race is that President Kennedy actually *sought* to collaborate with President

Khrushchev of the Soviet Union in order to achieve his vision of a man on the moon by the end of the decade. Kennedy put aside feelings of animosity and uncertainty in order to pursue a course of action that he believed essential to achieving this vision.

Indeed, on several occasions, Kennedy proposed a jointly manned lunar program to the Soviets. Arguably his most aggressive effort was made in a speech before the UN General Assembly on September 20, 1963. At the end of that address, Kennedy said, "In a field where the United States and the Soviet Union have a special capacity—in the field of space—there is room for new cooperation . . . I include among these possibilities a joint expedition to the moon . . . Space offers no problems of sovereignty . . . Why should the United States and the Soviet Union, in preparing for such expeditions, become involved in immense duplications of research, construction, and expenditure?"[8]

Kennedy signaled that the potential achievement of the ability to explore space could be a unifying goal, one that superseded the contest of sovereign supremacy. According to at least one report, President Khrushchev reached the decision to accept the collaboration proposal when Kennedy was tragically assassinated.[9] Imagine how different the past fifty years could have been if this collaboration had occurred!

Today there is no reason why we should not put aside our collective differences in order to unleash the energy of cross-nation and cross-sector collaboration to once again bring to life the achievement of a pursuit in our common interests.

As we have seen throughout *The Collaboration Economy*, there are private sector leaders wholly committed to this vision. Perhaps Unilever's CEO, Paul Polman, said it best during June's Rio+20 event: "Individually both governments and business have already mobilized significant resources to address the challenge of deforestation, but we all recognize that much more can be achieved if we align our efforts and work in partnership."[10]

Building on his view of his role as CEO of Seventh Generation, John Replogle explained that

> This orientation toward prioritizing the achievement of our company's mission moves you from compete-at-all-costs to collaborate in order to achieve your mission and increase the size of the overall pie and look after those things that are in the common. Ultimately the collaboration mind-set leads to not just thinking about peers as competitors but to thinking about how to further your mission by engaging with your competitors and the public and civil sectors.
>
> For example, Seventh Generation's mission is about reducing and removing toxins from our world. We are committed to being an advocate for individuals' health by reducing and removing toxins all around us. This mission means collaborating with the very best minds out there about what are the toxins. We work within our industry group. We collaborate with the ACI—the American Chemical Institute—which has virtually all of our leading competitors on the board of the ACI to review the ingredients we all use. Practicing self-regulation. We just had a major breakthrough with the ACI. Now all leading household chemical companies will not only disclose but also publish all of the chemicals they use.

Perhaps more provocative is Replogle's take on typifying Seventh Generation's "company" as

> a verb, not a noun. Most CEOs view the word "company" as a noun. A noun is definitive, implying a start and end point. We see ourselves in the center of a network. We actually view our organization as a verb, not as a noun.
>
> Seventh Generation is a living, breathing network. We are about partnering, collaborating, and amplifying our assets. Our company does not have boundaries—there are no start or end points with our company.

Therefore, there are no boundaries on our company—there is not a clear-cut start or finish to where Seventh Generation operates. Everything we do is done through a network. We work with our network to amplify our efforts. We embrace open innovation—not just product, but all facets of our mission. We have a network chart that measures the effectiveness of all our partnerships. This is a different mind-set from the traditional twentieth-century companies.

The Collaboration Economy is dedicated to showing why and how companies of all sizes are actively collaborating with entities in the private, public, and civil sectors. In lieu of recounting the reasons behind these companies' actions, I instead offer acid test number five: Which path do you believe will result in your company's accomplishment of its goals: going solo or solidarity?

Acting with Integrity, Guided by an Ethical Compass

In 'the past decade alone, we've witnessed corporate malfeasance on an historic level. Enron, Worldcom, HealthSouth, Tyco, ImClone Systems—all are examples of CEO-led malfeasance that destroyed lives, trust, and hundreds of billions of dollars in personal wealth and market value. Loyal employees at many of these companies had their entire retirement plans wiped out as a result of leaders' personal greed.

At best, an unethical CEO only saps employees' energy. At worst, a great company rots from the core as employees learn that it's OK to use their company as a personal bank account.

The benefits of being led by a CEO dedicated to acting ethically have been thoroughly dissected elsewhere. Rather than repeat common sense, allow me to say this: in the Collaboration Economy, where performance is determined by the strength of your network, the ethical CEO's company is more likely to operate with little to hide. As a result of this natural transparency, the CEO's company will find it easier to both nurture and maintain a vibrant network of private, public, and civil sector partners.

Here's acid test number six: If you ran a separate organization that had finite resources and a stellar reputation, would you want to partner with your organization?

Having an Iron Stomach . . . and Patience

Imagine that you are a CEO of a company in an industry that has seen little change over the past several decades. Incremental efficiency, not disruptive innovation, has been the source of growth. Entrenched rivals eye change warily. Making change takes time . . . and intestinal fortitude.

This is the situation Petter Heier and Grieg Shipping Group faced in 2010 when they created Grieg Green to change how commercial vessels are broken at the end of their useful life. As discussed in Chapter Five, fierce is an understated way to describe competition among shipowners. Differentiation is difficult to demonstrate, clients push for the lowest price, fuel costs can be volatile, and one accident can cause irreparable damage to reputation. Among decisions to make and risks to manage, disposal of an unwanted vessel does not rank high.

Heier and his colleagues at Grieg Shipping Group set out to change how this mature industry values the disposal impacts of unwanted vessels. His company, Grieg Green (a subsidiary of Grieg Shipping Group), is making headway against the tide. As Heier described to me, his advice to other leaders is to

> Recognize and accept that you have a long-term battle in front of you if you aspire to change a mature industry. The people who don't want change to occur are waiting for you to just run out of energy. Detractors at their kindest will simply say no. At their worst, they will dedicate themselves to resisting your desired change.

So it's in your best interest to demonstrate your belief to nonbelievers internally and externally. Then convince your stakeholders, including nonbelievers, of the worthiness of your mission. You will need allies, so invest your time and energy in the socialization of your ideas, beliefs, and mission.

Though he lives in Norway, Heier travels to Asia once every six weeks to meet with his partners and to show his unflappable commitment to changing how the shipping industry recycles its vessels.

Here's acid test number seven: Do you believe your company has the patience to work with others to increase the likelihood of a more prosperous future for your company?

Feeding Constructive Discontent

If necessity is the mother of invention, then reinvention is the father of survival. Technology and competition alone can erode the most resolute company's ability to survive. Equally adept at causing erosion is self-satisfaction—satisfaction with a company's own products, its leadership, and its performance.

Only 13 percent of the companies that appeared on the original Fortune 500 list in 1955 also appeared on the 2011 list. These companies—and their string of leaders—must have a secret formula for achieving prosperity in perpetuity. After all, they've navigated the disruption wrought by time, recessions, wars, technological upheaval, hypercompetition, and the rise of business imperatives such as the quality movement.

Coca-Cola is one of these companies. Muhtar Kent, CEO of Coca-Cola, demystified the secrets of the company's long-term success thusly:

First of all, innovation requires continuous investment. And not just monetary investments but investments of time and strategy and execution. Leading companies and organizations invest in tough times, as we've tried to do in recent years.

For inspiration, we've drawn on our company's experience during the Great Depression. While other consumer goods companies were cutting back on advertising and marketing, Coca-Cola Chairman Robert Woodruff charted a different path. Mr. Woodruff *increased* promotional spending—boosting brand strength, building our business and setting the company up for ever greater success.

Today, we're investing all over the world. In the U.S. and China and India and Russia and Mexico and Brazil and on and on. For the next five years, we've already announced plans to invest—just for starters—more than $30 billion in our brands and our infrastructure as we pursue our 2020 Vision for growth.[11]

Continuous investment—in good times and bad—is one part of the secret. It takes an iron stomach to make investments when times are tough. An equally powerful skill of the collaborative leader is *nurturing constructive discontent*. Again Muhtar Kent:

Leaders can't be complacent. We must keep moving forward, together with our colleagues and partners.

Personally, I feel my greatest legacy at Coca-Cola could be helping our company, our system and our people remain constructively discontent. I'm often asked what worries me, what keeps me up at night. And I'll tell you: arrogance.

Because any time anyone begins to think they've got it all figured out, that's when they get wiped out. By a competitor. A new environment. Or some other meteor, right out of the blue.[12]

Here's acid test number eight: What are your company's three competitive advantages? If you ran a rival company and your career was at stake, how would you compete against your company? Knowing this, what would you change about your current business? When was the last time you agitated for this change within your organization?

Call to Action

Our world, our society, and our economic system are changing. As the pressures mount on your company to adapt, one thing is clear: yesterday's leadership traits will not bring success tomorrow. My advice to you depends on your role:

- If you are a board member, carefully evaluate both your current CEO and your CEO's leadership team. Do they exhibit the traits needed to succeed in the Collaboration Economy? If not, now is the right time to consider whether you have the right leadership in place.

- If you are a CEO, do the leadership traits covered in this chapter resonate with you? Can you honestly say that these traits describe you, your messages to your company, and your leadership style? If not, now is the right time to deeply consider whether your skill set will enable you to effectively lead your company in our emerging economic system.

- If you are an aspiring CEO, grade yourself with these traits in mind. What changes would you make to your leadership approach and style? Does your company embrace these traits? Do you truly believe your company is on the path to success in the Collaboration Economy?

9

WINNING IN THE COLLABORATION ECONOMY

As we've seen throughout this book, strategy in the Collaboration Economy is governed by an overarching principle: your company no longer controls its destiny; now it can only influence it. Think about that for a minute. Your company's ability to achieve its enterprise-level goals, objectives, and aspirations is as likely to be determined by its stakeholders' actions as by its assets. This completely changes how your company should go about crafting and executing plans for long-term success.

Even though a basic premise of competitive strategy has changed—you no longer control your own destiny—what winning looks like has not. Performance will continue to be measured by your top- and bottom-line growth. Your ability to *influence* your top- and bottom-line growth will be driven by your portfolio of competitive advantages throughout your value chain.

But *how* you develop, nurture, and employ your portfolio of competitive advantages will differ in the Collaboration Economy. In particular, there is one "new" type of competitive advantage to which you should pay special attention: your portfolio of collaborative partnerships. The converse also holds true: a lack of collaborative partnerships will expose a weakness in your ability to outperform the competition.

The experiences of the trailblazing companies we explored in this book show us that companies will best be equipped to succeed in the Collaboration Economy after adapting their

- Corporate strategy—to answer the question, *How will we succeed now that we no longer control our destiny?*
- Corporate culture—shifting from a competitive mind-set to a partnership-oriented outlook
- Operations—to develop incentives for buyers to invest in creating long-term stability and development benefits in supply chains

Hardened by the fires of forming cross-sector collaborative alliances and carrying out your plans through such collaboration on core and strategic issues, your company will find its ability to adapt, to grow, and to become sustainable much stronger than it is today. This chapter provides you with pragmatic advice and replicable tools to win by operating in the Collaboration Economy.

Corporate Strategy

Corporate strategy in the Collaboration Economy differs from corporate strategy in the Waste Economy in several ways. For one, the corporate goal of strategy—maximizing the creation of value for stakeholders—is different from the twentieth-century goal of maximizing the creation of value for shareholders. Rivals can be irreplaceable collaborators nearly as frequently as they are competitors. Suppliers are partners, not merely vendors. And the very assumptions on which we've based our corporate strategies—assumptions such as unlimited availability of basic resources—no longer hold true.

To win in the Collaboration Economy, companies will need to integrate six skills into their corporate strategy management efforts. This section covers these six skills.

Employ the Buried Assumptions Exercise

Business has long created value for shareholders and customers by challenging assumptions and acting on their findings. For example, Starbucks developed into one of the world's most recognizable brands by challenging the convention that coffee was a boring commodity. The Collaboration Economy rewards companies for challenging assumptions within their value chains.

The Buried Assumptions exercise is an extension of traditional (but often neglected) scenario planning exercises. Specifically, Buried Assumptions focuses you on questioning your company's most closely held environmental and social assumptions. That is, by asking questions like the following, you identify exposed flanks and overlooked improvement opportunities by reexamining interdependencies in your business model:

- What happens if the public sector redefines, through legislation, product "ownership" to include external costs?
  - Product owners would own both the experience of using the product and the environmental and social impacts of that product's life, from manufacture, to use, all the way through to disposal.
- What if materials we rely on are no longer acceptable, either because of legislation or intra-industry action?
  - Sourcing of materials becomes more difficult and expensive.
  - Operations, procurement, and logistics activities would need to be reexamined.
- Within which of the local communities must we ensure that we retain the right to operate?
  - What are the issues each of these local communities cares most about?
  - What unique value can we bring to each of these communities to solve these issues and retain our license to operate?

As you work your way through this Buried Assumptions exercise, you will find that you have added numerous "to-do" items to include in your strategic and operating plans. This exercise will enable you to focus your short-, middle-, and long-term investments and initiatives.

Deploy Your Sustainability Department as an Innovation Department

When a company decides to become sustainable, it is deciding to broaden the scope of its responsibility. No longer is thinking of profit and loss sufficient; now you need also to think about the local communities in which you operate, the environmental impact of your actions, the expectations your stakeholders have of your organization, and so on. To the newly initiated, expansion of scope of responsibility would seem noncore at best and costly at worst. The topic of sustainability departments has been well covered elsewhere; suffice it to say that many companies are placing their sustainability departments at the forefront of these new demands on the corporation.

In the hands of a visionary company, a sustainability department can be so much more than a department that reactively responds to these new demands. It can be an epicenter for innovation. The pursuit of sustainability leads a company to examine tangential issues of strategic importance. The careful and intelligent exploration of these tangential issues expands a company's scope of the problems for it to potentially solve. As one chief sustainability officer describes the scope of his work: "We look at personal well-being in terms of people's health and wellness and active, healthy living—characteristics of a person's life that extend far beyond the consumer's use of our products. We look at economic empowerment of women and job creation for all ethnicities. We consider aspects of individuals' and communities' livelihoods because without healthy, vibrant communities we will not have employees, consumers, or community partners. So the scopes of our heretofore separate commercial and community involvement goals are now clearly intertwined."

As we've seen throughout *The Collaboration Economy*, high-performance companies are beginning to realize that they can make a larger impact by working with others than they can make alone. A roadblock to collaboration has long been institutional memory: "We historically have not worked with rivals. We won't start now." The sustainability department provides companies—even those hesitant to collaborate—with a safe outlet to experiment with partnerships. After all, for a company to ultimately become sustainable, it must resolve issues that are larger than it alone can handle. Partnerships are natural outcomes of the work of a visionary company's sustainability department.

When you combine an expansion of the issues you are willing to explore with collaboration that can enhance and broaden your capabilities, you have a powerful approach to pursue innovation.

Reconsider the Costs and Benefits of "Co-opetition"

There's a flawed belief that your only friends in business are the enemies of your enemy. At one time, this axiom held true. But in today's interdependent world, this flawed belief is proving a thorn in the balloon that would otherwise raise many companies' future commercial success. Indeed, the true paradox that smart, trailblazing companies are resolving is how to outperform their competition by *collaborating* with their competition.

Recently, the CEO of a very well-known consumer brand nearly scared the wits out of me. His company is quite respected in the sustainability community, both for its progressive social equity policies and for its green technology that limits the environmental impacts of its manufacturing activities. Curious about the growing divide I'm starting to see between traditional business competition and prospects for financial performance, I asked my big question: Do you foresee a time when you'd willingly provide access to your leading green technology to your competitors? His blunt response: no.

What scared me was not the answer itself; it's indicative of conventional logic. If you have a competitive advantage, you generally don't share it with rivals. Rather it was the ferocity with which the answer came forth. It was a simple no, but the manner with which it was delivered said, "There is no way my answer will ever change." That's unfortunate for this company's shareholders. This company is investing in biofuel facilities that turn the waste culled from the materials this company's manufacturing process consumes into usable and thus "free" material that it then feeds to its biofuel facility by way of its green manufacturing technology.

If the company did share access to its revolutionary technology with its competition, the company would gain financially in two, potentially three, ways. First, the company would increase the amount of free source material for its biofuel facility (assuming the competition does not have a similar biofuel facility, the competition would prefer to rid itself of the waste at the lowest cost possible), which would lead to lower per-unit cost of biofuel energy, expediting a positive return on the company's investment. Second, the company could decide to charge its competition for access to its proprietary green technology, leading to a new revenue stream. This tactic would be especially effective if the company priced access at the point just below the competitions' "go–no-go" price for developing similar technology. Third, the company could earn goodwill from the local communities in which it manufactures its products because it would be diverting the manufacturing process waste away from the communities' landfills or surrounding bodies of water.

There's a fundamental belief about competition that is becoming obsolete. The basic goal of competition—outcompeting in order to outperform—is now holding companies back from financial success. It is true that following this axiom has long enriched companies that showed they were different from their competition in ways that matter to consumers and then consistently delivered this differentiation. But it also overemphasizes the importance to companies of "going it alone."

The thinking behind this axiom began to be challenged in the mid-1990s, with the publication of smart, highly regarded competitive strategy books, such as *Co-opetition*, by Barry Nalebuff and Adam Brandenburger. By translating game theory into pragmatic business strategy, *Co-opetition* cleverly showed companies a new path to revenue growth: it's better to own 20 percent share of a $10 billion market than it is to own 75 percent share of a $2 billion market. This insight shaped and informed venerable brands' efforts to collectively develop new geographical markets while maintaining their competitive differences.

Stakeholders are scrutinizing the ways companies deliver value to consumers. Their voice, and therefore impact, is amplified by critical-mass adoption of social media as a shaping influence over individuals' decisions. As a result, companies are being held accountable for the ways they manufacture their products. Therefore, it's time to extend the concept of game theory to upstream activities, too.

Consider Nestlé Waters North America (NWNA), the owner of bottled water brands such as Poland Springs. The company's financial success is in part dependent on collecting and reusing as much recycled plastic as possible. But as we saw in Chapter Three, in the United States, less than 30 percent of used plastic bottles are collected from consumers. The other 70 percent winds up in landfills. NWNA and its rivals need plastic to keep their bottled water businesses afloat. If the industry can collect and process enough postconsumer plastic, it can drive the cost of manufacturing recycled plastic bottles below that of virgin plastic bottles, reducing costs for all involved. So NWNA is building a consortium of rivals to develop an alternative to the current fragmented and generally ineffective packaging recycling system.

By collaborating with rivals, NWNA will benefit from lower manufacturing costs while also reducing its environmental footprint. Companies within industries ranging from energy to food to pharmaceuticals to shipping are similarly beginning to reshape their industries' models of competition.

So what is the lesson to be learned from the efforts of NWNA and other trailblazing companies? Your company needs either to evolve its competitive strategy to embrace selective collaboration with rivals downstream *and* upstream, or to prepare to become obsolete.

Know When to Collaborate and When to Compete

The boundaries of competition are changing in myriad meaningful ways. Competition upstream in the Collaboration Economy is just as fierce as it is downstream. With resources limited, hard-edged competition for sourcing is a reality that will only become more complex. Indeed, the story of upstream competition is complicated by the fact that multiple industries rely on a variety of materials in common. This concept isn't new—nontraditional competitors like Coca-Cola and GE are (unknowing) rivals for fuel, for instance.

Interindustry competition for materials is heating up. NWNA competes with auto manufacturers like Ford for postconsumer-use plastic. (Ford uses recycled plastic bottles for the seats in its Focus electric vehicle.[1])

Curiously, interindustry competition for materials will likely lead to broader collaborative efforts. For NWNA and Ford, for example, ensuring as large and steady a flow of postconsumer-use plastic bottles is in both companies' best interests. So why not partner with one another to strengthen the packaging materials recycling system in order to get back as large an amount of reusable materials as possible?

Herein lies a complicated question: How will companies know when to collaborate and when to compete? Recognizing that every situation is unique, I offer these guidelines gleaned from the efforts covered throughout this book:

- Engage in cross-sector collaboration on natural resources.
- Compete when getting goods on and off the shelf.
- Collaborate again to get materials back into the manufacturing cycle.
- Compete for these materials once they are reprocessed.

As one senior executive explained to me, "If resources become scarce, then it's in everybody's interest to work together to make sure that the scarcity does not become a threat to your business. At the same time, there is the risk that it *will* become a threat to your business and then you will have to compete like crazy in order to get your hands on those resources."

Over time, more "collaborate or compete?" guidelines will become apparent. The four listed here will help you begin to make the necessary recalculations to your company's competitive strategy.

See "Supplier," Think "Partner"

The global economic crisis that took root in 2008 threatened the existence of many industries. The automotive industry was under tremendous pressure. Ford's two large U.S. peers, General Motors and Chrysler, were under such strong pressures that their survival was reliant on federal bailouts. The potential demise of two massive rivals would under normal circumstances be cause for great celebration by a company such as Ford. But this situation was quite different.

While the crisis was taking shape, Ford was gravely concerned about its own viability—not because the company was poorly run or in dire financial straits, but rather because Ford, GM, and Chrysler shared strategic suppliers in common. If GM and Chrysler were to cease to exist, what would happen to these strategic suppliers upon which Ford's future rested? Indeed, several were already on the brink of bankruptcy. Ford sprung into action, and Project Quark was born. It set up a supplier war room of sorts, identified the irreplaceable suppliers at risk under the worst-case scenario, and set about crafting plans to shore up these suppliers just in case.[2]

Although the full potential of Project Quark was not needed, Ford's focused efforts are illustrative of the Collaboration Economy's fundamental ethos: that we are so interconnected and interdependent that we no longer control our own destinies. Efforts like Project Quark that yield investments in partners and stakeholders alike are the best path to increasing your influence over your own destiny.

Engage Stakeholders in Your Decision-Making Processes

In my first book, *The Future of Value*, I illustrated society's emergent ability to trigger megatrends within the private sector. In brief, I traced the initial spark behind the business world's five most recent megatrends, starting with quality and ending with sustainability. Business competition was behind both the quality and business process reengineering movements. Business with a slice of society in the form of developing-world entrepreneurs were arguably behind the globalization effort. The public sector played an increased role in the dot-com revolution. (The roots of the Internet can be found in ARPANET, a military networking experiment.) The sustainability movement has been both sparked (Rachel Carson, Brundtland Commission, environmentalism, and so on) and colored by society.

With its voice amplified by social media (and the popular media—after all, controversy and debate sell news), society has become a formidable business stakeholder. So what does this mean for business?

Businesses that value nimbleness might just be able to move faster by involving more stakeholders at the decision-making table. There's no doubt that more megatrends will emerge. The likelihood that society will once again spark and shape these challenges to convention is high. Companies that build the bridges to bring society's input into the room today are more likely than their peers to be the ones that receive the early read on the megatrends to come.

Armed with this detection system and informed by the very people shepherding the change to come, these companies will have a head start on their peers when it comes time to change once again. In other words, by inviting more opinions starting today, these companies are likely to be more nimble than their peers come tomorrow.

There is at least one roadblock your company would do well to consider at the outset of adapting your approach to competitive strategy. By preemptively acting ahead of your peers, you might temporarily expose a flank. Consider the ongoing global sustainable development negotiations among nations. If a developed country agrees to curb carbon emissions without developing nations taking the same action, then businesses in developing countries might have a (temporary) cost, management focus, and operations advantage over businesses in the developed countries. That is to say, the businesses in developed countries would have to provide goods and services that adhere to more stringent rules than would their peers in developing countries.

Hal Hamilton is the director of the Sustainable Food Lab (and a coauthor of Chapter Four). He and his colleagues work with many of the world's food services companies, often running forums for these companies to openly discuss vexing environmental and social issues. Hamilton described the challenge to me as follows:

> Companies cannot add costs [that improve environmental or social conditions], in isolation, that make them less competitive. They would not survive. So some of the costs of sustainability require co-investment by other sectors, not only because of the challenges' scale but also to reduce the risk of opportunistic and asymmetric

competitive advantage that could come about as a result of nonaction.

Curiously, this is an issue that can lead to *broader* intra-industry participation in cross-sector collaborations. Few companies would dispute the importance of change to ensuring the likelihood that they will thrive over the long term. Which scenario is more aligned with this view: nonaction as a way to yield short-term asymmetric competitive advantage, or shared investment to lower the cost of the type of change that can increase the likelihood of your long-term survival? The answer should be obvious.

Corporate Culture

The common theme among my suggested alterations to your competitive strategy is the benefit of integrating collaborative thought and action into your calculations. But even the best-thought-out plans can succeed only when leaders and workers alike have bought into these plans and are capable of executing them.

This section covers alterations companies are making to their corporate cultures to succeed in the Collaboration Economy.

View Employees as Society's Ambassadors

There are people within your organization with whom you can set up cross-sector collaborations. After all, every one of your employees is also a representative of the civil sector (and, indirectly, the public sector, too). Critical-mass adoption of social media has increased the likelihood that how you treat your employees will inform society's view of your company.

Indeed, when the smoke clears, we might find that sustainability's most prominent impact on the business sector is the transformation of employees into stakeholders. So the greater value from working with your employees comes from the steady stream of information and feedback they can provide to you as society's ambassadors. And all you have to do is ask.

One of my clients recently benefited from this viewpoint. The company, which I'll disguise for the sake of its confidentiality, is a prominent member of the global financial services industry. This company often celebrated itself internally for being ranked among the world's top companies in the field of environmental sustainability. But it was unpleasantly surprised when its 2010 employee satisfaction report revealed that the majority of employees rated their level of satisfaction working at this company as "neutral" to "negative."

I was invited to give my opinion on this revelation, and I asked one particular question that resonated with my client. Specifically, I asked whether the company viewed its employees as labor or as representative slices of society. The company said the former, but my mention of the latter lit a lightbulb in this person's mind. Subsequently, the company asked its employees to identify which issues were of most interest and concern in the communities in which they live. Upon receipt of a collection of surprisingly common community issues, the company took action to work with many of these local communities. One step, for example, was to lower the amount of paper sent out to employees and clients alike, so as to reduce the amount of paper sent to local landfills. This step not only lowered an expense but also helped ensure that the company maintains its local license to operate in several communities.

The smartest companies are learning to engage employees, not just as employees, but also as consumers, influencers, citizens, family members, and idea generators. This 360-degree view of the individual behind the employee can spur growth and innovation, and increase corporate agility.

Feedback from this effort to engage individuals is likely to prove critical to the ability of companies to adjust to tomorrow's twists and turns. Society—and its ever more interconnected group of consumer-citizens—now has a loud voice in the creation and shape of megatrends (for example, the quality movement, globalization, and the sustainability movement, as noted earlier) that impact how the market operates and how companies compete.

Move Beyond the Mentality of Zero-Sum Competition

Zero-sum competition, in which one side wins by taking customers away from the other side, is an enemy of sustainability. Industry needs to rise above zero-sum competition by focusing less on who is right and more on approaches to achieve common environmental, social, and economic goals.

Spotting signs of zero-sum competition is easy; just look for industries locked in fierce price wars. Think of the electronics retailers of the 1980s. (Growing up in New York, I remember an electronics store called Crazy Eddie. The company's commercials featured a wild-eyed pitchman who looked into the camera and loudly proclaimed, "Our prices are INSANE!!!!") Consider the airlines of the 1990s. (One company would cut the price of a round-trip ticket to a destination; another company would lower its price for the same trip the same day.) For a more contemporary example, look to the online retailers of the early twenty-first century. (Amazon's Marketplace offers consumers several smaller retailers from which the consumer can buy a product; often the difference between retailers is one penny.)

Zero-sum competition is a fierce enemy of sustainability for at least two reasons. One is the pressure ultimately placed on suppliers by manufacturers (and their customers) to find ways to constantly lower their costs so that the companies selling these products can continue to lower their prices to attract and retain customers. Suppliers, often located in developing countries, managed by teams with rudimentary management skills, and barely breaking even, will find ways to lower their costs, often at the expense of the environment, society, or both. If you were one of these suppliers, would you make long-term investments to retrofit your factories to use renewable energy when fossil fuel energy is available and cheaper per unit of energy consumed?

The second reason zero-sum competition is the enemy of sustainability is that it reduces the sharing of best practices among competitors. If one competitor, focused on lowering costs, found a way to do so, what incentive does it have to share this new way with its competitors? Some will argue that this lack of sharing among competitors fuels innovation, ultimately leading to lower prices; in turn, this innovation produces a stream of new products, often making products sold last year obsolete. But where do these unwanted products land? All too often, they are thrown into landfills. Where's the innovation in that?

So how does industry move beyond zero-sum competition? I believe that one step is to agree on the destination before we design the journey. I propose the following as a destination for industry: endeavor to find a way to simultaneously grow and provide solutions to enable the global pursuit of sustainability.

Accept That You Can Only Influence Your Own Destiny

Jan Kees Vis, Unilever's global director of sustainable sourcing development (and a coauthor of Chapter Four), described the impetus for Unilever to realize that it can now only influence its destiny:

> Our impact on the world flows directly from the business model that we choose. So taking responsibilities that are clearly far beyond the traditional boundaries of the food production business comes with the realization that you have to look at your business model and you have to ask the question, "What parameters in the business world can we change or do we have

to change in order to be able to extend our influence across the entire economic chain?"

When we published the Unilever Sustainable Living Plan, we broke new ground by committing to take responsibility for the company's impacts right across the value chain, from the sourcing of raw materials all the way through to the consumer's use of its products to cook, clean, and wash. But Unilever's direct environmental impacts—manufacturing and logistics—together contribute only 5 percent of the total impact of the company's products.

This shows Unilever that it cannot meet its goals alone. In areas such as raw material production and consumer use, Unilever has a low degree of control but a high degree of influence. Unilever works with around eight thousand raw materials suppliers, and approximately 50 percent of the raw materials it buys are renewable. Harnessing the power of its brands and its supply chain partners to encourage consumer and business behavior change has therefore become a key focus.

Build Communities That Engage People Rather Than Hierarchies That Control Them

This point further underscores the emerging shift toward influencing your destiny. I borrowed this concept from Henry Mintzberg's 2011 *Harvard Business Review* article "To Fix Health Care, Ask the Right Questions."[3] Mintzberg's point applies equally well to all industries striving to realize the Collaboration Economy. That is, *something* called your employees, suppliers, and involved constituents to serve your industry. If you figure out *why*, beyond compensation, your employees and other stakeholders work within your industry, then you might discover commonalities upon which you can develop partnerships with the civil sector.

If your company remains intent simply on squeezing hours out of your employees, costs out of your suppliers, and concessions out of your constituents, you'll remain stuck in the Red Queen Syndrome—running faster and faster just to keep up. But if instead you cede the need to control these stakeholders and instead work with them to make their special *something* better, you might just find that you're progressing toward cross-sector partnerships you didn't know you were missing out on.

Adopt Systems Thinking as a Guide to Solving Problems

The internalization of external costs will challenge companies in many ways. One challenge is thinking in terms of systems, not just individual activities. It's easy to say, "Here's the amount of energy we used in plant X, here's what we did to reduce energy in plant X, and here's the evidence that we're sustainable." But this thinking (perhaps innocently) ignores all the other inputs that go into the plant's activities, as well as all the outputs of the plant's activities. The external costs that will eventually become internalized on income statements will include not only those that come about as a direct result of your actions but also those further upstream to enable your actions and those downstream as consumers use the outputs of your activities.

Each trailblazer featured in this book is employing systems thinking to both map out and then carry out the changes required to convert their visions into realities. Grieg Green, for example, realized that its commitment to responsible shipbreaking hinged on systems thinking. It did not stop at the question, *How do we ensure that Grieg Shipping Group vessels are dismantled responsibly?* Rather it asked itself questions outside its sphere of control, such as *What will it take to nudge competitors to move toward responsible shipbreaking yards?* and *How do we work with these competitors to overcome the institutional memory roadblocks that stand in the way of working with a rival?*

As the private sector becomes more used to the new reality that it can only influence its destiny, systems thinking will only become more prevalent. For an excellent book on systems thinking, I encourage you to read the fantastically insightful *Thinking in Systems: A Primer*, by Donella Meadows.

Adopt an Influence-and-Persuade Mind-Set

Companies that begin to transition to the "We can now only influence our destiny" way of thinking will likely ask, *How can we increase our influence?* My work with the companies in this book suggests one approach that will be useful: be seen as a consistent provider of meaningful value to your stakeholders. To get there, think about whether your business model is built on a zero-sum mentality or an "Our actions can benefit stakeholders, too" mentality.

Consider the perspective of Michael Washburn, VP of sustainability at NWNA (and a coauthor of Chapter Three), on the value to stakeholders of bringing extended producer responsibility (EPR) to the United States:

> EPR is something that does not just benefit NWNA. The benefits of EPR flow to citizens as taxpayers, as consumers, and as concerned local community members. The benefits flow to manufacturers and retailers. The benefits flow to local government entities. The benefits flow to market participants in the value chain on a range of materials. So it isn't like our being self-serving is happening in isolation. There's a common, shared benefit to EPR.
>
> I think the first order in developing our EPR coalition was to make that case. I'll say to my corporate rivals, "Hey guys. You're looking at me like I'm crazy trying to do some green initiative here. But let me tell you the business rationale for it, so that you don't think we're crazy." And then you have constituents responding to that by saying, "Well, OK, I get that."
>
> Then you go to local governments and you say, "We're going to take a cost off your taxpayers." And depending on who you're talking to, if it's the solid waste department, who feels threatened because you're going to take over their system, they don't like it. If it's the county commissioners who are looking at just trying to reduce cost, they love it. So it's establishing the common value set, sharing that with the people who are part of

that common interest, and then harnessing their energy to move the various pieces of the agenda over time.

Now up on the board are some ground rules. Number one, do not try to put one over on anybody. Number two, be humble and acknowledge that a lot of people will have a lot of questions. Acknowledge that you do not possess all the answers. When seeking to build your coalition, embrace your lack of complete answers to its fullest. So, for example, when our EPR coalition went to talk with another industry about recycling, we were asked tons of questions. We said, "That's great! They're legitimate questions. That's why you guys should put some money on the table. Help us answer those questions." And now that industry is preparing to do that.

Thinking in terms of value creation for all stakeholders is heavily reliant on psychology. A lot of the people I'm dealing with have been in their jobs for twenty years. My dad used to talk about teachers and he'd say, "There are teachers that have thirty years of experience, and there are teachers that have one year of experience thirty times." The latter frame is not useful anymore; it's obsolete. And teaching people to reset their frame is exactly what's at the core of cultural change.

———

Becoming an active participant in the Collaboration Economy will potentially necessitate changes in corporate culture. Although the task of adjustment takes time, there is little doubt that it will pay dividends, especially when your organization executes its new set of competitive strategies.

Alterations to Operations

In the Collaboration Economy, the most effective strategies are those that integrate social dimensions into competitive calculations and are carried out by companies that are culturally adept at working in tandem with others. But even in this scenario, the company's alterations to their operations will make the difference between visionary strategy and realized growth and prosperity.

This section covers alterations companies are making to their range of operations in order to succeed in the Collaboration Economy.

Roll Up Your Sleeves—There Are a *Lot* of Stakeholders to Reach

Influencing great change entails great effort. Common sense dictates that the more entities there are that support change, the more likely it is that change will occur. In the Collaboration Economy, every industry that is or will undergo change affects a minimum of thousands of stakeholders.

Think trailblazing companies are ignoring the need to roll up their sleeves? Think again. Coca-Cola rightly understands that water is essential to every community's health and development. GE is actively engaging with all sides of the energy debate. Grieg Green is working with hundreds of brokers of used ships, ship-dismantling yards, and shipowners. And Unilever is working to improve the lives of five hundred thousand smallholder farmers worldwide.

Here is how Michael Washburn describes the work he and his colleagues are doing to reach an impossibly large number of stakeholders in an effort to bring EPR to the United States:

> The challenge is rising to the enormity of the task at hand. There are thousands of brands in the U.S., and thousands more that sell into markets in the U.S. We've got to go to almost every leading brand. And mapping that out, understanding who the right people are to talk to is a challenge.
>
> Another challenge is figuring out who is the right person to start the EPR conversation at a company. We have started by connecting with companies' sustainability directors. But

ultimately we need to bring in a representative of practically every function at every brand owner. So engaging with each brand owner takes time. But we're committed to renewing the U.S. packaging materials recycling system, so we are going through this approach brand owner by brand owner and sector by sector.

Resist the temptation to be intimidated by the enormity of the task at hand. Map out the entities with which you ideally would collaborate. Then go one step at a time and keep an eye out for the opportunity to present your case by plugging in to existing forums or other groups that bring multiple target entities together.

View and Manage Your External Costs as Actual Expenses

It is one thing to say that your company will internalize external costs. It's another thing to actually start to track and report those costs. The vast majority of companies will not do so until a combination of stakeholder pressure and legislative policy requires it.

Courage is needed to overcome the limitations of voluntary action. Enter Puma. The company became an exemplar of the internalization of external costs in 2011 when it completed and published its first "Environmental Profit and Loss Account." The account places an economic value on the environmental impact of the company's actions. In November 2011, Puma valued its 2010 cost of environmental impact at €145 million.[4] For perspective, Puma's first-quarter 2012 revenue was €821 million.[5]

Puma is serving as a beacon in an age of uneven voluntary action. A CEO-track senior leader of a Fortune Global 500 company who is well known for his environmental sustainability expertise explained why other companies have not yet followed Puma's example:

What we've seen so far with most companies is parallel reporting that is, financial performance reported separately from sustainable development metrics like greenhouse gas emissions. Puma really tried to take it all the way home with its Environmental Profit and Loss Account. And I think it scares people. I think it scares CEOs a little bit. CEOs would have to say something along the lines of "We made all this money, but we did so at the expense of as much if not more degradation to natural resources on the planet. I wonder what my board will say to me about this."

Legislative action might be the elixir needed to overcome companies' reluctance to truly own up to the external costs of their business activities.

View the Elimination of Externalities as an Investment

An external cost of €145 million is a significant additional cost to ultimately be internalized. Other companies that calculate their external costs can be equally well equipped to estimate a return on investment for their potential initiatives that lower their external costs.

Hire Specialized Heads of Externality Management and Make Their Roles Matter

For most companies, the skill set needed for cultivating and then leveraging a portfolio of cross-sector collaborations will be a new addition. But pieces of this skill set probably already exist within your company, perhaps in your sustainability, legal, operations, or communications functions. Whether or not your company possesses this skill set, a very simple question remains: Who will oversee these interconnected collaboration activities?

Some companies are installing full-time teams to do just that. Consider Nike. The company has set up a team it calls Mobilize, which is a part of the company's Sustainable Business and Innovation unit. According to Nike's website, the Mobilize team is "set up to engage key business, sustainability and citizen constituents in the design of new ways of doing business. This includes a focus on collaboration, partnerships and open innovation to remove system barriers to sustainable growth and to catalyze innovation levers to take sustainability to scale. Such interventions ought to strengthen our business model resilience, reduce the cost of compliance, and open a space for disruptive innovation."

The Mobilize team consists of a senior lead and several direct reports. Recently, Mobilize sought a director to oversee the effort to mobilize Nike's networks of stakeholders. The following job description (from Nike's website) for the position of mobilization networks director is illustrative of the remit and qualifications for a person expected to lead a company's cross-sector collaboration efforts:

As our Mobilization Networks Director, you'll develop integrated network mobilization campaigns aligning public policy, business constituents, social and environmental networks, citizen influencers and citizen athletes to catalyze scale. You'll drive Mobilize campaigns from strategy and ideation through testing and implementation working closely with other strategists, technologists and interaction designers to make this happen. You'll lead external relations agenda, brokering Sustainable Business & Innovation's (SB&I) influence in the outside world. You'll mobilize NIKE's key networks and corporate constituents in support of our market transformation strategy and integrate Network Mobilization strategies at key moments and in key geos.

Qualifications

- Bachelor's degree in related field
- 10+ years' directly related experience including comprehensive experience as a business/process leader
- Experience contributing to the incubation of new movements and to business development
- Strong systems thinking acumen
- Ability to combine high-level strategy and analytical thinking with excellent management and consultancy skills as well as tactical creativity and flair
- Ability to develop strong working relationships across multiple functional areas
- Experience working with NGO's, non-profits, and/or public affairs a must. A combination of all three is highly desirable.

As companies like Nike continue to weave social consciousness into their business models, their businesses will reap benefits from stakeholder support for their actions. These benefits will likely yield growth, ripe innovation pipelines, and enhanced corporate agility.

Embrace a Longer-Term Time Frame

You make decisions faster when you are the sole decision maker. Collaborations consume time. There is no way around this fact. With collaborations come discussion, debate, and compromise.

The time involved is outweighed by the benefits of working in tandem. The reduction of external costs, the improvement of necessary infrastructure, and the better-assured access to finite resources are three reasons why collaboration is becoming an effective strategic tool for the smartest of companies.

Companies myopically focused on quarterly earnings cycles know well the tension between short-term performance and long-term investment. The Collaboration Economy does not call for the end of quarterly earnings cycles; it calls for courage from C-suites and boards worldwide.

For an example of the courage of conviction, consider Unilever. As discussed in Chapter One, soon after Paul Polman became Unilever's CEO, the company stopped providing quarterly earnings guidance to investors during quarterly earnings calls, a move that caused the share price to drop by 8 percent as worried investors pulled out their money. Polman said at the time, "I want people to focus on cash flow, which is a much longer-term measure than short-term profit, which doesn't take cost of capital into account, doesn't take capital investment into account . . . People always think that to do the right thing costs you more. That is not true at all. It can actually ignite innovation and lower your costs. The alternative of not having sustainable sourcing, of having to deal with the effects of climate change, is a much higher cost on business."[6]

The Collaboration Economy relies on the private sector's commitment to balance long-term thinking and short-term action. Polman's perspective encapsulates this mind-set perfectly.

Call to Action

The transition to the Collaboration Economy will be fueled by corporate changes to strategy, culture, and operations. Although the task of change might appear daunting, your new capabilities will outweigh the costs and temporary disruption involved.

Simple question: Do you want to be a high-performing part of the Collaboration Economy, or do you want to be on the outside looking in? Your answer will dictate your actions over the next twelve to eighteen months and your performance over the long term.

10

WHERE DO WE GO FROM HERE?

The Collaboration Economy is coming together. The partnerships being nurtured, the changes happening to industry business models, the public commitments being made by small and large companies alike are irreversible.

We stand at the brink of a new era of prosperity that will come about by *solving our most vexing environmental and social issues.* New technologies, new business models, and new relationships that quickly scale ideas into global solutions will emerge.

This book has looked at some of the ongoing efforts in the most foundational areas of our global economy. We've seen why no one sector alone can effect the kind of change that will increase the likelihood that we can achieve a state of sustainable development. And we've explored the pragmatic steps that disparate companies, agencies, and community organizations are taking daily to bring the Collaboration Economy to life.

But it's human nature to wonder, *What's next?* The lessons from our trip to the Collaboration Economy will enable us to ask a series of "What if?" "Why?" and "Why not?" questions. What is in our immediate future? What is in the middle- to long-term future? And what can each of us do right now to ensure a better future for generations to come?

This concluding chapter explores the future I see when I look through my cloudy crystal ball. We will look at the one regulatory change that I believe the United States needs to make today to drive innovation, growth, profitability, and sustainable development simultaneously. Next we delve into vexing social challenges not covered in this book that I (and numerous leaders in all three sectors) think can be solved by the mind-sets and frameworks presented in *The Collaboration Economy*. Then I lay out some of the additional thinking and research needed to bring the Collaboration Economy to life.

One U.S. Regulatory Change to Kick-Start Our Prosperity Engine

Volatility has become the new weather certainty. It is mild in the winter in places where snow is the norm. Torrential rain soaks one part of the world while another part accustomed to wet weather suffers from a never-ending drought. Regardless of whether you believe that there is an anthropogenic link to climate change, one thing is clear: spewing greenhouse gas (GHG) into our fragile atmosphere sure isn't helping to stabilize our weather patterns.

Human beings like certainty. We plan better with certainty, and we manage our resources better with certainty. So the global pursuit of GHG emission regulation as a way to stabilize the climate today and going forward appeals as a means of achieving certainty. As a result, the regulation of GHG emissions is at the center of sustainable development legislative interest worldwide.

The European Union's Emission Trading Scheme was designed and enacted as a legislative means of reducing emissions by putting a market price on carbon. The results have been encouraging enough for other regions to follow suit, including Australia.

The United States flirted with similar carbon regulation, but chose not to enact any. I believe that we are a minimum of one or two presidential terms away from revisiting the issue—the political will just isn't there.

So the leaders of the private sector have decided that their GHG policy must be one of action. More and more companies have publicly committed to carbon and other GHG emission reduction targets. And they are actively investing to hit their goals.

But such voluntary action must excuse neither Washington nor the rest of the world's public sector agencies from playing a consistent leadership role in the pursuit of sustainable development. Voluntary action alone can only take us so far.

I want us to cajole the world's public sector leaders to once again pick up the baton of sustainable development. Rather than pursue carbon regulation right now (for the record, I am convinced that carbon regulation is necessary), I propose that we dedicate our energy to the pursuit of a different regulation, one that can truly ignite the sustainable development, growth, innovation, and prosperity movement in relatively short order. I think the time has come to modernize U.S. antitrust regulation.

The Sherman Act of 1890 is the father of today's antitrust regulation. Simply put, it was enacted to "protect the consumers by preventing arrangements designed, or which tend, to advance the cost of goods to the consumer."[1] The legislation was well designed to meet the needs of the time; monopolistic behavior was not in the best interests of consumers (think Robber Barons and the like).

The prevention of monopolistic and pseudomonopolistic behavior is at the heart of today's U.S. antitrust regulation. We are correct in wanting to protect consumers' rights. But our vexing challenges necessitate an all-hands-on-deck mentality. The world has evolved, and we're in a different place: we have to create unique, innovative partnerships to protect our people and our planet. This is something that I think we're all starting to feel as the population grows, resources are stressed, and the economy changes very quickly, not just in the United States but around the world, too. I think it's time for certain rules and regulations to evolve in order to allow people to better work together to solve common issues.

Although antitrust regulation continues to protect the consumer, it runs the risk of doing so at the expense of the environment and at the expense of social and economic development. We must consider modernizing this regulation.

The companies featured in *The Collaboration Economy* described for me their guiding principles when working in local communities. The main principle each shared was common across the group: *Are we adding value? Are we helping enhance people's lives? Are we leaving these places in better shape than how we found them?* It is not surprising that this principle was commonly cited; it's illustrative of good common sense.

So one recommendation to legislators willing to determine whether the zeitgeist of current antitrust law is aligned with current conditions is to apply the aforementioned guiding principle to the evaluation of new partnerships formed by intraindustry rivals. There is too much at stake not to confirm that a well-intended and well-thought-through regulation is assisting, not hindering, our ability to achieve sustainable development.

The Collaboration Economy Can Enable Solutions to Other Vexing Issues

Food allergies among children seem to be more common today than ever before. Parents are more apt to bring their children to the doctor at the first sign of suspicious reactions. Doctors, perhaps consciously seeking to avoid litigious situations, are more apt to err on the side of caution and diagnose food allergies. I have seen this firsthand.

On the topic of health, one statistic in particular recently piqued my interest: in the United States alone, consumers spend $190 billion annually on health care services related to diabetes and obesity. The United Nations views diabetes and obesity as noncommunicable diseases. Evidence suggests that sociological behavior (such as eating patterns and exercise routines) serves as a significant contributing factor to the high incidence of these two noncommunicable diseases.

Food allergies, obesity, diabetes—what if these aren't outliers occurring in far greater numbers but rather indicators of the beings into which we are evolving? Do we want humanity to evolve into a state where these and related issues are the norm, not the exception?

Let's assume that our choices play a large role in determining whether we will experience these and related issues. These choices would seem to include how much and how often we exercise, what foods we consume, and what recreational choices we make. As an instant-gratification society, we want the most expedient "solutions" to our health problems, so we seek medications that potentially can provide quick resolution without significant, if any, additional modifications on our part.

We've explored the water-food-energy nexus throughout *The Collaboration Economy*. The food–behavior–health care nexus would appear to be another challenge that the ethos of the Collaboration Economy could help untangle. The food and pharmaceutical industries have flirted with each other before with, at best, mixed results. But as noted in Chapter Seven, previous results should be lessons to learn from, not excuses for avoiding collaboration between these two indispensable industries. This is why I call for the visionary companies in the food and pharmaceutical industries to once again explore collaboration that can at least mitigate social challenges while simultaneously leading to greater prosperity for both.

Help Wanted: Further Collaboration Economy Thinking Is Needed

My fervent hope is that *The Collaboration Economy* has illuminated questions and sparked ideas in your mind. The early work described throughout this book holds great promise for a better tomorrow. But this book is only the beginning of a long and arduous journey of discovery. It is an understatement to say that much research into and thinking about the Collaboration Economy remains.

So I call upon you, the reader, to join the leaders featured in this book and me on a journey to further shape and inform the Collaboration Economy. Here are two of the areas I believe require additional investigation.

Metrics

What gets measured gets managed. Until we integrate external costs—the value of renewed environmental conditions net of environmental degradation—into the most globally visible and widely publicized metrics, we will be fighting an uphill battle. Gross domestic product (GDP) is the one metric by which economic development is measured and economic health is publicized. With roughly two-thirds of GDP driven by individual consumption, a portion of social development and societal health is already folded into the GDP.

But everything we do, everything we produce, and everything we consume is completely reliant on environmental conditions. Without materials, there would not be products. Without energy, there would not be manufacturing and consumption. And without water, all else is moot.

The inclusion of a net environmental impact valuation in GDP would send a signal to the private and civil sectors that the public sector truly values sustainable development. This idea is already being explored in parts of the world. I've heard about at least one government in North America that plans to develop and test an environmental profit-and-loss account (E P&L), similar to Puma's, that it would publish alongside its financial accounts.

Speaking of Puma, I anticipate that more companies will move to develop similar E P&Ls. The pace of adoption of such accounts is unclear. To improve that pace, the private sector will need to create and agree to a standardized approach to valuing the externalities brought about by companies' business activities. This is a perfect opportunity for the private sector to reach out for at least civil sector assistance. Social sector experts could facilitate forums for intra-industry rivals to share codiscovery methods and best practices to precisely account for their environmental and social impacts in a way that would not be too arduous to regularly perform.

New Organizational Structures

My father-in-law has owned his own company for thirty years. A serial entrepreneur, he has also become a locally well-known philanthropist. He currently sits on more than a dozen nonprofit boards, such as the Perkins School for the Blind in Boston.

He is a leading indicator of what a Collaboration Economy future looks like. A veteran of numerous fundraising campaigns, he is now focused on enabling the Perkins School and many other nonprofits to become self-funding institutions. In particular, he is helping these organizations create for-profit entities within their nonprofit organizations. Who better to serve the needs of the blind by developing products for the blind than organizations that specialize in working with the blind?

A for-profit entity operating within a not-for-profit structure is one example of the new organizational structures emerging, representing a blurring of lines that I anticipate will accelerate in the near and middle term. As more companies integrate social dimensions into their business models, we will witness the birth of entirely new organizational structures. As rivals collaborate to protect resources and solve problems held in common, we might see a spate of joint ventures (JVs) emerge. One or more NGOs might well be involved, not only to provide local expertise but for management and oversight purposes, because although rivals might collaborate, they are neither willing nor able to simply follow one another's lead. So these community-level JVs may actually be led by an NGO that can navigate the politically tricky waters of JVs among fierce rivals.

GE's ecomagination accelerator hints at another form of organizational structure that might emerge. This form will couple an industrial giant with one or more entrepreneurs and social-impact nonprofits that "lease" the giant's scale in return for sharing revenue, technology, or expertise. The industrial giant, in this case GE, acts as incubator, investor, and stand-alone partner, and commits to not seeking to acquire the start-ups with which it partners. In return, the company or nonprofit organization is able to scale up quickly, thus having a measureable impact faster than it could have done on its own. The new organizational structure in this case might not be an organization at all; rather, it might amount to a new form of partnership agreement.

There is another new type of organizational structure that I sense but cannot yet describe in detail. At its core are employees and employers. The difference between this new organization and the typical organization of today lies in the nature of the employee–employer relationship.

I could continue speculating about new organizational structures that arise from among companies, start-ups, and citizens seeking work. Imagine the kinds of new structures that could emerge if companies were to enter true partnerships with the local communities in which they operate. The joint pursuit of such shared value could give rise to a structure owned by a for-profit (the company) and a nonprofit (the local community), through which the financial fruits of their joint labor were proportionately shared among all partners of the created entity. Replace local communities with local government agencies in that scenario, and yet another innovative organizational structure could emerge.

Indeed, we are on the cusp of a new age of innovation. We have to be; the extent of our challenges has far exceeded the capacity of our conventional approaches and existing technologies. Many of the younger generations' best thinkers and doers aspire to work with companies that serve the common good. They want to have as large an impact as possible as quickly as possible.

I've just scratched the surface of this emerging set of new organizational structures. New organizational structures that better reflect today's social realities will emerge. As these new structures take form, they will have to have rules, guidance, and oversight consistent with their unique design so as to optimize their efforts in a way that is consistent with local and global norms and expectations. This is one area of the Collaboration Economy that will benefit from further attention, research, and thinking.

———

We have just begun our journey. Much work remains. Let's not seek to sustain our current socioeconomic situation. Instead, let's work together to create a new era of prosperity that benefits our lives today while enhancing future generations' ability to meet their needs in perpetuity. The collective efforts of the many can and will lead to change we can all support. Thank you for joining my partners and me on this journey!

Endnotes

Introduction

1. MacKerron, C., *Unfinished Business: The Case for Extended Producer Responsibility for Post-Consumer Packaging*, As You Sow (July 24, 2012), http://asyousow.org/publications/2012 /UnfinishedBusiness_TheCaseforEPR_20120724.pdf
2. Brandenburger, A., and Nalebuff, B., *Co-opetition* (New York: Currency Doubleday, 1996).

Chapter 1

1. To learn more about the Matterhorn Group, visit its website, http://www.matterhorn-group.ch/en/matterhorn-group /company/, accessed March 5, 2012.
2. For far greater coverage of the "development and dispersion" of value to shareholders and stakeholders alike, please refer to my first book, *The Future of Value* (San Francisco: Jossey-Bass, 2011).
3. See Wikipedia's "Economy" entry, http://en.wikipedia.org /wiki/Economy, accessed September 22, 2012.
4. Department of the Treasury with the Council of Economic Advisers, *A New Economic Analysis of Infrastructure Investment* (March 23, 2012), http://www.treasury.gov/resource -center/economic-policy/Documents/20120323Infrastructure Report.pdf, accessed September 18, 2012.
5. Ibid.
6. Witters, D., and Agrawal, S., "Unhealthy U.S. Workers' Absenteeism Costs $153 Billion," Gallup (October 17, 2011),

http://www.gallup.com/poll/150026/unhealthy-workers
-absenteeism-costs-153-billion.aspx, accessed September 28,
2012.

7. My previous book, *The Future of Value*, chronicles these
companies' efforts and best practices.

8. Botelho, G., "Drought of 2012 Conjures Up Dust Bowl
Memories, Raises Questions for Tomorrow," CNN.com (September 15, 2012), http://www.cnn.com/2012/09/15/us/drought
-perspective/index.html?hpt=us_c2, accessed September 17,
2012.

9. Botelho, G., "By the Numbers: Today's Drought vs. the Dust
Bowl Era," CNN U.S. (September 15, 2012), http://www
.cnn.com/2012/09/15/us/drought-by-the-numbers/index
.html, accessed September 17, 2012.

10. OECD International Futures Programme, Strategic Transport Infrastructure Needs: Main Findings (2011), http://www
.oecd.org/futures/infrastructureto2030/49094448.pdf

11. See Wikipedia's "Public-Private Partnership" entry, http://
en.wikipedia.org/wiki/Public–private_partnership, accessed
September 18, 2012.

12. "Message from our CEO," Unilever (2012), http://www
.unilever.com/sustainable-living/ourapproach/messageceo/,
accessed September 28, 2012.

13. "Unilever Reports on First Year's Progress Against Ground-
Breaking Sustainable Living Plan Targets," Unilever (April
4, 2012), http://www.unilever.com/mediacentre/pressreleases
/2012/unilever-reports-slp-progress.aspx?name=Press13286
263Feature&item=6, accessed September 28, 2012.

Chapter 2

1. Gold, R., "Gas Producers Rush to Pennsylvania: Promising
Results There Spur Investment," *Wall Street Journal*, April 2,
2008, A2.

2. MacIssac, T., "As NY Turns to Fracking, Farmers Cash In," *Epoch Times*, March 11, 2012, http://www.theepochtimes .com/n2/united-states/as-ny-turns-to-fracking-farmers-cash -in-203580.html, accessed December 14, 2012.
3. Konrad, T., "Natural Gas Liquids Are Following Natural Gas off a Fracking Cliff," *Forbes*, July 3, 2012, http://www.forbes .com/sites/tomkonrad/2012/07/03/natural-gas-liquids-are -following-natural-gas-off-a-fracking-cliff/, accessed December 14, 2012.
4. U.S. Energy Information Administration, "Energy Explained: Energy in the United States" (May 2, 2012), http://205.254 .135.7/energyexplained/index.cfm?page=electricity_in_the _united_states, accessed July 11, 2012.
5. Ibid.
6. Union of Concerned Scientists, "How Natural Gas Works" (August 31, 2010), http://www.ucsusa.org/clean_energy/our -energy-choices/coal-and-other-fossil-fuels/how-natural-gas -works.html, accessed July 11, 2012.
7. Ibid.
8. For more information, see the Natural Resources Defense Council website, http://www.nrdc.org/energy/gasdrilling/, accessed December 26, 2012.
9. For more information, see Water Defense, "The Facts on Natural Gas," http://www.waterdefense.org/content/facts -natural-gas, accessed July 11, 2012.
10. U.S. Energy Information Administration, "Energy Explained."
11. Ibid.

Chapter 3

1. BlueGreen Alliance, "Report: Increasing Recycling Will Create Nearly 1.5 Million Jobs, Reduce Pollution" (November 15, 2011), http://www.bluegreenalliance.org/news/latest /increased-recycling-will-create-1–5-million-jobs-reduce -pollution, accessed April 25, 2012.

2. MacKerron, C., *Unfinished Business: The Case for Extended Producer Responsibility for Post-Consumer Packaging*, As You Sow (July 24, 2012), http://asyousow.org/publications/2012/UnfinishedBusiness_TheCaseforEPR_20120724.pdf

Chapter 4

1. International Fund for Cultural Development, *Climate Change and the Future of Smallholder Agriculture*, discussion paper prepared for the Roundtable on Climate Change at the thirty-first session of IFAD's Governing Council (February 14, 2008), http://www.ifad.org/climate/roundtable/index.htm, accessed December 2, 2012.

2. McKinsey & Company, *Resource Revolution: Meeting the World's Energy, Materials, Food, and Water Needs* (November 2011), available at http://www.mckinsey.com/Features/Resource_revolution.

3. Food and Agriculture Organization of the United Nations, *How to Feed the World in 2050* (n.d.), http://www.fao.org/fileadmin/templates/wsfs/docs/expert_paper/How_to_Feed_the_World_in_2050.pdf, accessed December 2, 2012.

4. Food and Agriculture Organization of the United Nations, *The State of Food and Agriculture 2008* (2008), available at http://www.fao.org/docrep/011/i0100e/i0100e00.htm

Chapter 5

1. Gambrell, J., "Abandoned Ships a Rusting Hazard in Nigeria Waters," Associated Press (May 1, 2012), http://finance.yahoo.com/news/abandoned-ships-rusting-hazard-nigeria-111458171.html, accessed June 21, 2012.

2. "Gaddani Shipbreakers Defy Death Everyday," *The News*, March 3, 2012, http://www.thenews.com.pk/article-38074-Gaddani-shipbreakers-defy-death-everyday, accessed April 19, 2012.

3. "Media Alert—Groundbreaking Ruling Shows Way Forward for Asbestos Victims," NGO Shipbreaking Platform (February 23, 2012), http://www.shipbreakingplatform.org/media-alert-groundbreaking-ruling-shows-way-forward-for-asbestos-victims/, accessed March 5, 2012.

4. "SC Asks HC to Examine Shipbreaking Rules," *Daily Star*, January 13, 2012, http://www.thedailystar.net/newDesign/news-details.php?nid=218147, accessed March 5, 2012.

5. Ethirajan, A., "Bangladesh Ship Breaking Workers Die After Inhaling Gas," BBC News (October 17, 2011), http://www.bbc.co.uk/news/world-south-asia-15334152, accessed March 10, 2012.

6. Yoshida, S., "Rio+20: In South Asia, It Is Survival That Counts . . . Not the Environment," *Asahi Shimbun*, June 14, 2012, http://ajw.asahi.com/article/economy/environment/AJ201206140070, accessed December 14, 2012.

7. "Media Alert—NGO Releases 2011 List of Top EU Companies Sending Toxic Ships to South Asia," NGO Shipping Platform (2012), http://www.shipbreakingplatform.org/media-alert-ngo-releases-2011-list-of-top-eu-companies-sending-toxic-ships-to-south-asia/, accessed April 24, 2012.

8. European Commission, "Environment: Commission Proposes Tighter Laws on Ship Breaking" (press release), Europa (March 23, 2012), http://europa.eu/rapid/pressReleasesAction.do?reference=IP/12/310, accessed April 24, 2012.

Chapter 6

1. Kim, W. C., and Mauborgne, R., *Blue Ocean Strategy* (Boston: Harvard Business School Press, 2005).

2. Kaskinen, T., and Mokka, R., "Green Markets Must Be Created by You," Low2No.org (September 13, 2011), http://www.low2no.org/essays/green-markets-created-by-you

3. For more information, see the Blue Ocean Strategy website's "Tagline" glossary entry, http://www.blueoceanstrategy.com/about/glossary/tagline/, accessed January 19, 2013.

4. Hawken, P., *The Ecology of Commerce: A Declaration of Sustainability* (New York: HarperBusiness, 2010), 79.
5. McDonough, W., and Braungart, M., *Cradle to Cradle: Remaking the Way We Make Things* (New York: North Point Press, 2002), 112.
6. Ellen MacArthur Foundation, "In Depth—Washing Machines" (October 9, 2012), http://www.ellenmacarthurfoundation.org /business/articles/in-depth-washing-machines
7. Vander Velpen, B.P.A., et al., "Implementing Service-Based Chemical Supply Relationship—Chemical Leasing—Potential in EU?" (May 9, 2012).

Chapter 7

1. Statistics are from World Business Council for Sustainable Development, *Water Facts and Trends* (August 2005), http:// www.unwater.org/downloads/Water_facts_and_trends.pdf, accessed August 15, 2012.
2. For more information, see Sidem, "How Much Water Comes from Desalination?" FAQ (2011), http://www.sidem -desalination.com/en/Process/FAQ/#c12260056211, accessed July 13, 2012.
3. UNICEF, "Child Survival Fact Sheet: Water and Sanitation" (August 24, 2004), http://www.unicef.org/media/media _21423.html, accessed August 15, 2012.
4. See Muhtar Kent's prepared remarks for Colorado State University, November 16, 2011, http://www.news.colostate .edu/content/documents/MuhtarKentSpeech.pdf, accessed August 15, 2012.

Chapter 8

1. See Paul Polman's speech at the Harold Wincott Awards for Financial Journalism 2012, May 24, 2012, http://www

.unilever.com/images/mc_speech-wincott-foundation _tcm13-288409.pdf, accessed December 1, 2012.

2. Ibid.

3. Riley, C., "100+ CEOs Promise No Campaign Donations," CNNMoney (August 26, 2011), http://money.cnn.com /2011/08/24/news/economy/ceo_pledge_donations/index .htm, accessed December 2, 2012.

4. Kaplan, D., "Howard Schultz Brews Strong Coffee at Star-bucks," CNNMoney (November 17, 2011), http://management .fortune.cnn.com/2011/11/17/starbucks-howard-schultz -business-person-year/, accessed December 2, 2012.

5. Mirdha, R., "H&M Chief to Visit Bangladesh," *Daily Star*, September 2, 2012, http://www.thedailystar.net/newDesign /news-details.php?nid=247989, accessed December 2, 2012.

6. Grankvist, P., "When a CEO Turns Activist: Why H&M Wants Bangladesh to Increase Workers' Wages," CSRwire (September 28, 2012), http://www.csrwire.com/blog/posts/558 -when-a-ceo-turns-activist-why-h-m-wants-bangladesh-to -increase-workers-wages, accessed December 2, 2012.

7. Strauss, L., "It's a Balancing Act," *Barron's*, July 28, 2012, http://online.barrons.com/article/SB5000142405311190434 6504577534861098874948.html#articleTabs_article%3D1, accessed December 14, 2012.

8. Kennedy, J. F., "Address Before the 18th General Assembly of the United Nations, September 20, 1963," John F. Kennedy Presidential Library and Museum, http://www.jfklibrary .org/Research/Ready-Reference/JFK-Speeches/Address -Before-the-18th-General-Assembly-of-the-United-Nations -September-20-1963.aspx.

9. Sietzen, F., "Soviets Planned to Accept JFK's Joint Lunar Mission Offer," SpaceCast News Service, *SpaceDaily*, Octo-ber 2, 1997, http://www.spacedaily.com/news/russia-97h.html, accessed August 14, 2012.

10. For more information, see Consumer Goods Forum, "Con-sumer Goods Forum and the US Government Announce a

Joint Initiative on Deforestation" (press release), Consumer Goods Forum (June 20, 2012), http://www.theconsumergoods forum.com/PDF/PressReleases/2012/2012-06-20-CGF-Us -Gov-deforestation.pdf, accessed December 22, 2012.

11. "Muhtar Kent's Keynote Speech at the Colorado Innovation Network," October 23, 2012, http://www.coca-colacompany .com/our-company/muhtar-kents-keynote-speech-at-the -colorado-innovation-network, accessed December 1, 2012.

12. Ibid.

Chapter 9

1. King, D., "Ford Uses Recycled Plastic Bottles for Focus Electric Seats," *autobloggreen*, January 8, 2012, http://green.autoblog .com/2012/01/08/ford-uses-recycled-plastic-bottles-for-focus -electric-seats/, accessed December 2, 2012.

2. For a great read on Project Quark, refer to Bryce Hoffman's article "Inside Ford's Fight to Avoid Disaster," *Wall Street Journal*, March 8, 2012, http://online.wsj.com/article/SB100 01424052970204781804577269410217101038.html, accessed December 14, 2012.

3. Mintzberg, H., "To Fix Health Care, Ask the Right Questions," *Harvard Business Review*, October 2011, http://hbr .org/2011/10/to-fix-health-care-ask-the-right-questions/ar/1, accessed December 14, 2012.

4. Puma, "PUMA Completes First Environmental Profit and Loss Account Which Values Impacts at € 145 Million" (press release), About Puma: News (November 16, 2011), http:// about.puma.com/puma-completes-first-environmental -profit-and-loss-account-which-values-impacts-at-e-145 -million/, accessed July 13, 2012.

5. Clark, P., "Puma to Kick Leather into Touch," *Financial Times*, June 22, 2012, http://www.ft.com/intl/cms/s/0/579f4512-bc62 -11e1-a836-00144feabdc0.html#axzz2F3AQEccD, accessed December 14, 2012.

6. Ahmed, K., "Davos 2011: Unilever's Paul Polman Believes We Need to Think Long Term," *Telegraph*, January 15, 2011, http://www.telegraph.co.uk/finance/financetopics/davos /8261178/Davos-2011-Unilevers-Paul-Polman-believes-we -need-to-think-long-term.html, accessed December 14, 2012.

Chapter 10

1. See Wikipedia's "Sherman Antitrust Act" entry, http://en .wikipedia.org/wiki/Sherman_Antitrust_Act, accessed December 14, 2012.

About the Author

Eric Lowitt is a globally recognized expert in the fields of competitive strategy, collaboration, and sustainability. A consultant and sought-after speaker, he is the author of *The Future of Value*, a critically acclaimed book that connects sustainability with competitive strategy and financial performance. Eric was named one of the Top 100 Thought Leaders in Trustworthy Business Behavior, and his work is regularly featured in the *Harvard Business Review*, the *Guardian*, and the *Wall Street Journal*, as well as news wires, industry publications, and other media outlets. He has worked for nearly two decades with Accenture, Fidelity Investments, and Deloitte Consulting, is fluent in Japanese, and earned his MBA from the Wharton School. To learn more about Eric, visit his website, www.ericlowitt.com.

INDEX

THE GHOSTS OF WAR

THE GHOSTS OF WAR

DANIEL COHEN

G. P. PUTNAM'S SONS   NEW YORK

G. P. Putnam's Sons, a division of The Putnam & Grosset Book Group,
200 Madison Avenue, New York, NY 10016.
Published simultaneously in Canada.
Printed in the United States of America.
Book design by Christy Hale

Library of Congress Cataloging-in-Publication Data
Cohen, Daniel. The ghosts of war / Daniel Cohen.
p.   cm.
Summary: Recounts supposedly true stories about ghosts
connected in some way with war, from haunted battlefields
to soldiers' premonitions of death.
1. Ghosts—Juvenile literature. 2. War—Miscellanea—Juvenile
literature. [1. Ghosts. 2. War—Miscellanea.] I. Title.
BF1471.C64 1990 133.1—dc20   89-27789 CIP AC
ISBN 0-399-22200-6
10   9   8   7   6   5   4   3

For Hope

Contents

THE GHOSTS OF WAR

INTRODUCTION

The Reader is Warned (Again)

THOSE OF YOU who have read the introduction to some of my previous ghost books may already know what I'm going to say. But some of you must be new readers, or if you've read other books you haven't read the introduction, or if you did you don't remember what I said. So I'm going to repeat myself, because I think it's important.

A lot of people say to me, "Oh, you write ghost stories." Well, not exactly. These accounts are about ghosts, and I guess you could call them stories, and I did write them. But I don't really "write ghost stories." That statement implies that I make the tales up. I don't. I wish I did, because there are some pretty darn good ones here and I would like to take complete credit for them. I can't.

These are accounts that I have heard or read elsewhere. I simply collect them and retell them. I report them. I don't make them up.

The next question is usually "You mean these are all true?" That's a tricky one. These stories are always "told as true." That is, the teller either believes they are true or wants you to believe it. Some people, probably a lot of people, do believe they are true, or at least that some of them are.

To be quite honest, some of these accounts are pretty clearly not true. Or they concern things that happened so long ago, or the evidence is so slight, that there is not good reason to believe that they are true. In other cases, admittedly a smaller number, there has been some investigation to determine what really happened.

So, though I didn't make these tales up, somebody surely made up some of them. In other cases, an ordinary or explainable event is made to seem extraordinary, even supernatural, because of poor memory, overactive imagination, and the unconscious embellishment that comes with retelling an experience. And then there are those cases which, well, make you wonder.

In this book I'm not trying to prove or disprove anything. I am quite simply recounting for your entertainment some tales that people have believed. Take them for what they are, tales meant to make you shiver, and perhaps wonder. Remember the best ghost tales are always supposed to be true—even if they aren't.

All the accounts in this book are about ghosts that are in one way or another connected with war. There are haunted battlefields, soldiers' premonitions of death—that sort of thing. War has often inspired ghostly tales.

While accounts of ghostly events have been known throughout history and in all parts of the world, a large percentage of the incidents in this book come from World Wars I and II, and they come from England. Why? Quite simply because there are more World War I and II ghost accounts, and the English have been the most diligent people in the world in collecting ghostly tales. The Japanese are also great collectors and tellers of ghost stories, and there is a famous Japanese tale in this book.

I once discussed the prevalence of English ghosts with the great spirit medium Eileen Garrett. I met her after she retired and was living in a huge villa in the south of France. By the way, Eileen Garrett figures prominently in one of the tales in these pages. I asked the medium why there were so many ghost accounts from England, and relatively few from France or other countries in Europe. Were there more ghosts in England? Or did the English just talk about them more often? She thought about the questions for a moment. Then she said she didn't have the faintest idea. I don't either, that's just the way it is.

There are very few ghostly tales from either the Korean War or the war in Vietnam. Once again I have absolutely no idea why. I'm not trying to ignore these wars. It's just that the information isn't there.

Perhaps these wars, particularly Vietnam, are still too recent. It often takes many, many years before a ghost appears. Or before those who have encountered one are willing to talk about it. Maybe in another ten or twenty years there could be a whole bookful of Vietnam War ghost tales.

In the meantime there are enough strange accounts of wartime ghosts to engage your attention for a while.

And just remember. If you want to repeat one of these accounts for your friends, be sure and tell them it's absolutely true. You know it is because you read it in a book.

1

Haunted Battlefields

DO PLACES WHERE violent deaths took place somehow absorb the horror of the events? Can these impressions be released again like photographs printed from a negative? Some people believe that is what happens. That's why ghosts are reported most often at places where people have died by violence.

If this is the case, then battlefields should be prime places for hauntings. And so they have been. From ancient times startled observers have reported seeing the ghosts of long-dead warriors and soldiers repeating the battles in which they fell.

One of the best known of all the haunted battlefields is located just seven miles outside the English town of Banbury. It is a place called Edgehill. On October 12 of 1642 the first major battle of the English Civil War between supporters and opponents of King Charles I was fought at Edgehill. Four thousand men were said to have died in the slaughter. Neither side really won the battle.

That Christmas Eve some shepherds in the area swore that they saw two armies of phantoms battle one another on the field at Edgehill. It was a reenactment of the battle that had taken place the _____ _____ _____ earlier.

The terrifie_____ _____ er. So the next night the minis_____ _____ itizens stood on a hill overlookin_____ _____ orted seeing the same mass of _____ _____ displayed, drums beating, musl_____ _____ arged and horses neighing. . ._____ _____ onsible observers said that the _____ _____ the ghosts. The entire ghostl_____ _____ the length of the original battle at Edgehill.

After that people from all over the countryside gathered to witness this astounding spectacle. Within a few weeks, news of the ghostly event reached the ears of King Charles. He was so impressed that he sent six trusted officers, headed by Colonel Lewis Kirke, to investigate. The six visited the spot themselves. In their report to the king they said they had seen the ghostly battle with their own eyes. Some members of Kirke's group insisted that they actually recognized among the ghosts men they had known who had fallen at Edgehill. One of those mentioned was the king's standard-bearer, Sir Edmund Verney. The king was very much moved by what the officers told him.

16

This, by the way, was one of the first actual investigations of a report of ghosts. King Charles thought the ghostly battle was a good omen, that the rebellion against him would be put down. He was wrong. Six years later he lost his throne and his head.

After these first reports hardly a year passed without people telling of an appearance by the ghostly armies of Edgehill. Usually the sightings were reported on October 12, the day of the battle, or at Christmas.

During World War II the War Department fenced off the Edgehill area, and there were no more reports of ghosts. Though the area is now unfenced, there have been few reports of the ghostly armies in recent years.

Two years after the battle of Edgehill another major battle in the English Civil War was fought nearby. It was at a spot called Marston Moor. Edgehill ended in a draw. Marston Moor ended with a complete defeat for the supporters of Charles I.

From time to time people have reported seeing a full-scale ghostly reenactment of this battle. But these appearances have been nowhere near as celebrated as those at Edgehill. Still, there have been some very unusual experiences recorded at Marston Moor.

In November 1932 a couple of motorists were driving on the road that runs right though the old battlefield. Ahead of them they saw a group of four ragged men stumbling along. The motorists slowed down in order to get a good look at the group. The men were wearing the wide-brimmed hats with feathers that were typical of the royalist armies in the days of Charles I. At first the motorists thought the four must be actors from some touring company still wearing their costumes. They soon found out differently.

A bus was coming the other way down the road. The four figures appeared to stagger into the path of the vehicle. The bus driver must not have seen them, for he didn't even slow down. The bus seemed to go right through these four strangely dressed men.

The motorists who had been watching the figures were horrified. They stopped their car and searched the road. They were convinced they would find the bodies of the four men. They found nothing.

From time to time even today travelers report seeing a solitary figure on the old battlefield. Usually it is the figure of a royalist soldier, still trying to flee the battle fought centuries ago.

In the 1930s at least one English traveler reported seeing a ghostly reenactment of a battle that took place in 1689. The place was the Pass of Killiecrankie in the Highlands of Scotland. It was there that the Scottish Highlanders and other followers of James II defeated the English troops of William and Mary. The defeat of the English was complete. But it was the only major victory the Scots were able to muster. Ultimately, the more numerous and better-armed English forces completely overwhelmed the brave but outnumbered Highlanders.

The visitor had bicycled out to the pass to look at the old battle scene. The ride was a long and exhausting one and she fell asleep. When she awoke she saw a crowd of red-coated English soldiers fumbling with their guns. They were surprised by a horde of fierce Highland warriors carrying shields and brandishing swords. The visitor watched in horror as the British were slaughtered.

She then saw the image of a young Highland woman moving silently among the dead and dying British soldiers. The woman quickly and efficiently removed all the buttons and buckles and other items of value from the uniforms of the men. Any man who was still alive was stabbed with the broad-bladed dagger she carried.

The young woman was a scavenger. Such people often were found on battlefields during that era. Once the battle was over, the scavengers collected what they could.

The terrified observer actually fainted at the gruesome sight. When she awoke it was morning. The pass was quiet and deserted. Had she simply experienced a vivid nightmare? Or had she really seen a vision of that awful battle? The woman was convinced that what she had seen was much more than a dream.

A different sort of haunting afflicted some more modern Highland soldiers during World War II. In June 1940 a company of Scottish Highlanders was part of the British forces fighting the Germans outside Dunkirk in northern France. The British troops had been taking a terrible beating. The Scots, who were always in the forefront of the fighting, had suffered exceptional losses. Finally they were pinned down by German fire in a little wooded area.

Normally the Highlanders were the bravest of the brave. But once inside the wood they seemed to lose all their will to fight. The sergeant major of the Scots came to his commander,

Lieutenant John Scollay, and told him they had to get out of the wood at all costs because it was haunted.

Lieutenant Scollay was astounded. He didn't believe in ghosts. And he didn't think his men would be frightened of anything.

But the sergeant major was clearly frightened, and he wouldn't change his mind. "The wood is haunted, sir," he said. "I know it and the lads know it. For the love of God, sir, we're not scared of Germans. If we have to we'll advance, or force our way through the Germans. But we can't stay here another night."

Foolish as the idea sounded, Lieutenant Scollay saw that his brave men were beginning to lose their nerve.

"It's just a presence, sir," explained the soldier, "but we've all felt it. It's a kind of force pushing us away. And it's something that none of us can fight, sir—something uncanny."

Eventually the Highlanders joined the other British troops in retreat. Once out of the "haunted wood" Scollay's men regained their fighting spirit. But they could do nothing against the overwhelming odds. Most were either killed or taken prisoner.

Lieutenant Scollay himself was taken prisoner and spent the rest of the war in a German POW camp. He often thought about the "haunted wood."

When he was released after the war, Scollay did some research in the library at Dunkirk. He found that in the summer of 1415, a few months before the battle of Agincourt between the English and the French, there had been another battle fought in that very same "haunted wood."

Scollay wondered if the spirits of those long-dead soldiers had somehow come back to torment their successors some five hundred years later. Or was the area just so filled with an aura of death that the Scots were able to sense it? There had been no previous stories of that particular place being haunted. Did the modern violence release forces that had been quiet for five centuries? Scollay didn't know.

The British are certainly not the only people to have tales of haunted battlefields. Reports of phantom armies come from every land and every age. The earliest ones that we know of come from the Assyrians thousands of years ago.

According to legends, ghosts have been seen at the battlefield in Marathon, where in 490 B.C. the ancient Greeks dealt a crushing blow to the invading Persians. It was said that anyone who visited the battlefield after sunset heard the clash of steel, and the screams of the wounded and dying, and that they smelled the odor of blood. Anyone who actually saw the ghostly warriors was reportedly dead within a year. It was not a place people liked to visit at night.

2

The Samurai Ghosts

BETWEEN THE YEARS 1180 and 1185 there was a great war in Japan. It was fought between two powerful warrior clans, the Genji and the Heike. The two clans had been enemies for many years. They had often fought before. The Heike had usually come out on top. The emperor of Japan came from the Heike clan.

As with many wars, the reasons for this one seem unimportant to us today. What was important was that both clans were controlled by powerful warriors called samurai. The samurai were loyal and unbelievably brave. They would die rather than suffer defeat or disgrace. To the samurai, battle was the only way of settling differences. They did not believe in compromise.

And so, in May of 1180, the war, called the Gempei War, began. It was to become the most celebrated of all samurai wars, and the most deadly.

For years the war dragged on. First one side seemed to have an advantage, then the other. Finally it all came down to a single battle fought on April 24, 1185. Both sides had gathered all their forces near a place called Dan-no-ura. The battle is considered the most decisive samurai battle in all Japanese history.

The samurai, like the knights of the middle ages in Europe, were heavily armored warriors. They fought with swords and bows and arrows. They were not really sailors. Yet the battle of Dan-no-ura took place at sea. Japan is a series of islands. The armies needed simple boats to transport troops from one place to another. The boats had no armaments of their own. They were just floating platforms for the samurai. These were the boats used at Dan-no-ura.

As the battle began, the Heike seemed to be winning. Their archers took a grim toll of the Genji warriors. Then the tide in the ocean changed and the advantage shifted to the Genji. Very soon it became apparent that the Heike were going to suffer a humiliating defeat. They could do nothing to avoid the disaster.

The Heike commander then went aboard the vessel that was carrying the eight-year-old emperor. He announced that the battle was lost. In accordance with samurai tradition he said that suicide was the only answer.

The grandmother of the boy emperor took the child in her arms and walked slowly to the edge of the ship. She offered a prayer to her imperial ancestors and to the Buddha. Then, still clinging to the child, she jumped into the ocean.

That began the most tragic mass suicide in Japanese history. Practically every one of the Heike samurai drowned himself. So did all the members of the imperial court.

The red banners of the Heike floated on the sea and washed up on the shore. The beach was dyed a scarlet color. One commentator on the battle wrote:

"The deserted empty ships rocked mournfully on the waves, driven aimlessly hither and thither by the wind and tide."

The battle of Dan-no-ura marked the utter destruction of the clan that had once been the most powerful in Japan. The name of the Heike simply disappeared from Japanese history.

The sheer scale of the horror left a profound impression on the Japanese. The story was told and retold many ways throughout the centuries. Poems and songs were written about the battle and its aftermath. And it has become a central theme for many Japanese ghost stories.

For centuries sailors avoided the area of Dan-no-ura. They feared that they might catch sight of the restless ghosts of the Heike, who had been condemned to wander the area for eternity.

Peasants reported seeing ghostly armies bailing out the sea with bottomless dippers. It was said they were attempting to cleanse the sea of blood, a task that could never be accomplished.

The ghosts were supposed to try to sink ships, or pull down anyone foolish enough to swim in such a cursed area.

Other tales were told about the Oni-bi, or demon fires. On dark nights thousands of ghostly fires have been seen hovering about the beach at Dan-no-ura or flitting on the surface of the water. These are supposed to be restless spirits.

The wind at that spot has a peculiar sound, like the shouting of thousands of voices or the clamor of battle.

Most singular of all the legends surrounding this terrifying event is that of the crabs that inhabit the area. They are called Heike crabs. The shell of the crabs appears to bear the image of a human face. The crabs are supposed to contain the spirits of dead samurai.

In order to put the spirits to rest, a large Buddhist temple was built near the site of the battle. A cemetery was also built close to the beach. In it were monuments to the dead emperor, and all the principal members of his court.

These signs of respect are supposed to have quieted the restless spirits somewhat. They were not seen or heard as often after the temple and cemetery were built. Still, the spirits had not found perfect peace. Hundreds of years after the battle of Dan-no-ura, it was still considered foolhardy to wander the beach at night, particularly in late April, the time when the terrible battle took place. Then the ghosts would appear, and there was no telling what they might do.

3

The Angels of Mons

SOMETIMES WE WANT to believe something so badly that we do, even when there is overwhelming evidence that what we believe is not true.

Nothing in the long history of ghostly lore illustrates this better than the case that has been called The Angels of Mons.

When World War I began, many of the people of Britain were very enthusiastic about it. They thought that they would win quickly and easily; that the war would result in a great and glorious victory for Britain. Of course, the other side, the Germans, thought exactly the same thing. As it turned out, the war wasn't quick and easy for anyone. It went on for years and was much more horrible than people on either side had imagined. Hope for a quick victory soon gave way to fear and despair.

There was an early indication of just how long and terrible the conflict would be. The war began in August 1914. On August 23, British soldiers in Europe faced their first major battle. It was outside the city of Mons in Belgium. The British were hopelessly outnumbered. They had to retreat. The retreat was a long and hard one. They had to go as far as the Marne River in France before they could join up with French forces and launch a counteroffensive.

News of the retreat from Mons hit the British public hard. Those who had been saying the war would be short and glorious now realized that it would be neither. People in Britain became very depressed.

A newspaperman and writer of supernatural stories, Arthur Machen, wrote an imaginary account of the British retreat at Mons. He said that ghostly archers had joined the British troops during the retreat. Several famous battles had taken place near Mons hundreds of years earlier. Most assumed the phantom soldiers were English bowmen from the Battle of Agincourt in 1415. The English had won a great victory in that battle. The story implied that their troops had been given some sort of supernatural aid by ghosts from the past. It was a reassuring tale. But it was entirely made up. Machen had never really tried to pretend that the story was true.

Yet the British public was so hungry for good news that many seized upon Machen's tale as a factual account of what had happened. The story grew day by day. Soon people were saying that the British had been saved by a ghostly army of sword-wielding horsemen. Some said the phantom army appeared in the sky. Others insisted that "warrior angels" had actually been fighting alongside the British troops.

Popular songs were written about the "Angels of Mons."

All of this surprised, even shocked, Arthur Machen. He had never imagined that his little story would provoke such a reaction. He had not counted on people's will to believe, particularly under the strain of war.

Machen began telling people that his story was just that—a story—something he had made up. He wrote letters to newspapers confessing what he had done. But that wasn't what people wanted to hear. They got mad at him. They wrote him angry letters. How could he be so unpatriotic? they said. The Angels were on the side of the British.

Others began saying that they had heard about the ghostly figures before Machen wrote his story. Some said that the sightings had been confirmed by their son, or nephew, or brother who had actually been at Mons and seen them.

Later some Germans claimed that the images were motion pictures projected on the clouds by German pilots. This they said was an attempt by the Germans to make the British think that the angels were on the German side!

None of this was true. The whole story came completely out of Arthur Machen's imagination. All the rest was the result of people's strong will to believe. Even today you can find some references to the Angels of Mons as something that people really saw. But they didn't.

Perhaps people were more likely to believe in the Angels of

Mons because they had already heard stories and legends about phantom armies.

So when Machen wrote his story he knew there was an old belief in phantom armies. But he didn't believe in the Angels of Mons, and nobody else should have either. But they did.

4

The Polish Mercenary

A MEDIUM IS a person who is supposed to have a special ability to contact the spirits of the dead. A medium will go into a trance and then his or her body is taken over by the spirit. The spirit often speaks through the medium. Typically a medium has a spirit guide or control who introduces other spirits. In cases of hauntings or other ghostly events, mediums are often brought in to contact and identify the restless spirits, and sometimes to lay them to rest.

It must be pointed out that an awful lot of people are convinced that there is nothing but fraud and wishful thinking in the whole idea of mediums. Many mediums have been caught red-handed in fraud, and have admitted to it. Just because a medium says that there is a ghost doesn't mean that there is. Still, mediums figure very prominently in many, many ghostly tales. Here is one of them.

In the early 1940s a popular New York City newspaper columnist named Danton Walker bought a house north of the city. He wanted to use it for weekends and vacations.

The house was old, and parts of it had been built in the days before the American Revolution. Lots of repairs were needed. It was located in a part of New York State where many Revolutionary War battles had been fought. The headquarters of the American Revolutionary War general "Mad" Anthony Wayne once stood nearby. The bloody battle of Stony Point had been fought just a few miles away. The house itself may once have been used to store equipment or house soldiers, or it may actually have served as a prison. There were no definite records from the time. But the house had certainly been there during the Revolution, and since there weren't many houses in the area at that time, it is reasonable to assume that it was used for something during the war.

Walker had heard rumors that the place was "haunted" even before he bought it. But all old houses are supposed to be haunted, so he didn't pay much attention to such rumors. It wasn't until 1944, when the house had been fully restored, that Walker began to go there regularly. Then things began to happen.

There were the familiar ghostly footsteps, mostly the sound of heavy boots tramping around empty rooms. There were unexplained knocks at the door when no one was there. Objects would disappear from one place and turn up in another days or weeks later. People who came into the house were oppressed by the feeling that there was something "unearthly" about it. A lot of people didn't like to visit Walker's country house. Finally Walker himself felt he couldn't even sleep in the place. He had his bed moved to a small building behind the main house.

Now, Danton Walker had a long-standing interest in ghosts. He had often written about the ghostly experiences of famous people in his newspaper column. Yet he never did anything about the ghosts that seemed to be disturbing his own house.

Then, in 1952, rumors of Walker's haunted house reached Eileen Garrett, one of the most famous mediums in the world. She lived in New York City and had built a solid reputation as a respected and responsible medium. She even started an organization to study hauntings and other phenomena that might be considered psychic. The famous medium asked Walker if she could visit his haunted house, and naturally he agreed.

On a stormy day in November 1952, Eileen Garrett and a small group of investigators from her organization drove up to the columnist's house in the country. They had cameras that would take pictures in the dark, and tape recorders to pick up any strange sounds. But the main tool was Mrs. Garrett herself.

Unlike many mediums, Eileen Garrett didn't go in for elaborate rituals. She looked around the house, then marched straight into the living room and sat down in a comfortable chair. The tape recorder was switched on and the medium fell into a trance almost instantly.

As soon as she went into a trance, her East Indian "spirit control," Unvani, began speaking through her. The voice of Unvani said that he was going to allow another spirit, the spirit that was haunting the Walker house, to take control. Unvani warned, "Remember that you are dealing with a personality very young, very tired, who has been very much hurt in life."

The change from the dignified and calm Unvani to this new spirit was startling. Mrs. Garrett's eyes popped wide open and she stared straight ahead in terror. But it was obvious that she saw nothing. Her body started to tremble violently and she began moaning and weeping. The medium fell out of her chair and dragged herself across the floor to where Danton Walker was sitting. When she tried to stand up, her leg gave way as if it had been broken. She lay on the floor shaking and crying. It was several minutes before any of the startled people in the room could make contact with the spirit that was supposed to be controlling the medium's body. Even then they could get little information, for the spirit seemed to be confused, in great pain, and spoke very little English.

What those in the room could figure out from the garbled speech was that the spirit was that of a Polish mercenary named Andreas, who had served with the Revolutionary army. He had been carrying some sort of map when he was trapped by British soldiers in that very house. They beat him horribly and left him for dead. But he did not die at once. He lingered on for several terrible, pain-filled days. The Andreas spirit also mentioned a brother, but at first no one could make head or tail of this.

Unvani once again resumed control of Mrs. Garrett's body. She got up off the floor, bowed, and sat down in a chair.

Unvani's calm voice explained the situation further. He said that Danton Walker resembled the dead soldier's brother, another mercenary, who had also been killed during the Revolutionary War. When Walker purchased the house, and started coming regularly, the resemblance triggered the haunting by Andreas' restless ghost.

Unvani suggested that everyone pray for peace to finally come to the troubled spirit of the Polish mercenary. At that, Mrs. Garrett awoke from her trance. As usual she said that she had no idea of what had happened while she was under the control of the spirits. The whole experience had taken about an hour and fifteen minutes.

A few months later Walker reported that the atmosphere of his house seemed much calmer. Perhaps the spirit of the unhappy soldier finally did find its rest.

5

A Hero's Ghost

STEPHEN DECATUR was one of America's greatest naval heroes. Handsome, charming, and fiercely patriotic, he was idolized during the early 1800s. Decatur is the man who popularized the saying "My country right or wrong."

Decatur had come from a family of seafarers. He had served on a variety of ships throughout the Caribbean and the Mediterranean. In 1803 he was given command of his first ship. He carried out a daring raid against pirates in Tripoli harbor in North Africa.

During his career he had faced death many times. In one encounter he had seen his own brother fall dead at his side. In another his best friend had chosen to be blown up in a ship-board explosion rather than risk capture.

But the encounter that ultimately led to Stephen Decatur's early death was one that he had not personally taken part in. Though the United States had successfully defeated the British in the War of Independence, there were still many hostile encounters between the two nations. Most of these took place at sea. In one the British frigate *Leopard* fired at the American frigate *Chesapeake*. The American commander, James Barron, did not fight back. He allowed the British to board his ship and remove four sailors who they claimed were deserters.

When Barron returned to Norfolk, Virginia, he faced a court-martial for not resisting the British. One of those on the nine-member board was Stephen Decatur. Barron was convicted and suspended from the navy for five years. The *Chesapeake-Leopard* encounter was part of the slow-burning fuse that finally ignited the War of 1812 between America and Britain.

Barron was bitter over what had happened to him. He believed he had acted properly. Barron particularly blamed Decatur for his conviction. His hatred was doubtless fueled by the fact that Decatur was made commander of the *Chesapeake*, his old ship. During the War of 1812, Decatur, aboard the *Chesapeake,* performed more heroic exploits. He became a bigger hero than ever before. Forgotten and embittered, James Barron plotted revenge.

After the war Decatur and his beautiful and soft-spoken wife, Susan, moved into an elegant new house on Lafayette Street in Washington, D.C. The Commodore, as he was often called, became one of the most popular men in Washington. He could have entered politics, or any other field he wished, and success would have been assured.

But in truth, Stephen Decatur was not a satisfied or happy man. He had spent most of his lifetime fighting at sea. It was the world he knew, and the world he loved. But now there was no war, and no prospect of war. He confided to a friend that he was ashamed that he might have "to die in my bed."

James Barron's suspension from the navy had expired. But he was always passed over for the posts he wanted. His naval career was effectively at an end. He was convinced that Decatur was the real source of his troubles, so he mounted a campaign to provoke Decatur into a duel.

Dueling was illegal, though it went on anyway. When he was young, Decatur had fought several duels. Dueling had become less respectable; however, it was still excused in young men who were considered "hot-blooded." Decatur was now a mature man. He did not seem anxious to fight another duel. Barron knew this and was persistent. Finally Decatur was goaded into reluctantly accepting the challenge. He wrote, ". . . if we fight, it must be on your own seeking."

Decatur did not tell his wife about the upcoming duel. The night before it was to take place, there was a party at the Decatur home. The guests knew nothing. Stephen Decatur, who was normally sociable, was gloomy and distracted that evening. He left the festivities early and went into his bedroom. There he spent a long time just gazing out the window.

Decatur was certainly not afraid of facing death. He had risked his life too often to have any fear. He knew, however, that even if he won the duel, his reputation would suffer. Perhaps he also had a premonition of how the duel would turn out.

Before sunrise of March 14, 1820, the Commodore slipped out a back door of his house carrying a box containing his dueling pistols. He met his friend William Bainbridge, who was to act as his second. The pair rode to a field near the small Maryland town of Bladensburg. The place was a notorious dueling field. A brook that ran nearby had been christened Blood Run.

The duel was to be fought at a mere eight paces—murderously close. It was certainly to be a duel to the death. The men were told that they were to take aim and could fire after the count of one, but not after the count of three. Witnesses reported that two shots rang out as soon as the count of two was reached.

Barron immediately fell, wounded in the hip. Decatur stood for a moment, but only a moment. He dropped his smoking gun, clutched at his right side, and fell. He had been mortally wounded.

Decatur was taken back to his home in Washington. His wife, Susan, was so grief-stricken that she was unable to bring herself to see him before he died. Decatur's last words were "If it were in the cause of my country, it would be nothing." They expressed the futility of his death on the dueling field.

Despite the manner of his death, the country mourned its hero. Flags flew at half-staff, and towns all over the country were named after him.

The Commodore's ghost didn't show up for a year. Then

some of the household staff at the Decatur home reported seeing his spirit standing at the window of the room that had been his bedroom. The spirit was doing what Decatur himself had done the night before the fatal duel—staring out morosely.

Once that story got around, the window was ordered walled up. It didn't stop the sightings. People passing the house, which still stands on Lafayette Street, report that they have seen the semitransparent form of the naval hero at the walled-up window.

People who have lived in the house also report that sometimes, early in the morning, they have seen his ghostly form slipping out of the back door. The figure carries a black box under its arm. Decatur would have carried his dueling pistols in just such a box when he left his house on the fatal morning of March 14, 1820.

Susan Decatur never really recovered from her husband's death. She fled their Washington home. Many considered her grief to be excessive. But it is said that at times she still can be heard weeping in the Decatur house. Perhaps she has not recovered from her grief yet.

6

"Rescue My Body"

ONE OF THE LESSER-KNOWN wars in American history is the conflict between the United States and Britain called the War of 1812. The war was fought primarily in the East and at sea. But one of the little-known facts of this little-known war is that there were battles fought along the Canadian border, between English troops in Canada, and Americans to the south.

At least one of these battles has produced a tale of love, death, and a ghost.

In the Canadian village of Windsor, just across the border from Detroit, lived a girl named Marie McIntosh. She was admired by all the young men of Windsor. No one loved her more than a British officer, Lieutenant William Muir. Marie was inclined to return the lieutenant's affections. But the style of the day required that girls remain reserved and coy. They could not express their feelings or appear to give in too easily. Muir himself was reserved, often very nearly tongue-tied in her presence.

Lieutenant Muir's regiment was selected to attack an American force at a place called Mongaugon on August 12, 1812. His troops were to lead the attack. It was a very dangerous assignment. It was one from which there was a good chance that he would not return alive.

This threat spurred the lieutenant to unaccustomed boldness. The night before the scheduled attack he went to Marie to ask, to very nearly demand, her pledge of love and loyalty. Marie was taken aback. He had always been so shy. Now suddenly he insisted on complete devotion.

Her reply was curt. She told him she didn't know whether she would be his or not. "It remains to be seen whether I might not find another more to my liking. After all, the life of a soldier's wife is not the best for a respectable young woman."

The young lieutenant said nothing. He simply turned on his heel and left. Marie was startled. She had expected some discussion, some argument. After a moment she ran outside, but he had already mounted his horse and could not hear her calling after him.

"Men are so foolish!" she shouted. "If a woman does not immediately say yes, they feel wounded."

Marie slept fitfully that night. She was oppressed by a feeling of doom. The sound of footsteps in her room woke her.

She saw the figure of Lieutenant Muir staring down at her. His face was a ghastly white, and blood ran from a terrible wound on his forehead.

"Don't be afraid, Marie," the form said. "I died honorably in battle. But I beg only one favor of you. My body lies in a thicket. Rescue it from the forest and bury it in a respectable grave." The figure then reached out and touched Marie's right hand. She collapsed and did not awake until morning.

Had the ghost of Lieutenant Muir visited her in the night, or had she only dreamed it? Then she looked at her hand where the figure of the lieutenant had touched her. There was now a deep red mark embedded in her palm.

Marie dressed quickly, saddled her horse, and rode to the British headquarters. She told the commander, an old family friend, of her experience. He arranged to have her escorted across the river to the battlefield.

Marie found her lieutenant's body in a thicket, just as the figure had said. There was a bullet hole through his head. His body was carried back to the British camp, where it was buried with full military honors.

The ghost of Lieutenant Muir did not make just a single appearance. For many years people walking in the forest near Mongaugon reported seeing the lieutenant marching through the woods toward where the American forces would have been. His arm was raised, a saber held firmly in his grip.

Marie McIntosh eventually married an English nobleman. But she did not forget Lieutenant Muir. Each August 12, the anniversary of the battle, Marie would dress in black and go out in the street to beg for money to help feed the poor. She regarded this as an act of contrition for her thoughtless rejection of the lieutenant before his death.

Marie always wore a black glove on her right hand. Very few knew the reason for this curious habit.

7

The Guardsman's Terror

ON JANUARY 3, 1804, nineteen-year-old Welsh-born George Jones, a private in the Coldstream Guards, was on sentry duty at Recruit House in the center of London. (The place was later renamed Wellington Barracks.) Sentry duty was not one of the more pleasant assignments for a guardsman. He had to stand stiffly at attention inside his sentry box. Every fifteen minutes he had to march smartly out of his box for two hundred yards, until he met the other sentry coming from the opposite direction. Night or day, it didn't make any difference, the routine was the same. Officers often prowled the area. Any sentry not carrying out his duties exactly as set down in the

44

regulations could be in serious trouble. No man at the barracks liked sentry duty. But none could avoid it either.

Sentry duty this particular night was unusually hard. It had snowed that day and the weather was extremely cold. Private Jones peered outside his box to make sure no officer was around. He then cradled his rifle in the crook of his left arm and rubbed his numbed hands together. The night was very quiet. The moon was full, and a silvery light shone on the trees in nearby St. James's Park. Despite the cold Private Jones felt oddly peaceful and contented.

The feeling of peace and contentment did not last for very long. As he looked out over the parade ground toward the canal, Private Jones saw a figure rise out of the earth not four feet away from him. It was the figure of a woman. The private could clearly see the make and pattern of her gown. It was made of cream satin with broad red stripes, and between the stripes were vertical rows of red spots. As the figure rose, it was surrounded by a glowing mist.

Jones was a brave man. Under normal circumstances he would have challenged the figure and called for aid from the other sentry. But there was something about this figure that absolutely froze him in terror and made him unable to move or to utter the slightest sound.

The woman had no head!

The stump of her neck stuck out of the lace-ruffled collar. The figure swayed a little, but made no attempt to move closer to Private Jones—much to his relief.

It must have stood there in front of him for fully two minutes. Then it turned and walked slowly and stiffly across the parade ground, toward the canal. When it had gone about fifty yards, it vanished.

At that moment Private Jones regained his voice and power of movement. Habit and training took over. Instead of running and screaming as most people would have done, he marched smartly out of his box to the halfway point between his box and that of the other sentry, Private David Rees.

"David, David," he called quietly. "Come here quick!"

Even speaking while on sentry duty was a breach of regulations. Rees was afraid an officer would hear them and they would both land in the guardhouse. "If you're fooling, George, I'll kill you," he said.

"I'm not fooling." Jones told him what had happened. Rees could tell that his fellow guardsman was not joking. He had been thoroughly terrified by something. But what? "It must have been a trick of the moonlight on the snow," Rees said sensibly.

Jones insisted it was no illusion. He knew what he had seen.

"You'll have to tell the sergeant of the guard, who is just coming up behind you," said Rees.

The sergeant of the guard couldn't image why his sentries were standing around talking that way. It was against all regulations.

"Private Jones says he's just seen a ghost, sir," said Rees.

The officer was not impressed. He wasn't any more impressed when he heard the private's story. "There are no ghosts in the Recruit House," the sergeant insisted. He told Jones to report to the guardhouse as soon as he was relieved.

As it happened, the officer in charge that evening was a

Welshman like Private Jones. He didn't particularly believe the young man's story. But he was not inclined to punish the Welsh private. He too had heard many ghost stories when he was a boy in Wales. He simply noted the incident:

"Private Jones, G., reported that while on sentry duty on No. 3 point, at about half after one in the morning, he saw the ghost of a headless woman on the parade ground."

He then sent Jones on his way and advised him not to see any more ghosts.

After Jones got some sleep, he thought about what had happened. In the cold light of day it all seemed too fantastic. He decided that Rees must have been right, it was the moonlight on the snow. In any case he wasn't going to say any more about it. Nor would Private Rees.

The whole incident would have been completely forgotten if it hadn't happened again three nights later. This time the sergeant of the guard found his sentry had fainted dead away in his box. When the man revived, he told of seeing the headless figure of a woman in a red-striped dress rise out of the ground just a few feet away from him.

A week later a veteran guardsman reported an identical experience.

Stories and rumors swept Recruit House. Things were beginning to get out of hand. The commanding officer of the base ordered an investigation. He hoped that this would put to rest all the rumors about headless ghosts.

Unfortunately for the commanding officer's hopes, the investigation turned up evidence that made the story more believable than ever. The investigators found that some twenty years earlier there had been a scandal attached to the Coldstream Guards at Recruit House.

A sergeant of the guards killed his wife. In a desperate attempt to make the corpse impossible to identify, he hacked off its head. The head was buried and never found, but the body was thrown in the canal near the barracks. That's where the ghost seemed to be going. The body soon floated to the surface. It was quickly identified because witnesses recognized the gown—of cream satin with red stripes and red spots between the stripes—that the body was clothed in. It was a dress that the sergeant's wife had owned.

No one could figure out a reason why the headless ghost suddenly decided to walk after twenty years. There was no record of the ghost ever having been seen before Private Jones reported it. And there seemed no way that Jones could have had any connection with the decades-old murder, or even know of it.

A clergyman was brought in. He spent a night in the sentry box, praying for the dead woman's soul. The ghost was never seen again. Just to be on the safe side, though, the sentry boxes at Recruit House were relocated so that none of them stood near the spot where the ghost had appeared.

8

Heard But Not Seen

IF THERE IS one characteristic common to all ghosts it's that they are elusive. They rarely appear on schedule in front of a large group of witnesses. They don't like to sit and have their picture taken. There have been a lot of "spirit photographs" since photography was first invented. But they are either so fuzzy and indistinct that they could be anything, or they are suspected, for very good reasons, of being frauds. For more than a century researchers and investigators have tried many methods of gathering solid scientific evidence of ghosts. These efforts have always fallen short. They may pick up some interesting bits of evidence, but no conclusive proof.

Some ghost hunters have used tape recorders. They have been able to pick up strange sounds that are difficult to explain. But they are not necessarily the sounds of ghosts.

In 1959 a man in Sweden gave the idea of recording ghostly sounds a new twist. He was recording the songs of birds in his garden. When he played the tape back he heard voices on the tape that he had not heard during the recording session. They were faint, difficult to interpret, but in his opinion very definitely there. So he tried recording under the same conditions again. He got the same results: strange and unexplainable voices when he played the tape.

These experiences started a worldwide interest in what has been called the Electronic Voice Phenomena or EVP. People from many different countries have reported picking up voices on tape that had not been heard during the recording session and should not be there. People who do this sort of thing often believe that the voices they hear are those of the dead.

It would be unfair not to point out that EVP is very controversial. Skeptics insist that what most people are hearing are really just scratches on the tape or some other sort of random noise. If the noises are amplified enough, or the speed at which the tapes are played is changed, then, with a considerable exercise of imagination as well, people can think that they are hearing voices. People once looked at photos where there was a blob of light or some other imperfection and thought they were seeing the faces of dead loved ones.

Imagination and wishful thinking are powerful influences on what we think we see, and think we hear.

Still, a lot of people do think that EVP means something. It has been tested in many places in the United States. One of the most interesting tests took place at a spot called Point Lookout.

Point Lookout State Park, in southern Maryland, is now a popular stop for tourists. During the Civil War, however, it was a scene of utter horror. Some say faint traces of this horror still linger.

The area was used by the government as a prisoner of war camp. It was officially known as Camp Hoffman. There were never any barracks. The prisoners lived in small tents. The land was low, marshy, and very unhealthy. There were regular outbreaks of smallpox, dysentery, scurvy, and other diseases. Between July 1863 and June 1865, over fifty thousand Confederate soldiers passed through the camp. Some four thousand of them died there.

Later some monuments to the Confederate dead were erected. In 1964 the land was purchased by the state of Maryland for a recreational area. It was then that the tales of strange and ghostly sounds began to circulate.

During the 1970s the park manager, Gerald Sword, lived in a large house on the park grounds. The building was called the Lighthouse. Sword swore the house was haunted. Doors opened and shut mysteriously; footsteps were heard in empty rooms and on deserted staircases. The sound of objects crashing to the ground would send people running to see what had happened. But nothing could be found.

Then Sword said he began hearing faint conversations. He could never pinpoint the source of the voices, nor could he hear what they were talking about. It was just the low and mysterious murmur of human voices. On other occasions he heard coughing and snoring. He felt invisible entities brush past him as he entered a room. And there was the constant feeling of being watched by unseen eyes.

Only once did Sword report actually seeing a ghost. He was sitting in the kitchen when he once again got that eerie feeling of being watched. He looked out the windows and saw the face of a young man wearing a floppy cap and a loose-fitting coat, looking back at him. He rushed to the window but the figure walked away and disappeared.

Sword thought that he could actually identify this particular ghost. It was not one of the Confederate prisoners. In 1878 a large steamer had broken up in a storm near Point Lookout. Thirty-one people were killed. The body of a young crewman named Joseph Haney was washed up on the beach at Point Lookout. He was buried near where his body had been found. Haney's description, printed in the newspapers of the time, matched exactly that of the young man Sword had seen at his window.

Another house on the property is located just across the road from the Confederate monument. It too has been troubled by strange and ghostly sounds.

A group of people interested in studying ghosts decided to try out the EVP procedure at Point Lookout. They figured that with so many reports of ghostly voices they had a chance at getting some on tape. Tape recorders were set up at places where the ghostly sounds had frequently been reported.

Though no voices were heard during the recording sessions, the group did believe they could detect faint voices and other sounds on their tapes when the tapes were replayed. One recording had what sounded exactly like the whistle of a steamboat. That would have been a common sound around Point Lookout many years ago, but steamboats have not operated in the area for a long time.

Men's voices on the tapes seem to use such phrases as "living in the Lighthouse" and "going home." Another interesting phrase heard on the tapes is "fire if they get too close." One woman's voice seemed to be using the word "vaccine" and another seemed to say, "Let us not take objections to what they are doing."

Do these tapes prove that there are ghosts at Point Lookout? They certainly do not. They are just another interesting bit of evidence about ghosts that has been collected. It's the sort of thing that keeps you wondering.

9

At the Moment of Death

PSYCHICAL RESEARCHERS—people who study ghosts and other strange events—speak of something they call a *crisis apparition*. A person sees the form of a relative or friend who should be hundreds or thousands of miles away. Then, after a few seconds, or a few minutes, the form disappears. Later the person learns that the individual he or she had seen had died, or was near death at the very moment the form appeared.

This is one of the most common forms of "ghost story." Thousands of these crisis apparitions have been recorded throughout history. They are particularly common in wartime, when men separated from their families often face sudden death.

Here are two examples from different wars.

Captain Eldrid Bowyer-Bower was a young British pilot. He was killed in action on March 19, 1917. That was during World War I. Three people in different parts of the world either saw him at the time he died or had some strong feeling that he had died. This happened long before they could possibly have known of his death by normal means.

The captain's half sister, a Mrs. Spearman, was in India when he died. She was sitting with her newborn baby on the morning of March 19 when:

"I had a great feeling I must turn around and did to see Eldrid. He looked so happy and had that mischievous look I had seen so often before. I was so glad to see him and told him I would just put the baby in a safer place, and then we could talk. 'Fancy coming all the way out here,' I said turning round again. I was just putting my arms out to give him a hug and a kiss but Eldrid was gone. I called and looked for him. I never saw him again."

At about the same time Captain Bowyer-Bower's niece in England, who was about three years old, also reported seeing him. Her mother described what happened:

"One morning while I was still in bed, about 9:15, she came into my room and said, 'Uncle Alley Boy is downstairs' (Alley Boy was a familiar pet name for the captain). I told her that he was in France, but she insisted that she had seen him. Later in the day I happened to be writing to my mother and mentioned this, not because I thought much about it, but to show that Betty still thought and spoke of her uncle of whom she was very fond. A few days afterwards we found that the date my brother was missing was the date on the letter."

The third experience did not involve an actual sighting. Just a feeling that something terrible had happened. The captain's mother received a letter from a Mrs. Watson, an elderly lady that she had known. Mrs. Watson had not written for almost two years. Then, quite unexpectedly, came a letter stating, "Something tells me you are having great anxiety about Eldrid. Will you let me know?" The letter was dated March 19, 1917, the day the captain was killed. At the time his mother did not know what had happened. Mrs. Watson later said that on the day she wrote she had an awful feeling the captain had been killed.

The second story comes from World War II.

Alexander Crockfield joined the navy just a few months before the attack on Pearl Harbor in 1941 that propelled the U.S. into the war. He took part in many of the early sea battles of the war in the Pacific.

His wife, Dorothy, had moved to California. She was expecting the couple's first child. Lieutenant Crockfield wrote regularly. He told his wife as much about what he was doing as the navy censors would allow. She knew that his ship was very active, and often in dangerous situations.

Mrs. Crockfield was naturally concerned about her husband's safety. But she was not overly concerned. Like many military wives she was able to keep from her mind the thought that anything could really happen to her husband. Tragedy might strike other people, but not her.

In due time the baby was born, a little girl, and Mrs. Crockfield filled her letters with details about the child. Her husband wrote back, eager for more information, even the smallest scrap. He also continued to be as informative as he could about what he was doing. His letters indicated that his ship was not in any unusually dangerous waters.

One evening she sat by herself rereading the latest letter from her husband. There was a noise in the child's room. Mrs. Crockfield immediately rushed to the door. Though the light in the room was dim, she could clearly see her husband standing by the baby's crib. He was wearing his tropical uniform and gazing down at the child.

Mrs. Crockfield tried to call out her husband's name. But before she could, the figure walked swiftly across the room and simply disappeared upon reaching the wall. A moment of joy gave way immediately to a sinking feeling of fear. It had not been her living husband in the room at all, but some sort of ghostly image.

When she went back to check on the infant, she noticed a pool of water near the crib, just where she had seen the figure standing. She dipped her finger in the pool and put it to her tongue. The water was salty. It was seawater. There was also something floating in the water, a piece of some sort of seaweed. She picked it up and carefully preserved it between two blotters.

A few days later the telegram from the Navy Department that Mrs. Crockfield had dreaded, yet expected, arrived. It informed her that her husband's ship had been sunk during a battle. He was missing and presumed dead.

When she had begun to recover from the shock, she took the bit of preserved seaweed to one of the large California universities. She found an expert on seaweed who was able to identify the curious and rare specimen. It was found only in the South Pacific, where her husband's ship had been lost. Legend had it that this particular type of seaweed grew only on dead bodies.

Not all crisis-apparition accounts involve a death. Sometimes, as the name implies, the apparition may appear when a person is in a grave crisis—possibly threatened with death. Would such an experience count as a "ghost story"? Most people think it does. Here is one, and you may judge for yourself.

In keeping with the theme, it is a military tale, and first appeared in a British army magazine called *Soldier*. It was written by James Simms.

On September 17, 1944, Simms, a British paratrooper, and others of his regiment were dropped into Holland. It was their task to capture a bridge in the center of a town called Arnhem. However, the Nazis had gotten information about the plan from a spy, and were waiting for them. The paratroopers were met with a deadly hail of gunfire. Many were killed, and most of the survivors, including Simms, were badly wounded.

The wounded were taken to a cellar in the town, where they had to stay for several days. Simms hovered between life and death. The men who were on either side of him in the cellar died from their wounds. But Simms hung on. He was finally shipped back to London, where he recovered.

When he was released from the hospital, Simms called a woman he had known since he was a boy. She told him that on September 19, while he lay nearly dead in that cellar in Arnhem, she had seen him. She had been sitting alone in her front parlor and suddenly had the feeling that someone was there. She looked up and saw the outline of Simms' figure. She accurately described how he looked at the time, right down to the thick bandages on his thigh. She said that he looked completely exhausted. He seemed to be holding on to the curtains on the window for support. It looked as if he were just about to step into the room. The woman had the feeling that something terrible was going to happen. She said out loud, "It's all right, Jim. It's all right." The figure then seemed to relax its grip on the curtains, and began to fade until it disappeared entirely.

According to Simms, the vision corresponded to the time that his condition took a turn for the better. On the 19th he had been very near death, but after that had begun to heal.

10

The Cursed Car

WARS RARELY START because of a single incident. Usually the tensions build up for a long time. There are a large number of potential points of conflict. Often different groups have different reasons for entering the same war. If the situation becomes bad enough, it may only take a spark to set off hostilities.

Nowhere in history can this be seen more clearly than in the start of World War I. The spark that set off that war was the assassination of the Archduke Francis Ferdinand of Austria by a young and fanatical Serbian nationalist. The assassination took place in the city of Sarajevo, in what is now Yugoslavia.

The war that exploded from this spark was fought primarily

between Germany on one side and France, Britain, and ultimately the United States on the other. Austria and the cause of Serbian nationalism played only a minor role in the war, which was responsible for some twenty million deaths.

But this is not a history book. This is a book about ghosts. Or in this case about how the aura of violent death may somehow be imprinted on an object so that others who come in contact with it may also be struck down.

In June of 1914 the Austrian Archduke and his wife were making what was supposed to be a goodwill tour throughout Central Europe, a region that was seething with unrest.

The royal couple arrived at Sarajevo, then capital of the state called Bosnia, on June 28, 1914. For his grand procession through the little city streets, Francis Ferdinand was given a blood-red, six-seat, open touring car. The car was impressive to look at, but provided absolutely no protection at all from potential assassins. The young fanatic, Gavrilo Princip, armed only with a small pistol, jumped out of the crowd, leaped onto the running board of the open car, and emptied his gun into the Archduke and Duchess, killing them both. Princip was captured immediately. He died in prison four years later.

Somehow the car survived the war. Afterward the newly appointed governor of Yugoslavia had the celebrated vehicle restored completely for his own use. However, after four accidents, one of which resulted in the loss of his right arm, the governor decided that the car was bad luck and should be destroyed.

However, the governor's friend, a Dr. Srikis, thought the idea of a cursed car was foolish. He bought the vehicle and drove it happily for six months. Then the overturned vehicle was found on the road. The doctor's crushed body was beneath it.

Another doctor bought the car. As soon as his patients heard about it they began to desert him. Perhaps they figured he wouldn't be around long enough to complete their treatment. Or perhaps they thought that the car's bad luck would rub off on them. Whatever the reason, the doctor's practice suffered greatly. So he sold the car to a Swiss racing driver. In a road race the driver clipped a stone wall, was thrown out of the car, and broke his neck. The car, however, needed only minor repairs.

The next owner was a wealthy farmer. The car stalled on him. Along with a friend, the farmer was towing it to a place where it could be repaired. Suddenly the stalled car started all by itself, killing both farmers.

Tiber Hirshfield, the car's next owner, decided it needed a new color scheme. Instead of blood red, he had it painted a neutral blue. Then, along with five friends, Hirshfield was driving to a wedding. There was an accident and four of the five were killed. The change of color hadn't helped a bit.

That ended the active life of the celebrated automobile. It was rebuilt and shipped off to a museum in Vienna, Austria. The car was so notorious that it attracted lots of visitors. The attendant in the museum, a man named Karl Brunner, used to regale visitors with stories of the "cursed" car.

In World War II bombs reduced the Vienna museum to rubble. No trace was found of the car. Or of Karl Brunner either.

11

Meeting in the Desert

CECIL BATHE WAS a Royal Air Force (RAF) mechanic. During World War II he was stationed in North Africa. He had driven a truckful of supplies from his base across the desert to another, about eighty miles away. He was returning to his home base when a sudden sandstorm blew up.

As the storm got worse, Bathe decided he had better wait it out. He knew such storms usually did not last long. He pulled his truck up alongside the wreck of a German tank that had been disabled in a battle about a month earlier. Hulks of this sort littered the desert after a battle.

Bathe didn't feel that he was in any real danger. The Germans had been decisively driven from the area. The storm would soon pass and he would be on his way again. He had a magazine with him, and a couple of bottles of beer that had been given to him by the Australian soldiers to whom he had delivered the supplies.

Bathe was sitting hunched inside his truck, reading and sipping his beer, when the whole vehicle seemed to be shaken by a strong gust of wind. He looked up and saw a lone uniformed figure standing amid the swirling dust and sand. Bathe opened the door to his truck and beckoned the man to come in quickly.

The stranger wore a ragged khaki uniform without any identifying insignia. He spoke English well enough, but with a rather strange clipped accent. None of this surprised Bathe. After two years of fighting in the desert, he was used to seeing men in ragged uniforms. As for the accent, well, there were a lot of different Allied troops fighting in North Africa. Bathe figured his companion might be Dutch, or perhaps a South African. He didn't know and didn't much care. Here was someone to share the loneliness of the wait in the desert with him.

Bathe gave the man a bottle of the beer the Australians had given him. The man accepted it eagerly. As he reached for the bottle, the Englishman noticed his companion had a large raw burn on his right hand and arm.

"That's a nasty burn," said Bathe. "You better have it attended to."

The man just laughed. "It's a bit late for that. Anyway, it doesn't matter." Bathe assumed that was simply a wounded soldier's show of bravery in the face of pain. He had seen that attitude many times before. He did not argue.

The two men chatted in an aimless sort of way. The stranger never gave his name or indicated where he had originally come from. But he did say that he had spent some time in England. When he was young he had been an enthusiastic Boy Scout, and he had attended an international scouting jamboree that was held in southern England. That bit of information caught Bathe's attention, for he too had been a Scout and had attended the very same jamboree. Perhaps they had met years before, Bathe said. "Perhaps we did," replied the man.

As night drew on, the sandstorm subsided. Bathe figured that it was time to make a run for his base. He wanted to get as far as he could before the desert became completely dark. The RAF man offered his visitor a lift, but the stranger shook his head. "I have to go in the other direction," he said. "But thanks for the beer."

The man stepped down from the truck and grasped Bathe's hand with surprising emotion. "God watch over you, fellow Scout," he said.

Bathe began to drive away, and glanced into the rearview mirror to see what the man was doing. He had disappeared. Bathe stopped his truck and got out to take a closer look. He could see nothing but the burned-out hulk of the German tank. The whole experience was an eerie one, and it troubled him all the way back to the camp. But he didn't dwell on what had happened. There was so much to be done that he quickly put the incident out of his mind.

Later in the week Bathe was making the same trip with his

supply truck. He passed the wrecked German tank again. Now there was a British salvage crew on the scene getting ready to haul it away. The wreck would be gutted for spare parts that might be of some use.

Bathe stopped to watch the salvage operation. The corporal in charge said that they had made a rather gruesome discovery. The driver of the tank had died at the controls a month before, when the tank had been hit by a shell. He was still inside the tank when the salvage crew arrived.

The body, which the corporal said had been pretty well preserved by the dry desert air, was laid out under a canvas next to the wreck.

A feeling of dread overcame Bathe. He didn't want to look under the canvas but knew he had to. The body was shrunken and partially decayed, but the features were quite clear. It was the same man he had shared a beer with a few days earlier. The burns on the dead man's hand and arm were clearly visible.

The corporal then said, "The strangest thing is that when we found the body there was a bottle of beer clutched in his hand. What's really strange, though, is that it was Australian beer. I wonder where a German tank driver got Australian beer."

Bathe said nothing. He just got back into his truck and drove away as quickly as he could.

12

A Visit to New York

DURING WORLD WAR II, a man named Oswald Remsen had a very strange experience. Later he never tired of telling his friends about it.

Remsen was a wealthy man. Every week or so he had to come into New York City on business. He had graduated from Harvard University. So when he was in the city he stayed at the Harvard Club, and he ate his meals there as well.

On this particular evening he was crossing Broadway at Forty-fifth Street near Times Square. In those days Times Square was still the heart of the theater district, not the sleazy dreadful place it became in later years.

Remsen had stopped to wait for the light to change before crossing the street. He was on his way to the Harvard Club, where he was going to have dinner alone. As he waited, two men in uniform stepped up next to him. He recognized the uniforms as those of the Royal Air Force, or RAF, from Britain. Remsen had seen RAF men in New York before. These two, however, appeared to be rather lost. They were looking around in wonder. They also seemed to be checking their watches against the large flashing sign on the New York Times Building.

One of the officers turned to Remsen and asked, "Is this Times Square?" Remsen found the question odd. Times Square was one of the best-known landmarks in the world. How could anyone not know he was in Times Square? Remsen assured the men that it was.

Remsen and the two Englishmen all seemed to be going in the same direction. They walked in silence for a few minutes. Then Remsen said a few friendly words. It was like a water faucet being opened. The two RAF men began chatting freely. They said they had never been in New York before, and they were full of questions. They commented on how exciting and alive the city felt after the grim restrictions that the war had imposed on England.

Remsen also recalled that every block or so one of the men would look at his watch. He wondered if they had an appointment of some sort. They said they didn't, that they were quite free for the evening.

"Then would you like to have supper with me at my club?" Remsen asked. The Englishmen seemed delighted at the suggestion. One of the men glanced at his watch and nodded to the other.

Dinner was excellent. The RAF pilots were lavish with their praise. They said they had not eaten so well since before the war. The three talked about the war, in a general sort of way. The two pilots, however, seemed unwilling to talk about their own experiences. Men at war often won't. Still, there was that annoying habit, as first one man and then the other looked at his watch.

"Are you sure you don't have an appointment?" Remsen said finally. "I don't want to keep you from anything important."

Once again the Englishmen assured the American that they were in no hurry to go anywhere. The conversation continued. They talked about the differences between England and America, and about the similarities. They talked about what the world would be like after the war. It was a pleasant and intelligent conversation.

Remsen had almost begun to ignore the men's habit of looking at their watches so often. Then, at five minutes to midnight, both of the men looked at their watches at once and rose from their chairs.

"Mr. Remsen," said one, "we would like to thank you very much. This has been a pleasant and unexpected evening. In many ways it's the strangest evening we have ever had."

That remark puzzled Remsen, and he said so.

"No, of course you don't understand," said the Englishman. "Let me explain. Just twenty-four hours ago, Bill and I were flying a mission over Berlin. We were shot down and killed. Now we have to be getting back. Thank you once again."

The two Englishmen started to walk toward the dining-room door and disappeared.

13

A Game of Billiards

BRITISH TROOPS WERE often quartered in large and stately old homes that the army had taken over temporarily. Many of the old houses in Britain are supposed to be haunted. Soldiers who stayed in them sometimes reported strange and ghostly encounters. None was stranger than that reported by Lieutenant Colonel Thomas O'Doneven.

In 1943 O'Doneven had taken some troops up to the Midlands—that is, the middle part of England—for training. They were staying in what he described as "a lovely old house, surrounded by parklands."

The owners had left the house. The only residents, aside

from the soldiers, were two old family servants. Colonel O'Doneven stressed to his men that they were guests in the house, not conquerors or invaders. They had to show respect for the property.

Dinner for the soldiers was at 7:45 P.M. each evening. One winter evening Colonel O'Doneven came down for dinner an hour early. He had not intended to be early. He speculated that he must have set his watch wrong. He looked at the hall clock and discovered his mistake. He decided that he would spend the hour sitting in front of the fire. Then he heard the sound of billiard balls clicking. The sound came from a room where O'Doneven had seen a billiard table. Being a keen billiard player himself, the colonel decided to investigate.

In the room the colonel saw a young man in uniform standing at the billiard table "knocking the balls about." He had never seen this particular fellow before, though he certainly should have remembered him. In the first place the uniform he wore looked strangely old-fashioned. Then the young man himself was bent over—slightly humpbacked. None of this seemed strange to O'Doneven. New men were always being moved in and out. He couldn't keep track of them, and didn't try. In 1943 the British were desperate for men. They might well have been taking people with handicaps into the army, particularly in noncombat jobs. As for the old-fashioned uniform, supplies were hard to come by, and perhaps that was the best they could come up with.

There was an hour to kill before dinner. Colonel O'Doneven asked the young man, "Want a game?" The man said nothing, but merely smiled agreeably. And so they began to play.

The game went on intensely and in total silence for nearly an hour. Both men were good and serious players. The score was tied. Then the colonel heard his officers moving around in the hall. He realized that it was almost time for dinner. He told his companion that this had to be his last shot. The young man nodded in agreement. The colonel took the shot—a good one that won him the game. "As I took my shot, he quietly put his cue back in the rack, gave me a smile and quietly walked through another door into what I afterwards discovered was a bathroom."

During dinner the colonel asked the other officers if they knew who his opponent at billiards had been. No one seemed to know him. "I was on the point of letting the matter drop, when I added, 'A nice lad, with a hump, I've just beaten him at billiards.'"

Upon hearing that, the old butler who was serving the dinner froze and went pale. "You've seen Master Willie, Sir," he said. The butler took a moment to recover, then he explained. "Master Willie" was the brother of the women who owned the house. He had joined the army during World War I. However, because of his deformity he was discharged and sent back home. "He came back here, Christmas 1916. He played a good game of billiards and shot himself in the room where he loved to play. We see him sometimes. . . ."

The colonel later told London reporter Dennis Bardens that during the game he had noticed nothing unusual. "It was all so natural," he said. "We just went on playing our shots as they came." They never spoke during the game. But Colonel O'Doneven said that he usually didn't speak while playing, and didn't like to be spoken to.

He reported that a couple of nights after the experience two of his junior officers saw the slightly humpbacked figure standing near a fireplace. Instead of checking more closely, they rushed upstairs to find some other officers as extra witnesses, and perhaps as extra courage. But when they got downstairs again, the figure was gone. However, the lights over the billiard table had been switched on.

After the war the house was sold to a new tenant. He dismissed the idea of ghosts. But Colonel O'Doneven recalled with some satisfaction that this new tenant did not remain in the house for very long. He sold it as quickly as he could, though he wouldn't say why.

14

The Haunted Air Base

ON THE SURFACE it was a simple enough assignment. A British film crew was going to make a management-training film. Much of the film was to be shot at a place called Bircham Newton in the county of Norfolk. Bircham Newton had been a Royal Air Force base during two world wars. More recently it had been turned into a school for students taking vocational courses.

The film project was to take only a few days. But from the start things began going wrong. Objects fell or were broken for no apparent reason. The scariest moment came when a heavy studio lamp nearly hit Peter Clark, a member of the film crew.

At the last second the lamp swerved, as if pulled away by an unseen force, and crashed harmlessly into a table. Clark had a narrow escape.

Just behind what was once the officers' dining room were indoor squash courts. Squash is a game very much like tennis. The courts had been built just before World War II and had been used by men at the air base. Another member of the film crew borrowed a tennis racket and a ball. He asked a few of his fellow workers if they wanted to have a game with him. No one seemed interested, so he went off to practice by himself.

There were two courts next to one another. The man from the film crew practiced first on one court, the one on the left. Then, for no apparent reason, he decided to switch to the other. As he began practice in the right court he heard footsteps behind him. At first he paid no attention. He simply assumed that another member of the film crew had come in to watch him. Then he realized that he had locked the door to the building when he came in. He was completely alone—or should have been.

For a moment he just kept hitting the ball off the wall. He didn't turn around. Then he heard a sigh. It was a sound that made him go cold all over. He turned around and saw a man wearing a World War II RAF uniform standing in the spectators' area. While he was watching, the figure vanished. That was enough for the film man. He ran from the building.

When he told his experience to Peter Clark, Clark had an idea. Why not go down to the squash court and try to record the sounds with the crew's tape recorder?

Later Clark explained, "It was a calm warm summer night

when we returned to the courts. We visited the left court, which felt completely normal. When we went to the court on the right, the atmosphere was so cold, so frightening, it was like stepping into another world."

The tape recorder was switched on and the men waited. But shortly an oppressive feeling made them so uncomfortable and fearful that they had to get out of the building. They locked the door and left the tape recorder running. By the time they came back the tape had run out.

When the tape was replayed it contained a lot of sounds that shouldn't have been there. There was the sound of aircraft and clanking machinery. These are sounds that would have been common during World War II, when Bircham Newton had been a working airfield. But such sounds had not been heard there for many years. Also on the tape was the murmur of voices, and what Clark interpreted as a strange and unearthly groaning. Both the tape and the machine were examined by an expert. There was nothing wrong with either one, nothing that could have accounted for the sounds.

Peter Clark had now become completely fascinated by the mystery. He got a group of his friends to go back to the old air base accompanied by a spirit medium. The aim was to find out what spirits were haunting the place. The medium identified the spirit of an airman called Wiley. As Clark continued to investigate the case he discovered that there had indeed been an airman called Wiley at the base during the war. He had committed suicide there.

As public interest in the haunting of Bircham Newton grew, others stepped forward with their tales. Some who had been students at the place after it had been turned into a school reported experiences common to many hauntings. They told of how the covers were torn off their beds at night, or how the curtains in their rooms were pulled down by an invisible force. There were those who said that unseen figures brushed past them or actually tapped them on the shoulder. One man claimed that he had seen a figure in an RAF uniform walk through a solid wall. He was so frightened that he dropped out of the school and left the very next day.

Finally the British Broadcasting Corporation (BBC) became interested. The BBC decided to do a special program on the haunting of the old air base. Two of Britain's leading spirit mediums were hired to help with the show. The mediums claimed that they knew little of the details of the case beforehand.

The mediums examined the squash courts. The left-hand one was normal. The right-hand court, however, held a "presence" according to the mediums. It was the spirit of a dead airman.

One of the mediums, John Sutton, fell into a trance. He began to speak in a different voice. His body had apparently been taken over by the spirit of a dead man. The spirit identified himself as Dusty Miller. He said he was a World War II airman who had been killed in a crash near the base along with two of his friends, Pat Sullivan and Gerry Arnold.

The spirit said that the three men had all been enthusiastic squash players, and that they had often used the courts on the base. They made a pact that if anything happened to them they would try to meet up again on the squash court where they had spent so many pleasant hours.

Shortly after making the pact the men were all killed during a training flight near the base. Now their spirits returned to the squash court just as they had promised.

The medium said that after the dead airman's spirit had been contacted, thus allowing the story to be told, the ghosts should finally be laid to rest. In fact, no more strange disturbances have been reported at Bircham Newton.

15

Return Flight

A LOT OF American pilots flew missions out of bases in England in World War II. One of them was an upstate New York man, Captain Charles "Brick" Barton.

Captain Barton was the pilot of one of the B-24s that carried out bombing missions over Germany during the spring of 1943. These missions were extremely dangerous. Many planes were lost to German antiaircraft guns and enemy fighter planes. Despite the dangers, morale among the American fliers remained high. Captain Barton himself was an incurable optimist. His good nature, supreme confidence, and great skill made him a real favorite with the others in his crew.

Though Brick himself had never been hurt, his plane had been hit several different times. His veteran copilot suffered an injury and had to be hospitalized. So when Barton's B-24 took off again, his backup was a young lieutenant on his first combat mission. And it was a tough one. They were to drop their bombs on the German city of Frankfurt, a well-defended target.

Though enemy fire was heavy, Barton's plane made it to Frankfurt, dropped its bombs on the assigned target, turned, and headed for home. But just a few minutes into the return trip, machine-gun fire from a German pursuit plane shattered the plastic glass of the cockpit. Brick was hit, his blood splattered over the instrument panel and around the cabin. Another burst of machine-gun fire ripped into the B-24's controls. The plane was flyable—but difficult to handle.

Brick said he was unable to fly the plane himself. His inexperienced copilot was forced to take over the controls. The young lieutenant very nearly panicked. Then he heard Brick's reassuring voice telling him what to do. Clearly the captain was badly hurt, yet he refused to be taken into the back of the plane where he might be able to lie down and be more comfortable. He remained in his seat talking calmly and quietly to his young companion. The copilot marveled at how clear Brick's mind was for a man who had obviously been seriously wounded and must have been in great pain.

The weather grew worse. The plane responded more and more uncertainly to the copilot's touch. Brick kept giving him helpful suggestions drawn from the experience of more than twenty missions over Germany. For nearly an hour the young copilot and the wounded veteran kept the plane on course back to its base in England.

As they neared base the copilot radioed for an ambulance. Brick had suddenly become silent for the first time during the return flight. The lieutenant worried that perhaps he had become unconscious from loss of blood.

The young man brought the balky and battered plane down to a safe landing and quickly climbed out to look for medical help. He almost bumped into the flight surgeon, who was running toward him.

"Good job bringing that plane in, young man," said the surgeon. "It looks to be pretty badly shot up. It couldn't have been easy to fly all the way back from Germany in that condition."

"I never would have been able to do it if it hadn't been for Captain Barton, sir," said the copilot. "He talked me through it all the way back from Frankfurt. He never complained about his wounds. He's the real hero. You better go and look at him. I think he's been unconscious for the last few minutes."

The surgeon climbed into the plane and the crew gathered around, waiting for word on Brick's condition. It didn't take long. After a moment the surgeon came out. He looked grim and color had drained from his face.

"Men, I'm afraid there is nothing I can do for your captain. He's dead."

The surgeon then took the copilot aside and asked him if he was sure about having talked to Captain Barton during the return flight.

"Of course I'm sure," said the young man. "I told you we

never would have been able to make it back if it hadn't been for his help."

"That's impossible," said the ashen-faced flight surgeon. "Captain Barton was shot in the head. He died instantly, and he's been dead for nearly an hour."

16

To Clear His Name

GHOSTLY LEGENDS OFTEN speak of the return of a spirit to correct some injustice. Perhaps to clear the dead man's name. That certainly seems to have been the case with Lieutenant Desmond Arthur.

On May 27, 1913, a little over a year before the start of World War I, Lieutenant Arthur was killed in the crash of his plane over the Scottish airbase of Montrose. Airplanes of that era were still crudely built and usually dangerous to fly. Lieutenant Arthur was piloting a BE2 biplane—that is a plane with a double wing. It seemed like a routine flight. He was gliding down from four thousand feet when one wing simply folded up in midair. The plane plummeted to the ground. Lieutenant Arthur was thrown out of the cockpit to his death. There were no parachutes in 1913.

A group called the Royal Aero Club investigated the accident. The conclusion these investigations reached was that somebody had botched a repair job. Just before Lieutenant Arthur's fatal flight a wing of the plane had been broken near the tip. The break had been repaired with a crude splice, and to conceal the shoddy work the man who did it put new fabric over the area. The repair looked all right but could not stand up to the stress of flight. That was the reason for the fatal accident. Lieutenant Arthur's friends said this carelessness amounted to murder. The guilty party, however, could not be identified.

In 1916 the war was on. There had been a number of fatal accidents to British planes. One member of parliament accused the government of doing nothing while men were "murdered . . . by the carelessness, incompetence, or ignorance of their senior officers or of the technical side of the service." It was a strong and very disturbing charge. One of the cases he cited was that of Lieutenant Arthur.

The government, however, was anxious to avoid any hint of scandal in the air service. They did not want public faith in the competence of those running the war effort undermined. So on August 3, 1916, the British Government issued its own report on the death of Lieutenant Arthur. The report said that the botched wing repair explanation that had been put forth by the Royal Aero Club was not correct. The obvious conclusion, said the government, was that Lieutenant Arthur had only himself to blame for his death. That conclusion enraged Arthur's friends, and may have enraged the dead man as well.

About a month after the government report was issued, strange things began happening at Montrose air base. One officer said that he was followed by a man in full flying gear. When he tried to get close to the mysterious pilot the figure vanished. A flying instructor woke up one night to find a strange man, again wearing full flying gear, sitting beside the fireplace in his bedroom. When the instructor challenged the intruder, he suddenly discovered that the chair was empty. Others in the base woke up with the unshakable feeling that someone else was in their room. But no one could be seen.

Stories of the strange occurrences at Montrose began to circulate around other air bases in Britain. Inevitably the name of Lieutenant Arthur was brought up. Was he the ghostly figure? Was he trying to encourage his pilot friends to help clear his name?

The stories also seemed to have some effect on members of the government commission who had issued the report blaming the lieutenant for his own death. A couple of them admitted publicly that they had never really studied the evidence. An engineer and a lawyer were called in to review the findings. Finally at Christmastime a new report was issued on the death of Lieutenant Desmond Arthur.

The report declared, "It appears probable that the machine had been damaged accidentally, and that the man (or men) responsible for the damage had repaired it as best he (or they) could to evade detection and punishment."

The guilty party remained unknown, but that conclusion

seems to have satisfied the restless spirit of Lieutenant Desmond Arthur. It made one more brief appearance in January of 1917—and was seen no more.

17

A Ghost of Yourself

In EUROPE, particularly in Germany, there is a strong belief in what is called the doppelgänger, or "double." A person suddenly encounters a ghostly image of him or her self.

Probably the most famous account of the doppelgänger comes from the great German writer Johann von Goethe.

"I rode on horseback over the footpath to Drusenheim, when one of the strangest experiences befell me. . . . I saw myself on horseback coming toward me on the same path dressed in a suit as I had never worn, pale gray with some gold. As soon as I had shaken myself out of this reverie the form vanished. It is strange, however, that I found myself returning on the same path eight years afterward . . . and that I wore the suit I had dreamt of, and not by design but chance."

Goethe's doppelgänger experience was a simple one. Most often the doppelgänger is associated with impending death or illness or appears to be a warning.

One of the most extraordinary doppelgänger accounts comes from an American, Alex B. Griffith.

In the summer of 1944, during World War II, Griffith was an infantry sergeant, leading a patrol in France. Part of the country through which Sergeant Griffith and his men passed was said to be filled with German troops who were well dug in and waiting to ambush the Americans. But Sergeant Griffith's men had been on patrol for several days and saw no signs of the enemy. As a result they felt quite relaxed. They had begun to believe that the stories of the dangers had been exaggerated.

Still, Sergeant Griffith and his men remained alert as they walked down the road. Suddenly the sergeant was startled to see a figure on the road ahead. The man was wearing the uniform of an American soldier, just like his own. As Griffith looked more closely he realized there was more than a similarity in uniform. The man in the road looked just like him. It was his double. Though Griffith did not know the word, it was his doppelgänger. The figure was waving its arms frantically. It was also moving its mouth as if it were shouting, but Griffith could hear nothing. While Griffith couldn't hear what his double was shouting, none of the other men in the patrol seemed to see it at all. Yet it was obvious to Sergeant Griffith that the figure in the road was signaling him to stop.

His men were quite surprised when Sergeant Griffith suddenly told them to halt and turn around. He couldn't tell them why he wanted them to stop. All he knew was that if they continued along the road they would be in great danger. He had been warned.

Griffith told his men to rest for a few minutes. As he sat on the ground trying to figure out what to do next, an American jeep filled with supplies passed the foot soldiers and headed down the road to the spot where the doppelgänger had given its warning. There was a sudden burst of machine-gun fire. The jeep went wildly out of control, for the driver had been shot. Somewhere up ahead was a hidden German machine-gun emplacement that had been set up to guard the road. If Griffith and his men had gone any farther, they would certainly have been gunned down. Griffith's vision of his double's waving and shouting in the road had saved their lives.

Some twenty years later Griffith experienced a replay of this lifesaving vision.

The war had long been over. Griffith, no longer a sergeant but a civilian, was out on a hike in the forest with his family. There had been a tremendous storm the previous night. On this day the rain had stopped, but the winds were still gusty.

While walking down the trail, Griffith saw his double again. But it was not the Alex Griffith of 1964. It was Sergeant Griffith. It was the same uniformed figure he had seen in France. And, as in the previous vision, the figure was waving its arms and moving its mouth as if shouting a warning.

No one else saw the figure. But Griffith had not forgotten what had happened in France. He immediately had his family stop and turn back down the trail. A few seconds later a huge tree, weakened by the storm, came crashing down into the clearing where Griffith and his family would have been had they not stopped.

Once again the doppelgänger provided a lifesaving warning.

18

Commander Potter's Vision

THE LIFE OF a combat pilot is always in danger. In World War II among the most dangerous missions were those flown by British pilots who were stationed in Egypt.

Bombers from Egypt flew out over the Mediterranean Sea to drop torpedoes and mines in the path of German ships bringing supplies to General Erwin Rommel's North African troops. The missions were too dangerous to fly during the day because the bombers had to fly low and close to their targets. There was a constant risk of being shot down, either by the German ships themselves or by German planes protecting the supply ships. So the British bombers usually flew at night.

The best time for them was during a full moon, so that they could use the moon's bright reflection off the water as an aid to navigation. Such periods of full moon were called a "bomber's moon."

A dramatic and eerie tale was told by Commander George Potter of the RAF. He was a squadron leader at the RAF base in Egypt.

Since the missions were so dangerous, the periods between them were very tense. The men often tried to overcome their anxiety and fear with an air of forced gaiety.

One evening just before a bomber's moon, Commander Potter and another officer named Reg Lamb were in the officers' mess having a drink. Also in the room at that time was a wing commander whom Potter identified only as Roy. Roy was sitting with a group of his friends, and as Potter and Lamb finished their drinks and got ready to leave, there was a burst of laughter from the group around Roy. The sudden noise caused Potter to look in their direction.

It was at that moment that Potter had a strange and terrifying vision. "I turned and saw the head and shoulders of the wing commander moving ever so slowly in a bottomless depth of blue-blackness. His lips were drawn back from his teeth in a dreadful grin; he had eye sockets but no eyes; the remaining flesh of his face was dully blotched in greenish purplish shadows, with shreds peeling off near his left ear.

"I gasped. It seemed that my heart had swollen and stopped. I experienced all the storybook sensations of utter horror. The hair on my temples and the back of my neck felt like wire, icy sweat trickled down my spine and I trembled slightly all over. I was vaguely aware of faces nearby, but the horrible death mask dominated the lot."

Potter had no idea how long the ghastly vision lasted. Finally he became aware of Lamb tugging at his sleeve and saying, "What's the matter: You've gone white as a sheet . . . as if you've seen a ghost."

"I have seen a ghost," said Potter. "Roy, Roy has the mark of death on him."

Lamb looked over to where Roy and his friends were sitting. He saw nothing unusual. Potter was still white faced and shaking all over. Both officers knew that Roy was scheduled to be flying the next night. Neither man knew what to do about it.

In the end Commander Potter decided to do nothing. He first thought of going to the group captain with the story and asking that Roy be taken off the mission. But he knew that Roy would certainly have objected and would have refused to be kept from his crew for such a reason. And if Roy said he wanted to go, the request to have him grounded would undoubtedly have been denied.

Potter came to believe that his final decision not to try to do anything was the right one. It was, he said, part of "a predetermined series of events." Besides, in reality there was nothing he could have done.

The following night Potter was extremely nervous and tense. He was expecting the worst. Finally he got the message that he had been fearing. Roy and his crew had been shot down and forced to ditch in the ocean. But the ditching apparently had gone well. Another plane in the squadron had seen the men in the water climbing into a life raft.

Potter was relieved for the moment. He convinced himself that the men would soon be rescued and that his vision had been a false or misleading one. But as the hours dragged on, no sign of Roy and his crew could be found.

"And then I knew what I had seen," said Potter. "The blue-black nothingness was the Mediterranean at night and he was floating somewhere in it dead, with just his head and shoulders held up by his life preserver."